A LEGACY OF SCOTS

A LEGACY OF SCOTS

SCOTTISH ACHIEVERS

Edited by
Charles T. Walker

MAINSTREAM
PUBLISHING

First published in Great Britain in 1988 by
MAINSTREAM PUBLISHING COMPANY (EDINBURGH) LTD.
7 Albany Street
Edinburgh EH1 3UG

British Library Cataloguing in Publication Data

A Legacy of Scots: Scottish achievers.
1. Scots, 1830—1987
I. Walker, Charles
920.0411

ISBN 1-85158-139-1 (cloth)
ISBN 1-85158-151-0 (paper)

Typeset in 11/12½pt Times by Pioneer Associates, Perthshire.
Printed in Great Britain by Billings & Sons, Worcester.

*In memory of Jane Haining who died
in Auschwitz sometime in the late summer
of 1944*

Acknowledgments

A great many people from all parts of the world have helped in making my dream of compiling a book come true. I am grateful to the contributing authors for their encouragement, their commitment, their time and their talent.

I ask to be forgiven for not crediting by name all those who assisted the contributors.

For their invaluable help at certain times in the book's evolution I acknowledge and thank Libby Horner, Dan Wilson, Drew Rennie, Kay Ramsay, Chan Yuen Ling, Pastor Tamás, Franciszer Piper, Kazimierz Smolén, Eszter Balázs, Louis Nagy, Kate Kelly, Joan and Keith Gordon, Lynn Lander, Harry Corrigan, Phillip Bruce, Dorothy Fraser, Tang Kit Han, Tong Kam Lai, Carol Westwood, Ena Bickett, Sandra Pope, and Judy Moir.

I should also like to extend thanks for permission to use photographs from: The *Glasgow Herald* (Bertie Forbes); The U.S. Naval Academy Museum (John Paul Jones); Pinkerton Inc.; Jardine, Matheson & Co.; The Church of Scotland Library (Mary Slessor); Ralph G. Burnett (Archie McKellar); The National Parks Service, U.S. Dept. of The Interior (John Muir); William Collins & Sons Co. Ltd.; James Fisher (Andrew Fisher); The House of Memories, Waipu, New Zealand (Norman McLeod); Baxters of Speyside; The Dairy Farm (Hong Kong) Ltd. (Patrick Manson); The Boys' Brigade (William Smith); T & R Annan & Sons, Glasgow (Rennie Mackintosh); British Aerospace plc (David MacIntyre); *The Economist* (James Wilson); Linda Hargreaves (John Clunies Ross); The Mitchell Library, Glasgow (Thomas Lipton); and The Auschwitz Museum (Jane Haining).

In the beginning I had a wife, four growing children and an ambition. My love and gratitude go to Liz, Stuart, Graeme, Ross and Amy for sharing me with *A Legacy of Scots*.

Charles T. Walker
Hong Kong 1988

Contents

Preface

'You haena been put intae this world tae enjoy yerself', was the advice given to the young Andrew Carnegie. Many individuals would agree with this maxim and indeed generations have prospered in many countries by excelling in its application. Advice such as this and influences that motivate people are by their very nature varied and complex. If when and where you are born has no greater significance than just time and place, or if genetic fingerprints pre-ordain you, or if your horoscope is set, what chance does a mere individual have of changing the course of life's path to achieve his or her particular ambitions?

In attempting to answer this, it should first be appreciated that everyone has a different definition of success. A baby's first steps can be as magnificent and valid to some as man's exploration of space, while others are fulfilled in simply attaining peace of mind. It is impossible therefore to quantify the effort involved in achieving one's ambition, as in the game of life, triumph depends not only on the circumstances but also on the quality of the player. History has shown repeatedly that when determination, conviction, and strength of character prevail, all things are possible and combine to create quite extraordinary people. Notable examples are Napoleon rising out of the chaos of the French Revolution, Gandhi from the poverty and prejudice of India and Hitler from a defeated, depressed Germany.

Fortunes could be made by those who capture and market the spark, the unquenchable flame that fires certain people to accomplish. Why should some be able to cope with adversity, disappointment and rejection and yet never lose sight of their dream? There is no known magic formula for this single-mindedness but certain trends and patterns are discernible.

In the case of Scottish people their Calvinistic heritage, with its philosophy of endeavour and sacrifice being both materially and spiritually rewarding, plays a significant part. The dour Scot knows almost instinctively that he is not put on this earth to enjoy himself. It is also recognised that this heritage helped create a nation that throughout history has wielded an influence over the world disproportionate to its population and size. What other country has produced such a galaxy of innovators, explorers, engineers, philanthropists and statesmen? But while Robert Burns was writing the words of *Auld Lang Syne*; when David Livingstone was exploring darkest Africa; when James Watt was perfecting his steam engine; when William Smellie was publishing the first edition of the *Encyclopaedia Britannica*; when Robert Louis Stevenson was penning *Dr. Jekyll and Mr. Hyde*; when Alexander Fleming was marvelling at penicillin spores forming in his petri dish, inspiration and determination of no less quality was being generated in other less well-known Scots.

A Legacy of Scots portrays the lives of others who exemplify this theme. It avoids the tendency to concentrate on popular subjects — those who have been analysed extensively. You will find no saints among them and how you rate their individual achievements depends on your own point of view, but all share a common thread — they are Scottish. They each reacted to a set of opportunities and challenges and in so doing, touched and altered the lives of their contemporaries and generations that followed. A few of these 'Scottish Achievers' will be known to some readers, but most are here rescued from obscurity.

You will learn of 20 lives that were colourful, dynamic, daring, and often caring. Those chosen, although from diverse backgrounds and different points in time, all exhibit a passionate drive and determination. The subjects can broadly be classified into those that are entrepreneurs, philanthropists or adventurers — some manage to combine all three qualities.

William Collins certainly combined the first two and the people of Glasgow and readers round the world have benefited from his endeavours. Another publishing magnate, Bertie Forbes, human-ised American big business with his philosophy that, 'business was originated to produce happiness, not pile up millions.' Mount Everest pilot David McIntyre had the foresight to establish aviation in Scotland. Ethel Baxter perfected the skills of jam-making and in so doing expanded a family firm worldwide. Gorbals-born Allan Pinkerton founded a detective agency that helped save the life of an American President. William Smith from Thurso although initially a business man, gave his philanthropic ideas priority to establish a movement that has since appealed to the youth of many lands. Norman McLeod on the other hand, ensured that his brand of Christianity flourished by moving his flock from Sutherland to Nova Scotia, then all the way to New Zealand. Another who came to the fore 'down under' is Andrew Fisher; tutored in the art of political debate, this Ayrshire miner put his expertise to use in a meteoric rise to become Prime Minister of Australia. Alternatively Jane Haining, a Dumfriesshire girl, had no political ideals. Her calling came when she tackled evil prejudice in Nazi-controlled Europe. The adventurers are, like the others, a mixed lot. There is Archie McKellar doing battle with the Luftwaffe in the skies over London; John Paul Jones sinking ships of the Royal Navy in the cause of freedom; John Muir trekking alone in the wilds of North America and Clunies Ross's swashbuckling adventures on a tropical island.

It would be partisan to claim that being born in Scotland is a passport to success, but I believe the country's location, landscape, climate, history and culture nurture and encourage a unique strength of character. This is often heightened when the Scot is transplanted to other parts of the world. Working abroad has made me more aware of different nationalities having discernible personality traits. A feature of the Scottish character for example is not to be as easy-going or forgiving as our English, American or antipodean cousins. P. G. Wodehouse put this rather well when he wrote, 'It is never difficult to distinguish between a Scotsman with a grievance and a ray of sunshine.'

The connecting thread for this book came to me as I browsed through a *Dictionary of Biographies*. This detailed 7,000 men and women of importance and interest in the contemporary and historical world. Out of nationalistic vanity, I decided to underline those who were in fact born in Scotland. I was rewarded to find an entry on every second or third page, many of them obscure. Further reading of the lives that appealed gave birth to *A Legacy of Scots*. Not having the detailed information to explore them fully, I coordinated the compilation by enlisting those who had. The 18 contributing authors are as diverse as their subjects, some already published, others in professions far removed from writing.

I am not totally blinkered into believing that Scots have a monopoly on individual success and would agree with cynics who will argue that other countries could compile such a list. However

I would contend that few could match the quality and depth of character and achievement these 20 biographies represent. Some of these, I hope, will enrich the mind, others gladden the heart and a few no doubt will surprise. Not all found happiness in the culmination of their dream, but their determination to realise their aspirations is both remarkable and inspirational.

Charles T. Walker
(Compiling Editor)
Hong Kong 1988

CHAPTER 1

Bertie Charles Forbes
Magazine Magnate
(1880—1954)

Jack Webster

The small farming community of Whitehill in the parish of New Deer, Aberdeenshire, might seem at first sight an unlikely starting-point for one of the great Scots-Americans of this century. Yet it was on that rolling Buchan landscape of well-ploughed fields, producing oats and turnips and black-cross cattle, that the seeds of success were sown for Bertie Charles Forbes, son of a poor country tailor, for whom any thoughts of fame and fortune in

America must have seemed like a distant dream in that latter part of the 19th century.

As the sixth child of Robbie and Agnes Forbes (in Buchan both vowels are pronounced in For-bes) he set out every day from that plain stone-and-lime cottage known as the *Cunnyknowe,* which stands today as a cottar house for Loanhead of New Deer but was then a combination of home for the Forbes family and a place of work for Robbie. Not only was he the local tailor but a purveyor of porter and ale, which could be consumed on a bench along the side of the house, making it a scene of some ribaldry among the farm servants.

The daily destination for Bertie Forbes and his brothers and sisters was the local school at Whitehill, more than 1.6 km (a mile) away, a typical establishment of its kind in the fine tradition of Scottish education, but more than normally blessed with the quality of its headmaster.

Gavin Greig had taken up his post as the dominie at Whitehill in 1878, at the age of 22, and throughout his career was to become known as poet, playwright, composer and collector of the *Folk Songs of the North-east,* more recently hailed as the finest collection of its kind in the world.

For a man of delicate health, that might have seemed more than enough to occupy his energies. But on top of all that, Gavin Greig (related to both Robert Burns and Edvard Grieg) was counted among the finest educationalists of his day, teaching the classics among other things to those country bairns who came pleitering in from fairm-touns, crofts and cottar houses.

Thus we gain the perspective of the small country school at the turn of the century, geographically remote perhaps but a settled seat of learning which sent youngsters like Bertie Forbes into the world with an education as broad and enlightened as you would now find at a much later age.

Bertie Forbes was a bouncing little butter-ball of a boy, eager, perky, inquisitive about life beyond Whitehill. His instincts were vaguely for a career in journalism but the best Gavin Greig could arrange in Buchan was an introduction to Dauvit Scott of the *Peterhead Sentinel*, who gave him a start as a printer's devil in 1894, when he was 14.

But his eye was still on that reporting option and the chance came with the *Dundee Courier,* for which he later ran the Montrose branch office.

Like the life of the reigning Queen Victoria, the century was drawing to its close. The Boer War was also advertising the existence of South Africa and it was to that distant land that the young Forbes set sail in his 21st year. There he teamed up with the thriller writer Edgar Wallace, who was taking over as editor of the revamped newspaper which was to be known as the *Rand Daily Mail.*

An energetic and ambitious young Scot was just what Wallace needed to assist in the editorial presentation of the paper and he gained such a regard for the lad that he went as far as to allow him to write the Wallace column under the master's own name.

Whitehill of New Deer must have seemed a long way from South Africa at the turn of the century. But among the new-found interests for the young Forbes was the game of golf and out there on the courses of Johannesburg he took to caddying for the wealthy diamond men, less for the financial reward than for the benefit of eavesdropping on their conversations about big business. His appetite was truly whetted. Stocks and shares became a major interest. With that kind of passion, there was only one destination and that was New York. Bertie Forbes sailed into Manhattan in 1904, considerably experienced in journalism at the age of 24 but quite unable to impress the newspaper moguls of the New World.

Who was this Scottish country bumpkin anyway? And where was Johannesburg? He was at the point of offering to work for nothing, an offer which could hardly be refused, when he was given a menial start on the *Journal of Commerce.* He had not progressed very far up the ladder when he took a bold decision to give up his lodgings and move into a room at the old Waldorf Astoria, which used to stand on the site of the Empire State Building.

He calculated that it was his best chance of rubbing shoulders with the men who mattered in American business life. A journalist who was able to live in that kind of style must indeed be of some consequence, they would think, totally unaware of the fact that his salary didn't even cover the cost of the room! Bertie Forbes had struck on a simple truth of journalism, which did not become commonly understood until a later stage, that people were mainly interested in reading about people.

He also carried into his journalism a searching, investigative streak which seems to have been strangely absent in American newspapers at that time. Even in those modest days he refused, for example, to accept the prices issued for publication by importers who were doctoring them to suit their own purposes.

The ethics of the honest, hard-working Scot were already drawing attention to the man who would become known as 'the great humanizer of American business'.

He was quickly snapped up by the most powerful newspaper owner the world had ever known, the legendary William Randolph Hearst, for his New York *American.* In later years, Forbes would relate how Hearst had offered him a blank cheque to sign his own salary. He chanced putting down a seemingly astronomical 20,000 dollars a year but Hearst had eventually confessed to him that he had taken the risk, believing the modest Scots would tend to undervalue themselves — and he had been prepared to pay a great deal more!

While still continuing to work for Hearst, Bertie Forbes decided that, as the most widely-read financial writer in the United States, his expertise should be put to better effect by starting his own journal. The original intention had been to call it *Doers and Doings* but he was persuaded to incorporate his own name in the title, the advice coming from Walter Drey, of the *Magazine of Wall Street,* who would join him as general manager on that condition. Drey knew that the power of Forbes's name would be an invaluable asset in attracting advertising.

So *Forbes Magazine* was launched on 15th September 1917, mainly on borrowed money, and setting the tone of integrity with a 'Fact and Comment' column (it survives to this day) which contained a quotation from the Bible as he had learned it in the family pew at New Deer Parish Church. 'With all thy getting, get understanding' became the guiding motto of *Forbes Magazine,* a message underlined in that very first issue when he declared that 'business was originated to produce happiness, not pile up millions. Are we in danger of forgetting this?'

In that same issue he took to task George Jay Gould of the mighty Jay Gould railroad empire, calling him a highly-placed misfit and blaming the dissipation of the Gould system on George's 'narrowness of vision, unreasoning jealousy, distrust of both subordinates and rivals'. He also offered $1,000 for the best essay on 'Who is the Best Employer in America?'

Though he was on first-name terms with the mighty men of America, like John D. Rockefeller and Frank Woolworth, he did not allow close contact to cloud his judgement or mute his criticism. In 1927 he took Henry Ford to task with a blunt exposé of the slave-driving in Ford factories. His attack on the R. J. Reynolds Tobacco Company lost him Camel advertising but left him with his self-respect, which mattered more.

Not that he could afford any loss of revenue. Indeed in those early days of *Forbes Magazine* he had to ask the staff to embark on a system of 'Scotch Weeks', which meant they received wages for three weeks in the month and nothing for the fourth week. Loyal employees, who knew the situation was genuine and that the boss was making similar sacrifices, went along with the request and were eventually rewarded for their support.

All that criticism of America's undesirable business methods sprang directly from Bertie's own integrity and had nothing to do with a vitriolic nature. On the contrary, he was a man of bubbling good humour, a pawky Scot in the traditional manner who could well have been impersonated by his fellow Aberdonian, that popular comedian Harry Gordon.

As the magazine grew in stature and financial stability, Bertie Forbes was also writing 11 books, founding the Investors League of America, receiving honorary degrees from universities and gaining the Freedom Foundation Award 'for outstanding achievement in bringing about a better understanding of the American way of life'.

But his whirlwind life in the United States did nothing to dim his memory of the little corner of Scotland which gave him roots, nor to blunt his gratitude to those who gave him a start in life. Every two years he returned to Whitehill to host a picnic for his old friends and their families. His old headmaster, Gavin Greig, the man he idolised above all others, had died prematurely at the start of the First World War but there were still Greig's children, who had been his childhood friends, not least of these Mary Jane Greig, a strapping lass much in demand among local farm servants.

At school little Bertie had pined for Mary Jane who, rather haughtily, had regarded his attentions with disdain. She remembered him as 'Patchy Forbes', a name deriving from the patches on his trousers which both indicated the poverty of the time and the fact that his father was, after all, a tailor. Mary Jane Greig, who became a widow in the First World War with four children to bring up, lived to ponder the different life she might have led if she had paid more attention to the baggy-breeked wee lad who longed for her hand.

At first those Bertie Picnics had involved a convoy of farm-carts from Whitehill to the beach at New Aberdour, but by the 1930s they were held in a field beside Whitehill School. By then Bertie was bringing not only his beautiful wife Adelaide but his five sons, Bruce, Duncan, Malcolm, Gordon and Wallace, all names carrying the ring of Scottish history about them.

They would settle in at the fashionable Cruden Bay Hotel, a railway establishment on the lines of the famous Gleneagles, with a branch line of the Buchan Railway running to the village and a tram-car bearing passengers to the main door. Those picnics were gloriously uninhibited affairs, with races not only for the children but their parents and grandparents as well, everyone joining in the fun and finding themselves recorded for posterity on that highly novel invention of the cinematograph.

For most folk in Buchan a meeting with Bertie Forbes was their first encounter with a millionaire, at a time when that financial status still carried the ring of glamorous wealth. He would cross the Atlantic on the Queen Mary and arrive by Rolls Royce from a world that was in stark contrast to the drudgery of farm life in the north-east of Scotland. But the gap was readily bridged as old friendships were renewed and Bertie became once again 'the loon fae the Cunnyknowe' and not the mighty mogul from Manhattan. Like everything else at the time, these picnics were interrupted by the Second World War but Bertie returned at the first opportunity and continued to do so until the 1950s.

The picnic was held as usual in 1952 and Whitehill did not expect to see him again for two years. But word went round that he was coming at Christmas time in 1953, breaking with his established tradition. He duly arrived, played Father Christmas at a party instead of a picnic, gave the children some words of advice about honesty and thrift and hard work — and seemed to take one last look round the scenes of his childhood.

Then his chauffeur drew up and Bertie disappeared over the horizon for the very last time. A few months later, in the Forbes Building in Fifth Avenue, New York, the elevator attendant was checking that all the lights were out when he came upon the founder, lying slumped by his desk, a pen still in his hand. Bertie Charles Forbes was dead, on 5th May 1954, a few days short of his 74th birthday, and was buried across the Hudson River at Englewood, New Jersey, which had been the family home for many years.

But the story and influence of Bertie Forbes can hardly be ended there. Of those five sons, Duncan had already been killed in a car crash. As the eldest, Bruce would succeed his father as the dominant figure in *Forbes Magazine* while the third son, Malcolm, would continue with his political ambitions. As a contemporary of John F. Kennedy, who was two years older, he was the bright young hopeful of the Republican Party, as much of a forecast for the White House as Kennedy on the Democratic side.

But fate had other plans. Malcolm Forbes took an unexpected defeat for the Governorship of New Jersey and veered away from politics. Then brother Bruce developed cancer and died in his forties, leaving Malcolm to head the magazine and turn it into the spectacular success it has become. As a highly prestigious financial journal, produced by some of the finest journalists in America, *Forbes* (as it is now called) runs to the length of a novel every two weeks and has a paid circulation of over 720,000, a glossy production with expensive advertising.

There is hardly a senior business executive in the United States who is not acquainted with *Forbes*, a name which has suffered not at all from the increasing prominence of its chairman and editor-in-chief, Malcolm Stevenson Forbes. In modern times, the personality columns of the world's press have had many a field day over his association with the much-married Elizabeth Taylor, following the ending of his 39-year-old marriage to Roberta in 1986.

But the colourful life had started a long time before that. After Princeton, Malcolm Forbes was fighting with the American forces in Europe during the Second World War, when he gained both the Bronze Star and the Purple Heart for bravery.

In charge of *Forbes,* he was soon extending the financial interests from the magazine to other areas like real estate, buying 174,000 acres of Colorado as one example and the whole of a Fijian island for another.

The properties acquired included the Chateau Balleroy in France, a sumptuous palace in Tangier, Old Battersea House in London, not to mention such trappings as the most spectacular yacht in New York Harbour (it is called *The Highlander*) and his own private Boeing 727, decked out in such luxury as to defy the imagination.

To many, all of that pales into insignificance when you mention the fabulous collection of Fabergé art, including the largest gathering in the world of those exquisite eggs, outnumbering those of the Kremlin and Her Majesty the Queen. To others, the most fascinating part of Malcolm Forbes's life is his ballooning, a hot-air adventure in which he set records for a flight across America and in which he has twice come close to death.

Motor bikes became a passion in his fifties and remain so in his late sixties, by which time he has led gleaming processions of Harley Davidsons across Russia and China and gained entry to the sanctums of Moscow and Peking, in much the same way that his friend, Armand Hammer, did a generation earlier.

'It's pretty hard to hate a balloon,' says Forbes as he leads his friendship tours around the world. He commissions a new balloon for every country. He took an elephant-shaped one to Thailand and a Sphinx to Egypt. In Japan it was a Golden Temple and there is a massive reproduction of his chateau in France. For his most recent adventure to Germany, he ordered a balloon in the shape of a Beethoven bust and caused some consternation to the Russians in June of 1987 when he raised it by the Berlin Wall.

But this was no spy-satellite or object of intended provocation, just a goodwill gesture to the German people for their friendship with the United States. On the day after that Berlin adventure, Malcolm Forbes flew his luxurious Boeing out of Germany and into Aberdeen Airport, just 48 km (30 miles) from his father's birthplace in Scotland. He did so for a very special reason.

In 1986 he was invited to Aberdeen University to receive an honorary degree, a capping ceremony of much pomp which left him deeply impressed. This was the land of his fathers and, in the hectic rush of life across the ocean, he had not been here as much as he might have wished. Friends noticed a touch of nostalgia for the native corner. Of course he had visited Scotland on numerous occasions but he had not been back at Whitehill since 1937, when he last attended his father's picnic as a teenager. Fifty years was a long time.

On that graduation day he took the first positive step towards resuming the picnic, which had once been such a feature of local life. A date was set for June 1987, a committee of local parents undertook to organise it and, on the appointed day, Malcolm

Forbes, along with sons Christopher and Bob, flew in from Germany to team up with daughter Moira and her husband, Ken Mumma, who were already in Scotland. Ten years earlier Moira had been a student of Aberdeen University. From Aberdeen Airport they were driven out past the Bridge of Don and into the Buchan countryside, where the Forbes story had started.

The party stopped off at the *Cunnyknowe* to see the cottage where Bertie was born and from which he had embarked on that daily journey to Whitehill School. Now they were travelling that same route to a school which was converted into a dwelling house but which still stood as a symbolic centre of a recognisable community.

Though they are now scattered to surrounding village schools, the children are still a definable group of 'Whitehill pupils' and this would be a special day for them and their parents and grandparents. Malcolm arrived to the skirl of the pipes and the greeting of a children's choir which had rehearsed a special song for the occasion. Miss Clubb, a former teacher at Whitehill, made a speech of welcome, explaining the Forbes story to a generation of children to whom it was but a vague legend — and pointing out to Malcolm that it was from scenes like these that talented Scots like his father had gone forth to make their mark on a distant world.

Like the scenes of the 1930s, country folk joined in the egg-and-spoon and sack races, heaved at tug-o'-war and enjoyed a cup of tea and sausage-roll in a big marquee. Malcolm and his family entered into the fun and took their seats on straw bales like everybody else enjoying the picnic fare. It was a memorable day for all concerned, not least for the man who is said to be worth around £500 million.

Fully conscious of his mortal state, Malcolm has adopted the motto 'While you're alive, LIVE'. That is something he has never failed to do, ever since he survived the battlegrounds of Europe, whether he is sampling the excitement of the balloons and the bikes, scouring the world in his Capitalist Tool jet, buying up the fabulous Fabergé or running a highly successful financial magazine.

Before he left Whitehill that day he visited the old school and, from its gateway, gazed out over the landscape of Buchan. Here is no scenic beauty of the Highlands but to him it was beautiful just the same, the rolling fields of fertility representing the soil from which his own heritage had sprung. He stood breathing in the fresh air, drooling over its invigorating properties, as if he were reluctant to leave it.

Malcolm Forbes had come home to the *Cunnyknowe* and left the trappings of unimaginable wealth behind. Now he was just a vulnerable human being, in reverie perhaps with the spirit of the baggy-breeked boy who trod those fields a century ago and dreamed dreams of life in a land that lay over the hill and far, far away.

AUTHOR

Jack Webster is an author and journalist who hails from the same parish as B. C. Forbes.

SOURCES

From conversations with B. C. Forbes himself, his son Malcolm and other members of the family; and people on both sides of the Atlantic who have known them.

CHAPTER 2

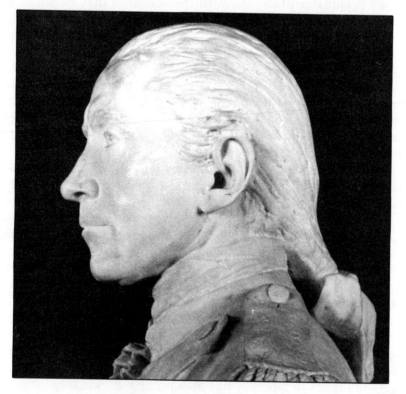

John Paul Jones
I Have Not Yet Begun to Fight
(1747—1792)

Roger Harding

Between the years 1953 and 1959, the Bath Iron Works, the Bethlehem Steel Company and two other manufacturers, built for the US Navy its first post-war class of destroyers. Eighteen ships in all were built, and, whilst heavier than the war-time classes they were to replace, no radical ideas were incorporated in their design. In 1965, conversion was started of four of the vessels to D.D.G., or guided missile destroyer configuration, but the conversion was not especially successful and did not extend to the remainder of the class. In the seventies they began to be allocated to subsidiary duties prior to being phased out of service and retired. One such retirement took place on 8th December 1982. The vessel was called the *John Paul Jones.*

The United States Navy is in the habit of calling its ships after its heroes and John Paul Jones was the US Navy's very first. Jones was not the name of his father, nor was America the land of his birth, but the sea took him, eventually, to the fledgling country, then still to be born of revolution, which is today the USA, and it made him famous.

As a small boy he was fascinated by the sea and ships, but like many sailors before and after him he did not come to love ships for their own sake; in fact, by his own account he saw his life in the merchant service as a means of making enough money to buy farmland and settle down in the style of a gentleman. And yet, his was a life of great adventure, stirring deeds, colour and controversy, amorous affairs, and service in the navies of both America and Russia, for he was first and foremost a fighting sailor of exceptional skill and daring and without peer in close engagements. He was charged with murder, sailed in the slave trade, put down a mutiny by running the leader through with his sword (and then fled from the subsequent impending trial), and handed a resounding defeat to the Royal Navy. He was by all accounts quick tempered, but also possessed, when he wished, great charm, something of a dandy in his dress, and a social climber before he became famous. So perhaps his stated desire to settle down was nothing more than self-delusion, for Jones was irredeemably a man of action, a practitioner par excellence in the art of war, and his canvas was the sea.

Jones was born in Galloway, at Kirkbean on the River Nith, in a cottage on the estate called Arbigland. The estate belonged to one William Craik, a local landowner and farmer, whom perhaps Jones wished to emulate when he later on in life talked of settling down in Virginia. Jones's father, John Paul, was gardener to the estate and came to Arbigland some years before Jones's birth. He married a local girl, Jean MacDuff, who was Craik's housekeeper, and after they were married Craik built them a four-roomed cottage near the sea. It was here, on 6th July 1747, that Jones was born, and was called John Paul after his father. He added the 'Jones' much later when he had left his homeland for good, but we will call him Jones now and throughout.

He was the fourth of seven children; the eldest was William, who also later went to Virginia, then came two daughters, then John Paul. After him were born two children who died when very young, and finally, another girl, Mary Ann, who married a sailor from Whitehaven, but he died suddenly, leaving her a young widow. She then married a local shopkeeper and had children; Lauden Richardson, a great, great, great grand-nephew of John Paul Jones lives in Dumfries today, a descendant of Mary Ann.

Galloway is not the Scotland of peat bogs, endless bleak heather moors, towering crags and remote lochs, but is a rounded, gentle and beautiful land of hills and forest, looking always to the south to the Solway Firth with its mud flats and sand, and where the tide goes out so far that the sea disappears. The River Nith flows into the Solway, and the sea was before Jones when he awakened in the morning and when he went to sleep at night. He fished in the Solway, and played by it, and whenever he could, he went to Carsethorn, a small port next to Kirkbean where ships of all kinds from all parts of the world would wait, beached on the flats if the tide had ebbed and they couldn't get up the firth to Dumfries. Here he would talk to the seafarers and explore the port and its vessels, and also dragoon his friends into simulated naval battles in their little cockle-shell rowing boats, while he shouted orders from the headland and set them on manoeuvre and counter-manoeuvre in prophetic adumbration of his destiny.

Jones left school in 1760 at the age of 13. He had attended the school attached to the parish of Kirkbean and must have been well taught, for later in life he was to spend a great deal of time in writing; indeed his own account of his most famous naval engagement, that against HMS *Serapis*, is very well written. At Carsethorn he took a boat across the Solway and down the Cumbrian coast to Whitehaven, where he was apprenticed into the Merchant Navy, to serve Mr John Younger, a shipowner, for seven years.

With influence and connections, and perhaps a sum of money Jones could have become a midshipman in the Royal Navy, and it would be fascinating to speculate what might have been had this come about. But Jones went to sea in the merchant service, and his first ship, the *Friendship,* of 180 tonnes, took him away from his home shores for the first time to the Caribbean and Virginia. *Friendship,* like many merchant ships of the day, was armed, as England and France were almost at war, and Jones sailed with her

25

to and from the New World until 1764 when the ship returned to Whitehaven to find its owner bankrupt. Mr Younger released Jones from his apprenticeship and the 17-year-old then became third mate on the *King George*. Two years later he joined the *Two Friends* in Jamaica as first mate. Both of these ships were slavers and soon after he joined the *Two Friends* Jones obtained his discharge in Kingston, Jamaica, having become sickened by the trade and vowing to have no more of it. Almost at once he met a fellow countryman, Mr Samual McAdam, of Kirkcudbright in Galloway, who was master of the brigantine *John*, bound for Scotland out of Kingston, and was offered a passage home. When at sea McAdam and his first mate died, and Jones brought the ship home. The owners offered him a command, and he took the *John* to and from the Caribbean at least twice; it was while in charge that one of several incidents that were to dog him for life befell him.

In late 1769, on a voyage to the Windward Islands, Mungo Maxwell, the ship's carpenter, was administered a lashing on Jones's orders, the reasons for which are not entirely clear. Maxwell complained to a marine court but had his appeal dismissed; he then returned home to Scotland, but died at sea, and Jones later arrived back in Kirkcudbright to find himself charged with murder by Maxwell's father, who alleged that his son had died as a result of the flogging. After being allowed out on bail and back to the West Indies to collect evidence, a court there found that Maxwell had died of fever not connected at all with his flogging, and Jones was cleared.

The *John* was sold in 1771, and after a job in charge of a packet plying between Galloway and the Isle of Man, Jones went back to the West Indies as master of the *Betsy*. It was on his second voyage with her that another more serious and far-reaching incident occurred. It began when Jones refused to advance wages to his crew, who grew nasty and tried to leave the ship to go ashore at Tobago in the ship's boat. After an altercation, Jones was attacked by the leader of the crew and Jones ran him through with his sword. Jones himself then went ashore and offered to give himself up, but was persuaded by friends to flee instead. This he did, to continental America, having first changed his name to John Paul Jones. For a while, he, to all intents and purposes, disappeared, and it was not until nearly two years later, on 7th December 1775 that a completely new way of life began for

Jones, one in which he was to become famous. He was commissioned as a first lieutenant in the Continental Navy, the navy of what was to become the United States of America and whose War of Independence had started against Britain some eight months earlier, in April 1775.

So what was he like, this new recruit into the newest of navies? Not yet 30 years old, he was an experienced seaman, ship's captain and navigator. He was a shrewd and successful trader and had at least part-ownership of the *Betsy*. He was a Freemason, having been accepted, in 1770, into the St. Bernard Lodge of Kirkcudbright, and this no doubt assisted him in his commercial and social endeavours both in Scotland and in America. Jones was a man of fiery temper, a smart dresser almost to the point of being a dandy, attracted by and attractive to women, although he died a single man and was perhaps only prepared to marry if the union would increase his social standing. And there was last, but by no means least, his fierce independence of spirit, which led him to declare his love of liberty, take up arms on behalf of the restless colony far across the Atlantic from his native Scotland, and eventually in its service to invade his homeland and secure a place in history. For of all the Scots celebrated in this book, Jones is surely the only one who returned as an enemy under arms.

Jones's first ship in his new country was the *Alfred*, and to her he was posted as a first lieutenant. Like all of the fledgling fleet she was a converted merchant vessel, with 30 or possibly 36 guns, a mixture of six and nine pounders, and Jones saw action in her the next year against HMS *Glasgow*. In May 1776 he was given command of the *Providence*, and in August of that year he was ordered on a cruise of up to three months against British shipping. A most successful time followed and Jones took many prizes of ships, but in October he was back on the *Alfred* and this time in command. Further prizes were taken off the eastern American seaboard, but Jones was then removed from command and fell foul, largely through his own doing, of naval politics. He was passed over for further command, and after a short hiatus, when attempts to get him across the Atlantic to France to take charge of a recently purchased ship failed, he was given command of the *Ranger* at Boston on 1st July 1777. *Ranger* was a new, square-rigged sloop of 20 guns, and it was with her that Jones really began to make his name. In November of that year he set off for France.

27

In early 1778 Jones received instructions to equip the *Ranger* for sea and to go out against the British; he proposed to raid an English port and perhaps destroy some shipping. He departed from Brest at the beginning of April and made his way up into the Irish Sea, where he had a brush with a cutter off the Isle of Man and sank at least two other merchant ships before arriving off Belfast Lough. There Jones discovered that a naval sloop, HMS *Drake* was moored, and he daringly attempted to board her by dropping his anchor on top of hers and then swinging around across her bow. This manoeuvre failed as the wind was too fresh and *Ranger* brought up well astern of the *Drake*. Jones promptly cut his cable and went out into the Irish Sea to prepare for a second attempt, but the weather again foiled him and he went across the sea to shelter off Galloway.

The next day he decided to enter Whitehaven harbour, which had about 300 craft in it, but yet again the weather intervened, this time when the wind dropped and left *Ranger* way out to sea. Jones put out two small boats and, with himself in command of one, they rowed to shore and arrived at daybreak.

Jones knew Whitehaven well from his youth, and this is probably why he chose it. The shipping in the harbour would have consisted of small fishing boats, cobles and the like for the most part, but the propaganda value of such a raid would undoubtedly outweigh any military considerations. By all accounts, however, Jones's crew was not impressed with the scheme, and would have much preferred to stay at sea and hunt for prizes, but nonetheless, at daybreak, Jones and the men of his boat went ashore at one of the two old batteries which guarded Whitehaven harbour and they spiked the guns. The men of the other boat were supposed to set fire to the shipping in the port, but went instead to the nearest tavern and set about the bar stocks with some gusto, so Jones himself spiked the guns in the other battery. He then set fire to a coble before setting off back to the *Ranger* who had meanwhile sailed in closer to shore to meet him. As Jones had hoped, the moral indignation exhibited by the British was immense. Nothing like this had happened in over 100 years, and even though the raid was, in military terms, a failure, and Jones was disappointed, he was recognised in Whitehaven and his name was brought before the public in the newsprints.

The incident was not yet over. The *Ranger* anchored a few hours later in Kirkcudbright Bay while Jones and a party of his

men went ashore on St. Mary's Isle with a view to capturing the
Earl of Selkirk and holding him as a hostage against the exchange
of American prisoners. This was on the 23rd April 1778 and the
raid foundered for the simple reason that the Earl was away from
home. His family and servants were present but on learning of the
Earl's absence Jones turned his party about and began to march it
back to the ship. This was too much for the men, who had signed
on in the first place for booty rather than ideals and the officers
with them demanded to be allowed to loot the mansion. Jones
agreed, and two officers and some men went back to the house
and took the family silver. No-one was harmed, nor anything else
taken, and the behaviour of Jones's men was apparently exemplary
throughout. Jones himself appeared to develop a twinge of
conscience about the whole business however, or else he wished
to ingratiate himself with the Earl and his family, and perhaps the
local community, (for the Selkirks knew Craik, Jones's father's
employer) as after the War of Independence he returned all the
stolen items having used his own money to purchase from his
men their share of silver.

One cannot help but wonder at what Jones himself felt when he
stepped ashore on St. Mary's Isle, which is, in fact, not an island
at all, but a long finger of land stretching into the bay of
Kirkcudbright. Not many men, before or since, can have raided
the playgrounds of their boyhood and youth under the flag of
another country, bearing arms and in a state of war. There can
have been little, presumably, other than revolutionary zeal, plus a
keen desire to get going again as quickly as possible, as pursuit
was inevitable and the *Drake* was just across the Irish Sea in
Carrickfergus. And yet, surely, he must have been not entirely
unmoved by his circumstances, for there is no indication that his
childhood had been unhappy and it was around Kirkcudbright
that he had made covenant with the sea. Anyway, whatever his
thoughts, they were swiftly concentrated at dawn the next day,
when he stood at Belfast Lough and engaged the *Drake* who was
leaving the lough to look for him. The engagement lasted an
hour. The sloop proved no match for the *Ranger* for while she
boasted 20 guns to the *Ranger*'s 18, the minutes of the court
martial investigating the incident reveal that *Drake* was on an
impressment mission and was manned by newly raised men, had
no gunner, had no cartridges filled and no preparation for
handling the powder. Her captain and first lieutenant were killed

and the ship herself was captured. After some repairs and some more minor adventures, Jones took her to Brest, with 200 prisoners. It was 8th May 1778.

In July 1778, open war broke out between France and England. Jones wanted another command, but despite his cultivation of members of the French naval hierarchy, and the American Commissioners in Paris, of whom Benjamin Franklin was one, he was to chafe at the bit until the end of 1778, when at last he was able to secure command of a relatively old East India merchantman called the *Duc de Duras,* purchased by the French from her private owner and fitted out by Jones at their expense. Jones gained permission to change her name, but it would not be until August 1779 that the *Bonhomme Richard* and its squadron would set off on the cruise that finally secured Jones a place in history.

Jones in the *Bonhomme Richard* was placed in command of a squadron. This comprised the *Alliance* a new American frigate brought to France with an American crew but commanded by a Frenchman, Pierre Landais, who was to prove a disastrous choice; and three French vessels. These were the frigate *Pallas,* the brigantine *Vengeance* and a cutter, the *Cerf* captured from the British. All these ships except *Alliance* were paid for and fitted out by France. All were well armed, but while *Bonhomme Richard* had 40 guns, they were of mixed calibre, some were worn out, and the ship was slow, so that Jones still did not have command of a vessel that could force a fast enemy to fight if the enemy did not want to. Jones was ordered on a raid round Britain which was to act as a diversion for a very ambitious invasion whereby almost 50,000 men would cross to southern England. The invasion was eventually defeated in equal parts by sickness (typhoid, scurvy and smallpox) and the slowness and bad organization of a Spanish fleet who were to partake in the operation. In the event it was Jones who was to provide the main attraction, while the invasion itself was abandoned, and after some preliminary escort duty the squadron set off under orders countersigned by Franklin, to raid shipping around the British coast with the addition, at the last minute, of two French privateers, the *Monsieur* and the *Granville.* These two did not last long, however, and left after a couple of weeks, so that by mid-August, the original squadron of five ships was all that remained as it passed to the west of the southern tip of Ireland on its way around the British Isles. It was here that an officer and some men took advantage of a fog to desert, and the *Cerf* also disappeared, while *Alliance* went off by herself. The remainder continued around Scotland, all the while doing a fairly brisk trade of capturing prizes and despatching them to various European ports with prize crews, eventually meeting up again off the Firth of Forth on 14th September 1779.

The weather was fine at this point and Jones wanted to sail up the firth into Leith and lay seige to it. It was hours before he could win over the captains of *Pallas* and *Vengeance,* however, and the next day the wind had changed and foul weather had set in. Nevertheless, Jones attempted to beat up the firth, but when he was almost at Leith a sudden squall blew the squadron back out to sea. By the time the storm had abated, Jones, having lost the element of surprise, decided to abandon the plan and pushed on south down the east coast of Scotland to where he would fight his most famous action.

On 23rd September 1779, after chasing prizes off the Yorkshire coast, Jones was approached from the north-east by a convoy of some 41 ships. He knew, from a captured pilot, that this was a convoy from the Baltic, escorted by two ships of war, HMS *Serapis* of 44 guns and the *Countess of Scarborough* of 20 guns. The captain of *Serapis,* Richard Pearson, RN, had been warned of Jones's presence by boats put out from the shore, so he sailed his convoy close to the coastline for protection, but in the evening came within cannon shot of the *Bonhomme Richard* and the two ships engaged while *Pallas* took on the *Countess of Scarborough.* The real fight however, lay between Jones and Pearson, and it must be said that the latter's vessel was superior, not only as a ship but also in terms of men and armament. Jones was quick to realize that if he was to have any chance he would have to board. Accordingly, after a series of dazzling close manoeuvres by both ships, they became lodged together, bow to stern. *Serapis* continued to blast *Richard* at point-blank range, but the former's decks were raked by musket fire from Jones's ship, so that all her deck guns had to be abandoned. It was during this manoeuvring that Pearson asked Jones to surrender, and received the immortal reply 'I have not yet begun to fight'.

By about 10 o'clock that evening the *Richard* was a wreck: on fire, its sails ablaze, the upper deck an open platform, as the ship's sides had been blasted away by *Serapis*'s cannon, many men dead, and the officers on the point of giving up. However, during the encounter, a seaman from *Richard,* lying out along the ship's main arm, had thrown a grenade down a hatch on *Serapis* and ignited a number of cartridges causing great carnage, so that when, just before 10.30 pm, the main mast of *Serapis* was hit, Pearson lowered his colours and surrendered to Jones. Less than half an hour after all had seemed lost, the *Richard*, although doomed, was victorious.

No thanks to Landais in the *Alliance.* Under the pretence of engaging *Serapis, Alliance* fired at least three broadsides at *Richard* before retreating. There seems little doubt that this action was deliberate, and Landais did nothing to help *Pallas* in her action. Pearson himself recorded his loss against two ships, but Landais had committed infamous treachery in a battle which was won almost by chance. At one point *Richard's* gunner had shouted for quarter (mercy), but was knocked down by a pistol thrown by Jones. Two days later the *Richard* was abandoned and sank and Jones transferred his flag to the *Serapis.* The Baltic convoy had long since made its escape, and Jones took his squadron slowly, because of damage to *Serapis,* to Holland and the Texel, an island in the Zuider Zee.

Jones's little fleet stayed in Holland until the end of the year, the victim of politics involving the French, Dutch and British Governments and the American Commissioners in Paris. The Dutch could not recognize the American flag, while the whole squadron was ordered to fly the colours of France. Eventually, Jones transferred his flag to the *Alliance,* which Landais had left, to go to Paris, and in December 1779 Jones broke through a British blockade and sped to L'Orient in France. From there, Jones went to Paris, to seek the money for his prizes and to pay off the *Alliance;* he stayed until May, but on return to L'Orient found that Landais had regained command of *Alliance* and taken her to America.

Jones was a hero in Paris, adored by female society, presented to the King, and it is no wonder he stayed as long as he did. At L'Orient he was given command of the ship *Ariel* and took her to America, where he was greeted in triumph. He was eventually ordered by Congress to take charge of the completion and launching, and then assume command, of the *America* a 70-gun ship which was to be the largest in the United States Navy. After launching, however, she was presented to France, but she was badly built, and was condemned in 1786. In 1783, he persuaded

Congress to send him back to Paris, to collect the prize money due to the *Bonhomme Richard* squadron, but the negotiations dragged on for three years and Congress did not approve the prize accounts until 1787. Jones meanwhile had returned to the United States and tried to get himself made up to Rear-Admiral, and when this failed he accepted a similar post in the Russian Navy in the service of Catherine the Great.

This sort of appointment was not at all untoward in those days. It was relatively commonplace for Army and Navy officers to enter the service of another country when their own was at peace, and as there was now no US Navy and the War of Independence was long over, this was a way for Jones to achieve his ambitions of attaining flag rank and seeing more action at sea. He served in the Black Sea fleet against the Turks in the second Russian-Turkish war, but fell foul of Potemkin, Catherine's lover and military commander, and was sent to the Baltic. On the way, in St Petersburg, he was accused of rape. It is unlikely he was guilty, and probably the incident, and more so the subsequent publicity, was contrived in order to attack his reputation. In this it was successful. Jones left Russia and, after an attempt to seek a commission in the Swedish Navy, went to Holland where he stayed until 1790. He wrote to friends that he was returning to America, but he never did, and instead went to Paris, the Paris of the French Revolution, where he died on 18th July 1792, of jaundice and nephritis, made fatal by bronchial pneumonia. He was just 45 years old.

An account such as this cannot really do justice to Jones's energy, industry, and ability as a fighting sailor, nor fully catalogue his flaws of character and temperament, of which the greatest was probably his immense egotism. It was this characteristic above all others that set him apart and, at the end, brought him to a lonely death. But he was not forgotten by his adopted America, and after several fruitless searches his remains, interned in a Paris cemetery and long built over, were in 1905 discovered and taken to the US Naval Academy, Annapolis, Maryland, where they were laid to rest in January 1913. It was Jones's misfortune that he had not been given a larger canvas to display his ability as a seaman, and he never really got the chance to show other than his skill as a tactician. But it was this skill that brought him fame and glory, and it was glory that was one of his passions, satisfied in the pursuit of freedom.

As well as the vessel described in the opening of this account, three other fighting ships were named after him. The first was a side-wheeler, a steam gunboat launched in 1862, the second, a torpedo boat destroyer which was laid down in 1899 and launched three years later, while the third, also a destroyer, was launched in 1920 and earned two battle stars in the Pacific in World War II. In 1956, USS *John Paul Jones*, on its first cruise, came to the British Isles, and to Kirkcudbright, where her commander, R. W. Hayler, Jr, presented to the people of Kirkcudbright the ship's emblem.

AUTHOR

Roger Harding is a chartered surveyor living and working in Hong Kong.

BIBLIOGRAPHY

Samuel Eliot Morison, *John Paul Jones — A Sailor's Biography*, Little, Brown and Company, 1959.

Commander Edward Ellsberg, USNR (Ret.), *I Have Just Begun to Fight — The Story of John Paul Jones*, Dodd, Mead and Company, 1966.

John Slinkman and the Editors of *Navy Times, Duel to the Death — Eyewitness Accounts of Great Battles at Sea*, Harcourt, Brace and World, Inc., 1969.

Dictionary of American Naval Fighting Ships, volume III, Navy Department, Office of the Chief of Naval Operations Naval, History Division, Washington, 1968.

Anthony Preston, *Warships of the World*, Jones' Publishing Company Ltd., 1980.

ACKNOWLEDGEMENT

The author extends thanks to the United States Navy and Naval Academy for providing and giving permission to use copyright material.

CHAPTER 3

Allan Pinkerton
The Eye that Never Slept
(1819—1884)

Elizabeth Walker

It was fitting, if not desirable, that Allan Pinkerton was born into squalor surrounded by violence, drunkenness and crime. These sins, born out of poverty and despair in the crumbling Gorbals in the early 19th century, were pitifully mundane compared to the organised crime he would be associated with in later life. He systematically crossed lawbreakers, social barriers and state boundaries to combat crime and in so doing, founded one of the oldest and largest private investigation firms in the world.

Hard times were familiar on Clydeside's left-bank, with its teeming tenements, unplanned children, noise and tension. Pinkerton escaped the fate of many weaker infants and survived the chronic diseases and epidemics commonplace at the time. What he lacked in vitamins he made up with an iron determination, and enjoyed a close if impoverished relationship with his mother and brother, Robert.

Allan's mother, a pretty mill girl from Glasgow, was the second wife of William Pinkerton. A reticent man and strict disciplinarian, William had followed the family tradition and become a blacksmith. Isabella bore him two sons whilst coping with his five surviving children from a previous marriage. Allan and Robert found life considerably easier once their unruly brothers and sisters had left home.

At eight years of age, young Pinkerton's formal education was abruptly halted. His father died and he was obliged to earn a living as a pattern-maker's apprentice, a dismal life for a confident and capable boy in his formative years. He worked from dawn to dusk for a pittance, yet seems to have had a stoical attitude and cared to recall the positive aspects of those deprived days, remembering, for example, his mother 'bringing home a precious egg'. Her efforts were later rewarded when as a journeyman 'tramp cooper', Pinkerton would live frugally and send the bulk of his wages home.

At the tender age of 12, he was enterprising enough to quit work in the pattern-maker's sweatshop, and began a seven-year apprenticeship with William McCaulay, a Glasgow cooper. He showed an aptitude for barrel-making, was eager and hard-working. On qualifying in 1837, he received his journeyman's cards and full membership of the 'Coopers of Glasgow and Suburbs Protective Association'. He worked for a time as a 'cooper tramp', travelling around the countryside fulfilling orders for barrels and casks.

Around this time in Britain, there was a highly motivated and volatile group rising up to fight social injustice and inequality. The Chartist Movement had many members ready to fight for freedom of the working classes, and Allan joined up without hesitation. As an earnest and militant member he was a popular choice from men on the cooperage floor to be their representative. He was unflinching in his efforts to have the 'People's Charter' reform bill accepted, and urged all Chartists to march, and to raise hell and funds for the cause. Fierce conflict over leadership split the beleaguered reformers into 'moral force' and 'physical force' reactionaries. The dynamic Pinkerton naturally fell into the latter group. When the government decided to make an example of well-known 'physical force' incendiaries, Pinkerton found his name on the King's Warrant list and was forced into hiding for several months. Before his retreat he had been enjoying the company of a young girl at many of the strikers' concerts. Now, with a price on his head, and forced to leave Scotland, he realised life would be pretty lonesome without her. Their courtship was brief and after the wedding ceremony on 13th March 1842, Joan Carfrae left friends and familiarity and with the help of Neil Murphy, Allan's old boss from pattern-making days, the honeymooners were smuggled aboard a ship bound for Canada.

A four-week voyage in rough seas ended in dramatic fashion when the ship struck a rock off the coast of Nova Scotia, and the Pinkertons took refuge in a lifeboat. Once safely ashore, they followed their plan to settle in Quebec, found that jobs there were few and far between, and moved on to Montreal. A temporary job here was a welcome stop-gap, but the ambitious Pinkerton quickly made plans to settle in the prospering frontier town, Chicago. He was surprised at his young bride's obvious distress when the hard-earned tickets were produced. She admitted to having put a small deposit on a 'wee bonnet' and the thought of losing her money and the millinery caused her such anxiety that Allan agreed to postpone their sailing for a week. They later found out that the earlier steamer had sunk, with no survivors. Pinkerton admitted, 'I tell you, my wee wife has had her way about bonnets ever since.'

They eventually settled in a sleepy little town, north-west of Chicago, aptly named Dundee. Thriving on hard work and devotion from Joan, he opened his own cooperage employing eight men.

Fate took a hand in Pinkerton's life in 1847 and his hidden talent for detection was revealed. Lumber was in short supply and expensive on the frontier so, to supplement his dwindling stock, he made regular trips to a small island in the Fox River, several miles from Dundee. This desolate little spot had wood ideal for hoops, staves and poles. On one such trip he was intrigued to see signs of a cooking fire. Naturally suspicious, he wanted to solve the riddle and returned several times. Late one night he saw the culprits leave their row boat and go ashore. He knew instinctively that no honest men would have nightly meetings in such a place, and he informed the sheriff. Gathering up a posse they raided the island and arrested a group of counterfeiters, collecting the illegal currency and tools of their trade.

News of the coup spread fast and Allan became a local celebrity, in demand for the second time when the area was flooded with fake banknotes. He collected enough evidence to be certain that one John Craig was a ringleader and working on a theory that 'to catch a thief, you set a thief' he wormed his way into Craig's confidence. In conversation, Pinkerton gave the counterfeiter the distinct impression that he was not averse to earning more, albeit crooked money. The plan worked, a meeting was set up and Craig was duly arrested. The tenacious crime-solver would not be content with barrel making much longer. It was obvious that there was more potential, more job satisfaction and more financial gain to be had solving crimes. Pinkerton had all the qualities of a successful sleuth — and his native cunning, tact, integrity and a supreme confidence of always getting his man, established him as a sheriff in Chicago, feared and respected by the city's criminals.

At that time the biggest city in the midwest, Chicago boasted fashionable hotels, new churches, theatres and some 16,000 residents. Fast on the heels of this boom came a dramatic increase in crime. The railroads were being crippled by vandalism and theft almost daily. Law and order was breaking down as described in Horan's biography of Pinkerton: 'the police were either too busy, paid off, politically dominated or restricted by local jurisdiction in their pursuit of thieves'. The countryside was crying out for determined, honest law enforcement, and overwhelmed by demand, Pinkerton opened his own detective agency in 1850.

During the next few years he became almost paranoic in his zeal to track down criminals. He drove himself to exhaustion, believing he had a patent on success. Joan Pinkerton had little time or inclination to think about bonnets as she stood by her husband in those empire-building years. The 'bonnie days' she remembered from Dundee sustained her in accepting the typical Victorian régime imposed by her husband. She endured the birth of six and death of three of their children with a courage and serenity common to many of her generation and background, and suffered in silence the fastidious ways of the complex man she loved. This unromantic man who maintained order at home, as he did in business, believing that the end justifies the means, sowed the seeds of resentment and bitter frustration in his children. Once her brothers were married, Allan's only daughter, Joan, became more openly defiant of her father in his belief that 'women belonged in the kitchen, in bed and with the children'. Caustic familial quarrels lay ahead before he would mellow a little and take time to appreciate his wife who had supported him from the Chartist days in the Gorbals, to the elaborate luxury of *The Larches,* their palatial estate and symbol of his triumph over humble beginnings. For the time being, however, hard-nosed practicality was more to his bent and the trivialities of family life concerned him little.

Pinkerton's trademark of an open eye with the slogan 'We never sleep' was known to all. Criminals nicknamed him 'The Eye' which in turn caused any detective to be labelled as a 'private eye'. He founded a profession on integrity and zeal, and made certain his employees followed suit. They had to be 'men of high order of mind and possess clean, honest, comprehensive understanding, force of will and vigour of body'. He wanted stalwarts with a true sense of vocation, men who would be relentless in the pursuit of crime. With an uncanny knack of spotting a maverick, he chose his original team of operatives after much strict vetting and interrogation, and also had the foresight to employ the country's first female detective. Kate Warne, a young widow, was chosen because Pinkerton realised she had the confidence and guile needed to 'worm out secrets in many places to which it was impossible for male detectives to gain access'. Her loyalty to him never wavered in the 12 years she served the agency, and she eventually headed and trained his team of female detectives. Another renowned Pinkerton employee was the debonair and devoted George Bangs, who would become the agency's first general manager. A small group, comprising Kate Warne, George Bangs, three other detectives, a secretary and a few clerks formed the nucleus of a dynasty that would become synonymous with professionalism and integrity. It was a comforting thought to the honest citizens in America to know that 'The Eye never sleeps'.

Their innovative 'rogues' gallery' although unsophisticated by today's standards, was a forerunner for the classification files used by the FBI of today. Crudely taken 'mug shots' were added to dossiers containing ludicrous parochial descriptions of known suspects. The files show: 'A bank robber who had a scar on his left hand, "speaks Mex" and lives with a hooker named Frisco Ann' or 'A forger who spits frequently as he talks, "works East St Louis, and is a friend of the Scratch." (Charles Becker the world-famous forger of banknotes.)' This was 19th-century criminology at its best, and prisoners were stripped of clothing and dignity as Pinkerton's men studied, classified and described in detail their physical abnormalities. The early 'Pinkertons' used code names for each other, and built up a reputation for protecting informants whilst keeping on the best of terms with the police. As a gesture of goodwill, the agency never collected a reward. This fact did not go unnoticed by the city fathers.

Today we would describe Allan Pinkerton as a workaholic who demanded total dedication and loyalty from his staff. New employees were quickly made aware of his fierce and surly nature. Indeed he wrote to one of them: 'I rule my office with an iron hand, I am self-willed and obstinate . . . I must have my own way of doing things.' His agents became masters of disguise and were highly skilled in infiltration and interrogation techniques.

Contradictory to the agency's view of strict adherence to the law, Allan Pinkerton seems to have had no conscience when it came to the hiding of runaway slaves. Fervent abolitionists from the early days in America, he and Joan made their home in Adams Street a refuge for the bonded — sometimes the house held more than had the Dundee cooperage. Committed to the Unionist cause, he readily gave of his resources and talent needed in the crisis of the Civil War. As thousands donned uniform, he helped the war effort by tracking down rebel conspirators using every clandestine method he knew to hinder secessionist plots of sabotage.

His operatives loosened many a boastful tongue using a well tried technique of subtle probing and bar-room whisky. In Baltimore during one of these drunken sessions, they uncovered a plot to assassinate the president-elect Abraham Lincoln as he passed that way for the inauguration in Washington. According to Pinkerton, the risk to Lincoln's life would be considerably lessened if he could be persuaded to travel through secessionist-inflamed Baltimore under cover of darkness. Lincoln was finally convinced of the danger, and under protest agreed to Pinkerton's schedule. Lincoln's enemies would denounce him 'for his undignified flight' from Harrisburg to the capital. He was publicly humiliated by the press and 'ultimately regretted having arrived at the nation's seat of power unannounced'. For the practical Pinkerton it was reward enough to be able to send the dramatic coded message back to Harrisburg, 'Plums delivered nuts safely.'

In the early days of the war General George McClennan who had had business dealings with Pinkerton in Illinois, now called on him to help with intelligence work in the field. Making several trips behind enemy lines, Pinkerton made an important contribution by giving the strategists detailed information on rebel defences and supplies. As a spy he was certainly courageous, but once promoted to Chief of the Secret Service, his methods were found to be sadly lacking. He made an incredibly poor military officer, perhaps because of his civilian approach, adopting the same methods he had used as a railroad detective. This period was an inglorious chapter in Pinkerton's life, and one that undoubtedly did little to hasten the end of the war.

The cinema has created a near-mythical notion of the American wild west but in reality the recession following the Civil War brought financial ruin to many. The country was in the grip of panic and depression and morale was at an all time low. Legend has glorified the bandannaed desperados as scores were settled by the law of the gun, and time has done little to change the public's empathy for the bandits on horseback.

The expanding West meant trains often carried huge fortunes. Gold was hauled in one direction and cash — for payment — in the other. The collar and tie image of the Pinkertons was quickly, if uncomfortably, changed for boots and saddles as they became the nemesis of outlaws and train robbers. They advertised their involvement by flooding towns with 'wanted' posters offering handsome rewards for information and caught many of the most renowned criminals of the day.

The Reno Gang was recognised as the first organised band of train robbers and put Seymour, Indiana, on the map as a town shamed by ruthless killings, gambling kings and whorehouses. The gang's presence, and the sizable band of thieves and cutthroats it attracted accelerated the violence and degradation in the town. Although Allan Pinkerton had plenty of evidence against them, gaining a conviction was another matter. Fears of reprisal from the gang gripped the entire community. Despite this, Pinkerton continued to investigate the increasing number of robberies perpetrated on the Adams Express Company by the gang. Hit men made two attempts to kill Allan Pinkerton, before he put three of the Reno Gang brothers and a key member of the gang behind bars for the last time.

The townspeople eventually took the law into their own hands, honest men joined ranks and the vigilante group stormed the jail. The four lynchings that followed drew the curtain on the Reno brand of outlawry in Indiana.

The legendary James brothers and their sidekicks the Younger brothers were achieving even greater notoriety than the Reno gang. The public was largely hypnotised by their bravado and willing to help them. It proved an insurmountable task for the Pinkertons and lawmen alike to have them convicted. Through persistent attempts to 'get their man' Pinkerton agents, thinking they had found the gang's hideout, opened fire on a cabin and killed Jesse and Frank James's eight-year-old half-brother, and severely wounded their mother. Allan Pinkerton was the prime target for Jesse's vengeance until his dying day. Jesse James is, of course, legendary; he died with his boots on, gunned down by a member of his own gang. Frank's image was tarnished somewhat, as he ended his days telling tales of past glory and coaxing 50 cents apiece from visitors for a guided tour of the family farm.

The motion picture industry made gods out of Butch Cassidy and the Sundance Kid. In reality they certainly had charisma and something of a conscience when it came to killing innocent people. As a teenager Harry Longabaugh, alias the Sundance Kid, spent 18 months in jail for stealing a horse. This harsh sentence, at a time when robber barons were grabbing every acre of good land and ruthlessly gobbling up the wealth of the country, embittered Longabaugh and he turned to a life of crime.

He met up with Robert Le Roy Parker, better known as Butch Cassidy, when both men were in their thirties. By then Butch had discarded his stable upbringing and this colourful pair formed the legendary 'Wild Bunch'. Their hallmark of a well executed raid showed 'no loss of life of train crew or outlaws, no molestation of passengers, and the use of inordinate quantities of dynamite', as discussed in Voss and Barber's book, *We Never Sleep*. Sophisticated bandits, they always seemed one step ahead of the Pinkertons, even though each agent had photographs and drawings of the gang. Ironically, a photograph the Wild Bunch had taken of themselves almost caused their downfall. A spending spree followed a successful raid on the First National Bank in Winnemucca. Resplendent in fashionable clothes, the group posed for a photograph. The supremely confident Butch sent one copy to the bank, thanking them for the finery. William Pinkerton sent copies of the flamboyant photograph plus serial numbers of the stolen bonds to banks throughout the country. An alert teller in Nashville spotted one of the bonds and Pinkerton agents caught two of the Wild Bunch. The subsequent trail of Butch Cassidy and the Sundance Kid across South America is as difficult to substantiate by historians today, as it was for Pinkerton's men at the time. This marked the end of an era in American criminal history and the name Pinkerton was as intertwined with the name of western banditry as the outlaws themselves.

The Pinkerton agency was slowly recovering from post-war financial difficulties when Bangs was instructed to drum up business and renew acquaintances in Philadelphia with Franklin Benjamin Gowan, President of the Reading Railroad. It proved an opportune time as violence was escalating in the coalfields of Pennsylvania.

In 1873, Allan Pinkerton chose one of his newest recruits to take on an extremely delicate and dangerous assignment. Twenty-nine-year-old James McParland had brains, brawn and had kissed the proverbial blarney stone. The fact that he was Irish and Catholic would allow him some access to the 'Molly Maguires', but it would take great skill and deft play-acting to stay alive and on the right side of the law once he had gained their confidence.

The name 'Molly Maguires' instilled fear into the hearts of the luckless miners in the dingy coalfields around Pennsylvania. This secret society was spawned from the Mollys' supposedly altruistic feelings for their immigrant brothers, but quickly deteriorated into an élitist group of hoodlums, hell bent on robbing, terrorising and murdering on a wanton scale. Posing as James McKenna, McParland drank, laughed and sang his way into the inner circle of the Mollys, but was never too befuddled to write detailed notes for the agency, quoting names and dates of upsurges planned in the anthracite coal mines. For almost three years McParland lived in constant fear of being 'tumbled' and came precariously close to leading marauding groups in acts of sabotage and murder. He became secretary of the society, and the confidante of Jack Kehoe, the undisputed 'King of the Mollys'. James had been instrumental in frustrating many plots. The search for the informant was closing in, but he evaded premature death by escaping to a safe county. The reign of terror ended in the winter of 1877, when the brave McParland strode into a courtroom in Pottsville and gave enough evidence to convict 20 ringleaders, including Jack Kehoe. All were sent to the gallows and Kehoe endured a 'particularly horrible death when the noose slipped and he slowly strangled'.

Atrocities had been committed by the 'Molly Maguires' in the name of Christian brotherhood and it is a sad historical fact that even after this carnage and brutality, the lot of the miners did not change. Praise was heaped upon McParland and Pinkerton, and indeed one journalist heralded their achievement as 'one of the greatest works for public good that has been achieved in this country and in this generation'.

During the next few years Allan Pinkerton became obsessive in his zeal to track down criminals. Business continued to flourish, but the gruelling, self-imposed demands took a toll on his health, and he suffered a stroke in the summer of 1869. Typically, he denounced the doctors' prognosis and set himself a régime of exercises and therapeutic baths. After many months, for all his boasting of having regained his health, his letters reveal a signature similar to the laboured efforts of a small child.

He now turned over the administration of his beloved agency to his sons William and Robert. Records of the time show that the operating expenses for the Chicago, New York and Philadelphia offices, plus two fifths of the general expenses of the entire business exceeded $1,000,000. Allan now spent much of his time supervising the building of *The Larches*. Restricted by a speech impediment and rheumatic-ridden bones, both legacies of his stroke, he was irritable and often irrational. He insisted 85,000 larch trees be shipped from Scotland to line the driveways of his new home. The first load of saplings died due to neglect on the journey, and the fierce weather. Undeterred, Pinkerton ordered another batch. He was still determined to 'have his own way of doing things'. This grandiose estate of 254 acres would soon boast guard houses, complete with armed guards at each entrance, a racetrack, expert horsemen and grooms for the stables, stately rooms adorned with chandeliers and original oil paintings.

Pinkerton's love for the estate was obvious in his will. 'He requested that the showplace be kept in its present condition, be worked for seven years, then another seven, and if possible to remain in the family forever.' He never fully recovered from the stroke and died on 1st July 1884 with his wife, William, Robert and Joan, his daughter, at his bedside. He was buried in Graceland Cemetery, Chicago, beside other family members and Pinkerton employees.

In life he had fled his beloved Scotland as a fugitive radical, a champion of the exploited working man, but he became a respected household name in America. His sons continued his tradition of fidelity and service to the public, and sustained a remarkable loyalty from their operatives. Today the company has over 35,000 employees offering a broad spectrum of security and investigative expertise. Many of the principles that Allan Pinkerton laid down over a century ago are still in use today, and the expansion of the present firm shows there is little need to change that philosophy.

AUTHOR

Liz Walker is a gregarious Aquarius who prefers marathon running to housework.

BIBLIOGRAPHY

James D. Horan, *The Pinkertons*, Bonanza Books.
Frederick Voss and James Barber, *We Never Sleep*, Smithsonian Institution Press.
Francis P. Dewes, *The Molly Maguires*, Burt Franklin, 1966.
Charles Van Doren (ed.), *Webster's American Biographies*, 1975.

ACKNOWLEDGEMENT

The author extends thanks to Pinkerton Inc. for access to company literature and photographs.

CHAPTER 4

William Jardine
Mercantile Viking

(1784—1843)

Charles T. Walker

In the early 1800s the expansionist power of the British Empire came into headlong conflict with the bamboo wall and ancient Confucian logic of the Celestial Empire, China. A figure central to the unfolding events in those exhilarating times was not a diplomat, soldier or statesman but a Dumfriesshire-born entrepreneur, William Jardine. His commercial acumen and sense of high adventure empowered Jardine to orchestrate and found a vast business conglomerate and to play a crucial part in the establishment of the Crown Colony, Hong Kong. His story has in fact formed the basis of James Clavell's best selling novel, *Tai-Pan*.

How then did a farmer's son come to play this role and what chain of events took him from humble beginnings in south-west Scotland to the cut and thrust of life among the pirates, Manchu warriors and opium dens of China? To answer these questions we have to examine his life, not only in the context of the times in which he lived, but also to appreciate the factors that brought western ideology on a collision course with the oriental east.

He was born on the 24th February 1784, at Broadholm, a farm near Lochmaben in Dumfriesshire. He was the fourth child of Andrew and Elizabeth Jardine, the family being increased to five by the birth of a girl in 1786. The other son and elder brother had been named David. When William was nine years old his father died leaving the close-knit family to mourn his loss. At 16 he was attending classes in medical practice, anatomy and obstetrics at the medical school of Edinburgh University. He was partly supported at this time by his older brother and it is thought he was apprenticed to a surgeon. The advantages of this method of study were twofold. By being in the service of a surgeon, the student would be acquainted with hospital practice, as well as being provided lodgings by his employer. The need to live frugally and eke out the occasional remittance from David, plus the realisation that only by his own efforts would he succeed, were to prove powerful influences on the young William. He was later to write to a nephew in 1830, 'I have the strongest objection to extravagance and idleness.'

Throughout his life he remained deeply grateful to his family and acknowledged this by ensuring that their descendants held the key positions in his company. This blood bond was to pay many dividends over the years, and is one of the many strengths of the present-day firm.

On the 2nd March 1802 he received his diploma from the Royal College of Surgeons, and shortly after travelled down to London to be interviewed for the post of surgeon's mate on one of the ships of the East India Company. This London-based organisation was a large quasi-governmental trading combine holding a royal charter for the sole franchise of trade between Britain, India and the Far East.

He was leaving behind a Scotland of the Clearances, of Robert

47

Burns's *A Man's a Man for A' That* and a Britain reeling from the consequences of the American War of Independence (1775-1783), the French Revolution (1789-1799) and of Thomas Paine's *The Rights of Man.* So it was that the young 18-year-old found himself on the pitching deck of the 1,200-tonne *Brunswick.* He would soon be familiar with the tortuous route through the Bay of Biscay, rounding the Cape of Good Hope, surging through the Indian Ocean and running before the mighty typhoons of the tropical South China Sea. During the next 15 years William was to make six round trips between the Thames and Pearl Rivers. He was promoted to surgeon after the first voyage and, allowing for port calls and time trading at Canton, he was away from home for more than a year at a stretch. His duties included full responsibility for the health and welfare of the crew and passengers. Conditions were primitive and his doctoring would have been rough and ready, though no less skilful as disease, sickness and injury struck perhaps weeks from the nearest port and at the mercy of the winds and tides. In such circumstances a man learned to rely on his own judgement, make decisions, act upon them and live with the consequences. The strict upbringing of a Dumfriesshire farm boy was being overlain with the disciplines of seafaring and the responsibilities of life and death decisions taken alone.

These were the years of the Napoleonic wars — of Trafalgar and Waterloo, with French and British ships cruising the sea lanes looking for war prizes. It was to be on William's second voyage, again aboard the *Brunswick,* that he came face to face with the enemy. They were on the homeward leg off the Sri Lankan coast in the Indian Ocean, when they sighted the sails of two French war ships. The slow moving *Brunswick* was no match for these cruisers and they were soon within firing range. What thoughts must have raced through the 19-year-old's mind as he prepared to receive the first casualties? He would hear the discharge of the French guns and feel the recoil of the *Brunswick's* in reply.

This, however, was to be the extent of the battle as his commanding officer, Captain Grant, lowered the colours as a token of surrender. William witnessed this and later saw a contingent of armed Frenchmen come aboard and sail their prize to a neutral port on the Dutch protectorate at the Cape of Good Hope. At the court of enquiry held to determine responsibility for the loss of the *Brunswick,* Captain Grant was severely censured and banned from future captainship in any of the company's ships.

About one month later, the ill-fated *Brunswick* ran aground near Cape Town, but thankfully all hands were saved. These events are significant to our story, because one passenger on this troubled voyage was an Indian merchant called Jamsetjee Jejeebhoy. The shared misfortune of these two young men started a friendship that would last a lifetime. From vastly different cultures and backgrounds, they recognised in each other an integrity and shrewd awareness of business matters that would later manifest itself in each helping the other form successful trading empires.

As surgeon's mate and later surgeon, William's rates of pay were £2.50 and £3.25 per month respectively. Not a princely sum, but this could be increased dramatically, as one of the few perks of being a ship's officer on these treacherous waters was the entitlement of *privilege tonnage.* In addition to his salary, an officer was allocated a certain amount of cargo space in the ship, which he could fill with goods on his private account. A captain, for example, was allowed 56 tonnes on the outward journey and 35 tonnes on the homeward trip. It is recorded that the average return from a China voyage for a captain was approximately £6,000 plus sea pay. William quickly learned to take advantage of the situation and always made sure he fully utilised his allowance of three tonnes. Indeed, many officers retired after several voyages to enjoy the benefits reaped from shrewd investment of their *privilege tonnage.*

During his seafaring years between 1802 and 1817, William Jardine established contacts in London, India and China. Never married, he had no family commitments to detract from the time-consuming activities of his expanding business. His dealings alerted him to the vast profits to be made buying boxes of tea, bales of silk, cases of oriental curios and possibly a chest or two of Chinese porcelain, *china,* for the eager public back in Britain. He also realised there was one item the Chinese treasured more than anything — opium. To appreciate the significance opium played in historical terms in general and William's career in particular, we should examine the overall trading picture at this time.

In the preceding century the British had perfected a most advantageous trade arrangement. British piece goods went to Africa, slaves to the Americas and on the last leg of the triangle, cotton, sugar, tobacco and rum back to the homeland. Industrialisation in Europe and impending abolition of the slave trade were threatening this trading cycle so India was targeted for manufactured products. China too, in the eyes of the merchantile machine, was ripe for the outpourings of the industrial revolution. China had the tea, silk and porcelain but, much to the consternation of the traders, was not much interested in what they had to offer in return. The Emperor Chien Lung wrote in 1796 to King George III in reply to a proposal for more trade, 'We possess all things. I set no value on things strange or ingenious and have no use for your country's manufactures.' What then was to be done with this Celestial Kingdom that restricted all contact to one port, Canton, on the Pearl estuary? The gentlemen of the East India Company resolved this by the export of opium from India to China. Another trade triangle had been created to the financial advantage of the industrial heartland of Britain albeit that the item of trade was an hallucinatory drug obtained from the dried juice of the unripe seed head of the poppy plant. In 1781, after carefully organised cultivation and preparation, the Company sent its first consignment to Canton, from the port of Calcutta.

In this insidious fashion the Chinese people were handed a prescription for disaster. Over the next 60 years the opium traffic increased dramatically and in 1833 the number of addicts had escalated to over four million. A Shan-si provincial administrator wrote at the time:

> The officers, scholars and people, soldiers and servants, the women and girls are all involved in this vice. Six-tenths of the people in the villages, and eight-tenths in the cities are infected by it. They look like ghosts. They get up late, they are indolent. If in an office, they neglect their duties. If they belong to the labouring class, they shirk their tasks. Things grow worse every year. The poor grow poorer, the weak grow weaker. What will be the future of Shan-si province in a few years? Only ruin is to be expected.

A generation was being sabotaged and systematically destroyed and one of the leading participants in supplying the cancer was the Presbyterian Jardine.

Opium's hallucinatory effects had been known for centuries but how and why China should succumb so willingly to this narcotic, is again a matter of history. It was a period of major degeneration in this inward looking society. The people's discontent came to a head with the White Lotus Rebellion (1796-1804). This uprising exposed the ineffectiveness of the corrupt governing bureaucracy and undermined the prestige of the Manchu dynasty. The people retreated into opium abuse as a therapeutic relief from the mental anguish of their country's decline. After some 20 years of this increasing addiction, economic problems began to surface due to the huge outflows of capital to fund the purchasing of the drug. Such was the scale of the damage, both social and financial, that the Emperor banned the importation of opium with the death sentence imposed on any Chinese found dealing in or smoking the drug. By this time however (1800) major industries in both Britain and India were being oiled by this celestial money. The British government via the East India Company resolved their moral conflict yet maintained the trade by withdrawing the monopoly rights and banning the Company's ships from carrying opium. The East India Company did, however, actively continue to produce opium for public auction.

William Jardine quickly saw the potential for enormous financial gain in this chain of events and resolved to exploit it fully. Leaving the service of the East India Company in 1817 he established himself as a China Trader. Based in Macau and Canton he traded in a variety of goods but concentrated more and more on the opium business. Some years later he was to make the acquaintance of a fellow Scot, James Matheson, who, although 12 years younger, had considerable experience and detailed knowledge of the China Trade. On the 1st July 1832, this enterprising pair opened for business under the name Jardine Matheson and Company in the tiny Portuguese enclave of Macau. Macau was ideally situated at the mouth of the Pearl estuary, some 160 km (60 miles) south of Canton. By uniting their considerable financial assets and organisational skills they rapidly became the leaders in this ignoble trade, acquiring a merchant fleet of the fastest ships, employing the best captains and crews.

The outflow of bullion became a torrent. By the late 1830s the trade in opium was probably the largest commerce of its time in any single commodity anywhere in the known world. The financial strain was likely to prompt the rulers in Peking to act. Skirmishes between the westerners and locals became more frequent and more serious. Forty-four-year-old Jardine anticipated trouble and knew his cause would be best served by lobbying where the real power lay — the Houses of Parliament, in London. In January

1839 he sailed for Britain for the last time leaving the firm in the hands of his partner, his nephews Andrew and David Jardine and a nephew of James called Alexander Matheson. On the 27th September of that year he gained an interview with the Minister in charge of the Foreign Office, the Irish peer Lord Palmerston. Men of similar age but from different backgrounds, they shared an awareness of the overall situation.

Back in Canton events were moving fast. In March (1839) High Commissioner Lin Tse-hsu had arrived from Peking. His brief was to flush out all corrupt officials and stop the drug trade once and for all. This tough, astute, 54-year-old mandarin distrusted all round-eyed barbarians and warned that foreigners and Chinese would be sentenced to death if they concealed that *dirty mud,* his description of opium. On his orders all trade came to a halt; ships were stopped and searched; access to food and servants was withdrawn from the foreign community in Macau; 20,283 chests were confiscated; the price slumped dramatically in India. Jardine and his industrialist cronies predicted a major recession. It was Lin's harsh treatment of the foreign nationals — which today would appear expedient and morally justified but in the 19th century was construed as arrogant — that in fact, prompted Lord Palmerston to listen seriously to what Jardine had to say. In a detailed confidential report Jardine explained how a military operation might be mounted to teach these infidels a lesson. This report not only made use of the Jardine Matheson Company charts, but detailed the layouts of the fortifications around the Pearl estuary. On the 19th March 1840 Lord Russell announced to a packed House of Commons that a military operation was at hand for reparation for insults to British subjects in Canton, payment for 20,283 chests of opium, and pressure for a firm treaty of security for the China Traders. The assembled naval force that Jardine and Palmerston planned consisted of 16 men-of-war, four armed steamers, and 27 transports carrying 4,000 Scottish (Cameronians), Irish, English and Indian troops. On the 7th January 1841 this armada struck the main defences south of Canton. The *Bogue Forts* fell in less than 24 hours. The assembled Manchu fleet was annihilated. Admiral Kuan sued for a truce. The British demanded and got the island of Hong Kong, an indemnity of $6 million Mexican dollars (approximately £30 million at 1987 prices) and trade re-opened at Canton. Gunboat diplomacy had worked! A few months later Jardine Matheson and Company erected the first stone building on the new British colony.

If we are to judge this Presbyterian entrepreneur who manoeuvred the war (later to be called *The First Opium War*) and founded a commercial conglomerate that today has interests worldwide and a turnover (in 1986) of US $1,335 million, we must avoid the temptation to assess him with the benefit of hindsight. His was a world of De Quincy's *The Confessions of an Opium Eater*, and of Coleridge's *Kubla Khan*, openly admitted by the poet to have come to him in an opium-induced dream. Perhaps he justified his empire funded at its conception from drug trafficking, knowing that temperance societies were as much against gin abuse as the twopenny packets of opium powder readily available over the counter in Britain. How else was the working man to escape his often dreary existence but with a few glasses of wine laced with opium? Laudanum, as it was called, was drunk by many as Britain at this time imported 300 chests annually. Since the use of narcotics was perfectly legal throughout the British Empire it is reasonable to expect this God-fearing Scot would view addicts as many today see alcoholics, believing their behaviour to be a sign of weakness and not a symptom of disease.

It should also be realised that in common with most of his peers, he would view the non-Christian Chinese nation with contempt, and the Chinese with their overt posturing would reinforce this view. The aware Jardine, however, should have known better. He had after all spent most of his adult life in the Far East. He would know about Chinese culture, how it had evolved and how it had served the people well. He would be aware that when opposing factions came into conflict a traditional face-saving formula was employed. Warring armies, rather than actually engage in physical combat, preferred to bang gongs, wave flags and fire cannon shot overhead in a great show of aggression. After such prevarication the weaker side would realise the hopelessness of their stance, pay over some *squeeze* and leave the bloodless battlefield, threatening to return should there be further trouble. Such were the ways of the inscrutable, accommodating orientals. Initially strange to the definitive logic of the western mind it would have a certain appeal to old hands like Jardine. As a doctor he would also be aware of the long-term effects of smoking opium, the emaciated bodies, the black teeth, the hollow dull eyes, sights common in 19th-century China. Back in London he would have heard the young Gladstone speak with some passion against his trade as his own beloved sister Helen was now a hopeless addict after taking the ubiquitous laudanum to dull a minor ailment. He would also read how Disraeli described him thus: 'Oh a dreadful man! A Scotchman, richer than Croesus, one Mr. Druggy, fresh from Canton, with a million in opium in each pocket, denouncing corruption and bellowing free trade.' Jardine's conscience it seems was not particularly troubled by this criticism. Buying opium in India was legal and sailing it off the China coast was legitimate. It was only when on sovereign Chinese territory that it became contraband. When called to give evidence to a House of Commons select committee he stated, 'When the East India Company were growing it, and selling it, and there was a declaration of the House of Lords and Commons with all the bench of bishops at their back that it was inexpedient to do it away, I think our moral scruples need not have been so very great'.

The latter years of William Jardine's life were tame compared to his tumultuous days in the East. He bought Lanrick estate in Perthshire, became a member of Parliament for Ashburton and succumbed to a terminal illness on the 27th February 1843. So ended a life that took full advantage of the 'Victorian Viking' ethics of commerce and industry. He succeeded in building his empire at the expense of many lives and never publicly atoned for being the leading perpetrator in the least defensible war Britain ever fought. However his contemporaries in the China Trade saw few shortcomings in the man. A eulogy written shortly after his death stated, 'His truth and honour were ever unsullied and unsuspected. No one who knew him could associate with his character anything unworthy. You saw in a moment that such things as meanness or pettiness were altogether unknown to him, and were evidently foreign to his nature, and such qualities could clearly find no entrance into his mind.'

In appreciating that no man is wholly good or wholly evil can anyone be viewed objectively, without some benefit of hindsight? The realistic Commissioner Lin had no such help when he risked great face by writing a pleading letter to the 'Queen over the water', Queen Victoria, 'Since a Chinese could not peddle or smoke opium if foreigners had not brought it to China, it is clear that the true culprits are the opium traders.' It must be one of the supreme ironies of history that this appraisal was addressed to a queen who, of all the long line of sovereigns, prided herself upon her Christian convictions and moral principles.

Commissioner Lin's letter was written at the second moon of the 19th year of Tao Kuang (1839). What might have happened had his logic won the day?

AUTHOR

Charles T. Walker is a civil engineer who has worked in the New Territories of Hong Kong for the past 11 years.

BIBLIOGRAPHY

Peter Ward Fay, *The Opium War*, Chapel Hill, 1975.
Jack Beeching, *The Chinese Opium Wars*, Hutchinson, 1975.
Geoffrey Robley Sayer, *Hong Kong 1841—1862*, Hong Kong University Press, 1980.
Dun J. Li, *China in Transition*, Van Nostrand Reinhold, 1969.
Captain A. R. Williamson, *Eastern Traders*, Printed privately for Jardine Matheson & Co. Ltd., 1975.
James Steuart, *Jardine Matheson & Co. (1832—1932)*, printed privately for Jardine Matheson & Co. Ltd., 1934.
J. Edkins, *Opium*, American Presbyterian Press Shanghai, 1898.
Israel Epstein, *From Opium War to Liberation*, Joint Publishing Co., Hong Kong, 1980.
Maurice Collis, *Foreign Mud*, Faber, 1946.
Colin Crisswell, *The Taipans*, Oxford University Press, 1981.
Nigel Cameron, *Hong Kong the Cultured Pearl*, Oxford University Press, 1978.
W. Scott Morton, *China Its History and Culture*, Lippincott Crowell, New York, 1980.
A. Wally, *The Opium War through Chinese Eyes*, Allen and Unwin, 1958.
Maggie Keswick (ed.), *The Thistle and The Jade*, Octopus Books Ltd., 1982.
The Opium War, Foreign Languages Press, Peking 1976.
Journals of the Hong Kong Branch of the Royal Asiatic Society.

ACKNOWLEDGEMENT

The author extends thanks to Jardine, Matheson & Co., for access to company literature.

CHAPTER 5

Mary Slessor
Eka Kpukpro Owo
(1848—1915)

James Buchan

It was September 1888. The young woman pegged down spreadeagled in the market-place of Ekenge township in the Calabar forests of West Africa would have known that nothing could save her. The chiefs had sentenced her to have boiling oil poured over her.

She would have been as amazed as everyone else when the torch-lit circle of onlookers silenced their excited chatter and the robed official, who was to carry out the sentence, turned away from the pot on the fire to face whoever had caused the silence. By straining against the cords that tied her she would have been able to see that it was only a frail-looking white woman. Hope of rescue would have vanished instantly.

The official went towards the interfering white woman. He was swinging a heavy iron ladle round his head. The white woman walked towards the official. At that moment her own life was more at risk than that of the condemned woman. But instead of showing fear, her eyes were bright with anger.

If, when they met, the official had struck her down with his ladle the white woman's body would have been thrown out to the scavenging leopards and that would have been that. But what was happening was entirely outside his experience. Women were third-class citizens. They had no rights except through their husbands or fathers. They had no say in anything. Yet here was one defying tribal law. He could not have been more surprised if the sun had appeared in the night sky.

This woman claimed to be a messenger from the white man's special God. Everyone knew that power and protection came from the gods. The knowledge was bred into them. In the month which she had spent with the tribe she had already shown amazing courage and she had been given healing powers no one else possessed. If he killed her then her God would take a terrible revenge. He stood aside.

Mary Slessor walked past him to where the head chief, Edem, was sitting and, fluently in his own language, told him what she thought of a tribal law which sentenced a woman to torture for giving food to a slave in her husband's absence.

Edem agreed to look again at the 'palaver' (case). Mary took charge of the prisoner. But the case was soon forgotten. The fate of a mere woman was nothing compared to this latest demonstration of the power of the white man's God.

Later, Mary, lying in her mud hut, went into the bouts of trembling which usually followed occasions when her sense of duty and her temper drove her to risk her life. 'Courage', she had written to a friend, 'is only the overcoming of fear by faith.' But although this was true for her in the long term, often in the short term it was explosions of the flaming temper, which back in the Dundee slums had won her the nickname 'Fire', that now both got her into dangerous situations and got her out of them.

That night, the relief of having survived her most dangerous encounter since she joined the tribe, was mixed with the excitement of seeing for the first time that perhaps her dreams were going to come true; that after spending 10 years training herself in Calabar to go out into the forests and live the primitive life of the townships, she was perhaps going to win enough influence over her chosen tribe to change its way of life and help it to make peace with its neighbours.

That her work in the forests would continue for another 28 years and her influence would spread over 1,000 square miles, and that when the British moved in to govern she would be their adviser on how to handle the chiefs as well as the chiefs' adviser on how to handle the British, would have been beyond her wildest dreams.

If anyone had told her that Mary Kingsley, the anthropologist, would describe her as having an influence over the tribes 'which is hers and hers alone,' and that the eminent historian, Margery Perham, would describe her as '. . . one of the greatest women of her generation,' Mary Slessor would have laughed her head off. For another of the personal assets which was essential to her in her work was a strong sense of humour.

But how had tribes, which had once traded contentedly together become so cruel and so dangerous? And how did a mill-lassie from the Dundee slums come to be in Calabar?

Calabar is now a province in the new Nigeria with a modern city of the same name. But at the beginning of the 19th century it was one of the most unattractive places on earth. It was not typical of the rest of Africa but only of those places on the continent which had been infected by the iniquities of the slave trade, and where the chiefs, far from doing away with ancient customs like human sacrifice — as practised in ancient times by several white nations — had made the treatment of their own people even more cruel.

In order to 'tell the truth' about Mary Slessor it is necessary to describe what Calabar was like immediately after the era of slave trading. Anyone who may consider this 'racist' is advised to read the books recommended at the end of the chapter which themselves contain bibliographies for further study.

For over two centuries the estuary of the two great rivers, the Cross and the Calabar, had provided a sheltered anchorage for the European slave-traders, who waited in their ships until the

Efik tribe, which owned the anchorage, had brought enough prisoners down the rivers to fill their holds.

The prisoners were first herded into stockades along the banks of the estuary to be examined by the ships' surgeons. Those who passed as fit for the voyage to America or the West Indies were then taken out to the ships in canoes and manacled to the benches in the holds on which most of them would remain for the voyage. Those who were considered too frail for the voyage were taken away by the Efiks, butchered, and their bodies left for the leopards and the birds.

It was an extremely profitable business both for the Europeans and the Efik chiefs. For the Europeans it had to be, because the mysterious malaria fever sometimes wiped out whole crews while they lay at anchor. No white man in his right senses would go near the place except to get rich. And for the chiefs there was the barter of enough guns to hold back the other tribes and force them to accept the Efiks as middlemen in the trading. They could also keep some of the best of the prisoners to form a warrior élite manning scores of war canoes for the tribe.

By the beginning of the 19th century the Efiks were one of the richest tribes along the Guinea Coast. But the cruelty of the trade had spread through their whole society and up the rivers also, and was destroying the cultures of the tribes of the interior. Before the slave trade set tribe fighting tribe for prisoners to sell, they had generally traded with one another in peace, but now no tribe could trust any other and no family could trust another family.

The Efiks had no ancestral ruler but were governed by the Egbo Order, a council of chiefs, which the Nigerian historian Professor Onwuka Dike describes as, 'the supreme political power in Calabar' at that time. It ruled by terror and he gives a list of the punishments which it meted out to offenders. These included '. . . crucifixion round a large cask . . . suspension by the thumbs . . . impaling on a stake . . . driving a steel rod through the body until it appeared through the skull . . . '.

The slave trade not only destroyed the culture of the Efiks, but it also perverted their religion. At the funeral of a chief it had always been the custom to kill a few wives and servants to accompany him into the spirit world so that he would be recognised as a chief. Now these ceremonies became orgies of killing. An Efik trader, Antera Duke, writing between 1785 and 1788, describes how 50 slaves were beheaded in one morning.

By 1810 Britain, which had been one of the greatest of the slave trading nations, had been forced by public opinion to oppose it. By then the Royal Navy had begun to seize slave-ships off the Guinea Coast and soon the slaves in the West Indies were set free. Their freedom gave a group of Scottish missionaries, who had been working among them since 1824, the idea of taking some of them back to West Africa to set up an African branch of the Presbyterian Church and attempt to undo the appalling damage which the slave trade had done to the tribes.

Since the Calabar chiefs were known, as Professor Dike writes, to have '. . . an avid desire for Europeanisation' and were petitioning London for a Protectorate and for 'God and Book', they were asked to invite a Scottish mission to join them. This they did. The Protectorate was refused but the mission, composed of Scots and Jamaicans, arrived in 1845.

Over the next 40 years, however, it failed to get beyond the towns round the anchorage. The Efiks had made an exception for the white missionaries and allowed them, unlike the white traders, to live ashore, but the chiefs would not let the missionaries go up the Cross River to the other tribes. And Beecroft, the British Consul for the area, who lived on the island of Fernando Po, warned them that if they tried to go up the Calabar River their lives would 'not be worth a moment's purchase'. He had tried to go up it himself and had been driven back by the Okoyong, a tribe of mercenary warriors.

The mission worked patiently on in the estuary towns and, with the help of the British, managed to get the chiefs of the Egbo Order to do away with cruel old customs like the killing of twin babies — one was thought to be the child of a devil and no one knew which one. They also practised the killing of wives and slaves at the funerals of chiefs as human sacrifices to the gods. But the missionaries could not reach the other tribes up-river who were still living in the appalling state to which the slave trade had reduced them.

Twenty-eight missionaries died during those first 40 years and even more were invalided home with their health ruined by the still mysterious malaria. James Luke, a mission historian, wrote, 'For years as each new worker arrived, he was absorbed at the base, played out, and sent home or fell; and the passing days were marked by new graves in old ground.'

Only a few missionaries gave up and went back to Scotland for reasons other than those of health. Most stuck it out until they died. But recruits understandably soon became few and the key to the forests for which the pioneers were praying was as elusive as ever.

Of course when in 1876 it arrived in the shape of a young woman with red hair no one recognised it. That an ex-slum-lassie would one day be described as 'dragging a great church behind her into Africa' by that same mission historian, would have seemed too unlikely even for a God who was known to have extraordinary ways of doing things.

Mary Mitchell Slessor was born in Aberdeen in December 1848. Her father, Robert, was a shoemaker. Her mother, also named Mary, was a weaver. They had seven children and when three of them died, the struggle to rear the surviving children Mary, John, and Susan, — Janie was born later — became too much for Robert and he took to drink. By 1859 he had drunk himself out of his job. The family moved to Dundee where Mrs. Slessor could find work and where Robert could make a fresh start.

In Scotland the 1840s were 'The Hungry Forties'. Crops were poor. The harnessing of steam was destroying the old cottage industries. To escape starvation people were packing into the cities in search of jobs. In Dundee the mill owners were beginning to make fortunes out of the new power-driven looms and the city was booming. Its population doubled and doubled again. Its Historical Society reports that in the 1850s the city was an insanitary place with heaps of animal manure, human excreta, and rubbish piled in the lanes and backyards. 'Adequate social services and accommodation simply did not exist.' Whole families, totalling over 30,000 people, were crammed into one-room homes called 'single-ends'.

This was the squalid, single-end world into which Mary Slessor arrived at 10 years of age. This was the world which taught her to endure the squalor of the forest townships, which, without her background, no white woman could have endured. When she was 11, Mary became a 'half-timer' working in the morning from 6 a.m. to 11 a.m. in the mills, then from noon to 6 p.m. in the evening in school. She wrote, 'at this time I was wee and thin and not very strong.'

Her father took to drink again, tried for a year to fight it, failed, and lost his job. Soon he was unemployable. Mrs. Slessor was a deeply religious woman. As her husband went steadily downhill she found more and more comfort in her Church, which distributed a magazine, *The Missionary Record,* carrying reports from overseas, especially from Calabar which in the 1860s was very much in the news because of the courage of the missionaries and their high casualties from fever. It was common practice for British children to take pennies to Sunday school to help the courageous in Calabar.

Mrs. Slessor would read these reports to her children and encourage them to play at teaching black children. She had an ambition for her son John to work in Calabar as a tradesman. The women who worked for the mission as teachers were usually drawn from the professional classes. An uneducated mill-lassie would not have been wanted. But Mary, like John, grew up knowing about the mission, about the problems which it faced, and about the climate.

However, by the time Janie was born, and she had moved into her teens, Mary's health had improved and on her own admission she had become 'a wild lassie'. Dundee mill-lassies were tough. They had to be. In the mills a mistake would bring a clout, and in school, to fall asleep, a strap over the hand. Then her father died suddenly and Mary, remembering the man who had played with her, was miserable. She too began to find comfort in religion. She tried talking to this Jesus of Nazareth and, to her surprise at first, she found he seemed to be listening. Soon she was chatting away to him in her mind any time, any place.

By now she was a full-timer, but an idea began to pester her: she was to go to night-school and improve her education. Her teachers found her exceptionally intelligent with a keen logical brain which quickly went to the heart of a problem. Soon she was reading about how her hero, David Livingstone, who had already survived hair-raising adventures, was back in Africa and about to set off on a new expedition to Lake Tanganyika.

James Logie, an elder of her kirk, was impressed by her intelligence. He began to lend her books and he and his wife began to teach the uncouth mill-lassie proper manners and speech. By the time she was 20 she was teaching in his Sunday school and helping him to run what we would call a youth club. She was also helping women with large families who could not cope. After her death, a member of the parish described Mary as, at this time, 'an angel of mercy in miserable homes'.

Then, in 1874, when she was 25, Mary heard of Livingstone's death. He had written, 'I direct your attention to Africa . . . I know that in a few years I shall be cut off in that country which is now open . . . . Do not let it be shut again. Do you carry out the work I have begun. I leave it with you . . . .'

Mary read the words again and again. A new and appalling idea began to flash up on the screen of her mind. She had known of her mother's ambition for John. But he had died two years earlier. All along it had been she, Mary, who was being directed to Calabar. The idea was ridiculous and, knowing what the mission faced, it frightened her stiff. She prayed about it and for a year she fought it. But there was no escape. From now on Mary Slessor would be in the grip of an ideal from which, 38 years later, only death in a mud hut in the forests would her part.

In 1875 Mary Slessor applied to join the mission. She was strongly recommended by Logie and, at her interview, impressed the mission board. She arrived in Calabar in September 1876. She wrote to a friend, 'I am now living among an entirely different class of people.' There were four ordained missionaries, four men teachers, and five women teachers, including Mary. At first she was tongue-tied and very conscious of being 'lower class'. She quickly took a 'scunner' (dislike) to Duke Town where the mission had its headquarters, in a white house outside the town.

By now the palm oil trade had replaced the slave trade and the traders who had been known as 'The Palm Oil Ruffians' were calling themselves 'The Gentlemen of the River'. The African chiefs, some of whom had adopted the titles 'King' or 'Duke' were also very much on their dignity. Mary found the protocol and the stuffy tea-parties, which the mission gave each week for the senior officers of the ships, a waste of time.

But when she was given three of the African staff to guide her and sent on a tour of the out-stations round the estuary she cheered up considerably. The forests with blossoms cascading from the huge fronds which dangled from the giant trees, the antics of the monkeys, and the brilliantly coloured butterflies and birds, fascinated the young woman from the mucky, smoky, streets of grey Dundee. On this tour she fell in love with the Calabar forests and she never fell out of love with them. They were to become the only home she knew.

However, she found the mission uniform of sun helmet, white blouse, voluminous black skirt, petticoat, stockings, and snake boots, as insufferable as she found the protocol. This was not surprising since the rivers, creeks, and swamps made the climate humid. The temperature sometimes soared to 35°C and never fell below 20°C even at night.

Back in Duke Town, she was so bored that she took to running races and climbing trees with the school-children in her petticoat. She hated the round of visits to the snooty wives of the chiefs and much preferred to work among the domestic slaves, whose ailments worried her. In her letters home she described how some of the slaves' children were covered in sores. Since the slaves did not speak English she quickly began to learn Efik. Her colleagues were surprised at how soon she was beginning to speak it.

After a few months she went down with malaria as did every missionary in Calabar. It was still thought that malaria was carried by the thick mists from the swamps and there was no preventative. Mary took it very badly and was delirious for days. It began to look as if she was going to be yet another of the recruits who would die in their first bout. It was some months before she could go racing and tree-climbing again.

Now she knew that to be a Calabar missionary meant fighting countless bouts of fever and by the end of her third year she was so run down that the mission sent her home to Scotland. It may not have expected to see her back again.

Mary, however, was determined to go back, and it seems that it was in Dundee that her keen mind examined why she had been so unhappy in Duke Town. She could see of course that the mission was still doing important work round the estuary towns. So what, for her, had gone wrong? Back in the slums she got her answer. The people there had always confided in her, whereas they had been tongue-tied in front of 'better-class' visitors, who sympathised, but had no idea what it was like to live in the slums.

Living up in the white mission house on the hill, wearing her mission uniform, eating imported food, and drinking water which had been boiled, she was no African: she was the equivalent of the well-meaning visitor to her slums. To have the same relationship with the people of Calabar as she had with her own people she must become an African. Before she left Calabar she had already been talking about going up-river to live in the forests. But only she had taken the idea seriously. Now, as she prayed about the idea, it became a definite plan. She would train herself to go up into the forests and live under the same conditions as the tribes who lived there.

She had heard a great deal about the Okoyong mercenary tribe; how they were at war with their neighbours; how they were of better physique and better fighters than the Efiks; how when there was no one else to fight they fought among themselves, just like the old Highland clans.

For some reason which she never really understood herself, she knew that her first task was to go and 'straighten out' the Okoyong. But when she mentioned her plan to Hugh Goldie, one of the mission's pioneers who had also come to Scotland on leave, he was horrified. He told her that the risks for a woman were appalling and that the mission would never let her run them. He was wrong.

By 1880 Mary was back in Calabar and in charge of the Old Town out-station. It had been closed because of lack of staff. In helping to repair the building she began to learn the methods which she would use to build her own huts in the forests. She had of course to discard her sunhelmet, cut off her sweat-soaked ringlets which got in the way, and began to wear a cotton dress and canvas shoes.

Next she took to eating only native foods and drinking water direct from the river. She began visiting villages deep in the forests, spending nights on mud benches in the huts which they lent to her. Sometimes, with her African team carrying her medicine-chest and food-box, she had to make journeys through the forests at night. When she heard the leopards snarling she prayed her special prayer, 'Oh Lord of Daniel shut their mouths.'

But in 1883 she nearly died of malaria and the mission put her on a ship for Scotland as her only chance of survival. Her return to Calabar was delayed until 1885 by the death of her sister Susan and the illnesses of her mother and Janie, both of whom died the following year. Mary told the mission, 'Now there is no one to worry about me if I go up-country,' and she pleaded to be allowed to go and join the Okoyong whose reputation for fighting was still as bad as ever. The mission had persuaded them for the first time to accept an African teacher, who had only just managed to escape from being chased for his life.

It took until 1887 for the mission to agree to her plans and until 1888 for the Mission Board in Edinburgh to agree. Then it took three visits to the tribe by Mary to get them to agree. The chiefs of the Ekenge township said they would have her on a trial basis. She was still very much on trial when she rescued the woman from the boiling oil.

Edem, the head chief of Ekenge, had allotted land to her and had said that the tribe would build huts for her on it. But for four months nothing had happened. Then one morning he sent for her and she found the land already cleared and an excited crowd waiting to hear just what she wanted. In her mind and in theirs she now belonged to the Okoyong. The women took to wearing cotton dresses like hers, and she went bareheaded and barefoot as they did.

She was determined to break down her tribe's isolation by getting it to trade with the other tribes. Her friend Chief Eyo of the Creek Town Efiks sent an invitation for the Okoyong to send a delegation with samples of their produce. But it took weeks for Mary to get them to accept it. Indeed when the day came, because they were warriors not boatmen, they overloaded the canoe and when they tried to launch it, it turned on its side. It took an explosion of the Slessor temper, in which she slung the swords at them, which she found among the produce, for them to ignore the warning of the river God and go with her.

The visit was a success. Peace was declared between the tribes. The Efiks and the Okoyong began trading, and soon acquiring European goods became more important to them than fighting. Instead they brought their disputes to her for arbitration.

By December 1889 Mary had completed her four-year term and was due for leave. But since no other missionary would risk taking her place with her unpredictable tribe, she 'drudged on' fighting off bout after bout of fever. In that year three more missionaries died. Dr. Rae, the latest of a succession of medical missionaries, wrote, 'An under-manned mission in such a climate means a high death-rate.' Within months he had himself died.

Sometimes Mary was so ill that the tribe had to bring her to Duke Town for hospital treatment. On one of these visits she met Charles Morrison who had joined the mission to train African teachers. He was a delicate, sensitive man who wrote poetry and was working on a novel. Like her he was a loner. They got on well together. They both loved books, and on her visits he used to read to her in hospital. When she went back to Ekenge they wrote long letters to each other.

By now it was not so much that she belonged to the tribe as that the tribe belonged to her. Any unusually beautiful grove or huge tree was special to them as a place of the spirits. The white messenger from God was also now special to them. Until she became special to the whole tribe the Ekenge warriors guarded her wherever she went. Now she could stop battles and riots simply by walking into the middle of them.

In October 1890 she had to accept leave to Scotland because she was so ill that she could hardly walk. Before she left Charles Morrison asked her to marry him and she agreed. But when she returned in March 1892 she found that Charles had been told that to remain in Calabar would kill him. The mission had ordered him home. He wanted Mary to marry him and to sail with him. She prayed about it and then decided that this she simply could not do. By now she and her ideal were one. She said goodbye to him and a year later heard that he was dead. Her colleagues thought that she had forgotten him. Events proved them wrong.

At Duke Town before rejoining her tribe, Mary had discussions with Sir Claud Macdonald, the Consul-General for Calabar, who had taken up residence there, when in 1891 the British had at last accepted the chiefs' invitation to move in and govern. He was in the process of appointing Vice-Consuls to supervise the work of the new native courts and he made Mary the first woman Vice-Consul in the whole of the British Empire.

Within five years, six more missionaries had died and five had been invalided home. The Mission Board decreed that there was to be no more expansion up the rivers. But the British had opened up the opposite bank of the Cross from the Okoyong territory. When Mary visited Itu, one of the principal trading centres on the other bank, the chiefs invited her to come and set up one of her mud church-cum-schools. They too wanted 'God and Book'.

Chiefs from as far as 100 miles away were now visiting Mary to get advice on handling the British and she had already met those from Itu. She felt that she must press on and open up as much territory as possible to the influence of Christianity. Two other missionaries went to live with the Okoyong, who said goodbye to the woman whom all the tribes now called *Eka Kpukpro Owo* (Mother of All The Peoples), with much weeping and wailing and too many gifts for the mission launch to carry.

On the other bank some of the tribes were still hostile to the British, whose officers always travelled with a military escort. They were soon amazed to see a barefoot white woman trudging along the new roads, which they were building, accompanied only by a group of orphans whose lives she had saved.

For the next 23 years Mary went deeper and deeper into the

forests, depending most of the time on the food which the Africans gave her. Twice she came out in crops of boils which were agony. Once all her hair fell out, but luckily grew back in again. By 1905, when she was 57, she could hardly walk and had to be pulled along by her orphans in what she called her 'rickshaw'. Three times she collapsed and the British doctors saw no hope of recovery. But each time the old leopardess proved them wrong.

Eventually towns from Ikot Ekpene to beyond Arochuku had copied her Itu 'spirit-house' and sent messages that now they were ready for her. Because she knew that, given the chance, the Africans could look after their own affairs, she trained teachers for them, and left them to run the schools themselves.

At last, in January 1915, time ran out for her. She died in a mud hut at Use near Itu. Over the years and the miles she had kept only what she and the orphans could carry. Among the treasured things which she carried down the years, the mission found the books *Eugene Aram* and *Sketches By Boz* in which she and Charles Morrison had signed their names side by side.

Mary Slessor is buried in the mission cemetery at Duke Town. When, in 1956, Her Majesty Queen Elizabeth visited Calabar she laid a wreath on the grave. The Calabar Church which the Scots founded is now one of the most flourishing in Africa. On their white choir-robes some of the women have a stencilled photograph. It is the face of *Eka Kpukpro Owo*.

AUTHOR

James Buchan is the author of two books on Mary Slessor and *Thatched Village,* the story of his boyhood in a primitive village between 1920 and 1935. He has also been a television writer and producer since 1951.

BIBLIOGRAPHY

Onwuka Dike, *Trade & Politics in Niger Delta*, Oxford University Press, 1956.
A. J. Latham, *Old Calabar*, Oxford University Press, 1973.
J. Buchan, *The Expendable Mary Slessor*, St. Andrews Press, 1980.

CHAPTER 6

Archie McKellar
The Forgotten Ace
(1912—1940)

Jim Foley

By September 1940 the Battle of Britain had reached a critical stage. Each day, swarms of enemy bombers and their fighter escorts were assembling over Calais and Boulogne, before setting course to bomb and strafe targets in southern Britain. Crossing the Kent coast they would encounter fierce opposition from the waiting Hurricanes and Spitfires of the RAF. Both sides suffered grievously.

The RAF, unable to train pilots quickly enough, was sending

inexperienced flyers into action, some with only a few hours' flying time in fighters. Since many airfields were under almost hourly attack by the Luftwaffe, heroic ground staff were performing miracles in the repair and maintenance of aircraft, often under battlefield conditions, and suffering heavy casualties.

From Manston came reports that airmen had locked themselves in the air-raid shelters and were refusing to come out, despite threats from their officers that they would be shot if they didn't. As a result, exhausted pilots were having to re-arm and refuel their own planes.

On 7th September, Air Marshal Sir Keith Park was stubbornly refusing to obey an order from the Air Ministry, instructing him to commence the immediate destruction of all his airfields, to prevent their use by invading forces. Instead, he wanted to use them to defend Britain to the end.

On that same, grimly anxious day, Archie McKellar was flying south with 605 Squadron, to be based at Croydon, a front-line airfield in the defence of London. . . .

Archibald Ashmore McKellar (the birth certificate records only Archibald McKellar, the Ashmore being added later) was the ideal height and build for a fighter pilot. Only five feet three inches tall, he had the stocky, fit body of a man keen on all forms of sport, and accustomed to hard physical work.

He was born in Paisley, Scotland, on 10th April 1912, at 4 Southpark Drive, the only son of John and Margaret McKellar. Less than three years later John McKellar moved his family to Glasgow, where he and his brother had established a plasterer's business.

Archie first attended Shawlands Academy as a primary pupil, and is remembered by former classmate James F. Brown, who thought him a 'great wee scrapper', who never looked for trouble, but when it came always gave better than he got. During one fight blood was pouring down his face from a cut above his eye, but young Archie still wouldn't give up — and eventually gave the bully a good hiding.

Archie was tough from an early age. He was born with both legs broken, and spent the first few months of his life enduring the discomfort of plaster casts. Growing up, he was an adventurous boy, and a cousin, John Fairley, remembers one of his escapades. Archie arrived home early from school one day to find his mother out and the door locked. At that time the family lived three floors up in a tenement block in Pollok. Undaunted, young Archie simply shinned up a convenient drain-pipe and got into the house through a window.

Hector Maclean, a fellow pilot on 602 Squadron, told me that Archie wasn't a keen scholar. 'This didn't surprise me,' he said, 'since Archie was essentially a man of action, who quickly grasped how many beans made five in a given situation.'

It was at Shawlands Academy however, that Archie's great interest in sport was fostered and encouraged. He eventually became a fine wing three-quarter, and is remembered by the Craiglea Rugby Club as having a dashing and spectacular style, combining quickness of the eye and mind with excellent co-ordination, and showing all the grit and determination to win that would later make him one of the RAF's greatest fighter pilots.

Archie's great wish on leaving school was to become a plasterer like his father. But John McKellar would have none of it. Instead, he got his son a job with a firm of stockbrokers, Miller and Cooper, who had their offices at 48 West George Street, Glasgow. Also working there as an office-boy was David Turner, now a retired farmer. He found Archie great company, and the pair had many laughs together. He has a vivid recollection of several impromptu rugby scrums conducted on the office floor when the boss wasn't around. David found Archie a hard man in a scrum, and says he had the bruises to prove it! One night, it seems, they went to the Plaza Ballroom. As David explained, those were the days when you could hire a partner for sixpence a dance, and he remembers Archie, immaculately dressed in his evening suit, going over to a girl and handing over his sixpence. What followed was the best exhibition of the fox-trot he'd ever seen. 'He was a great dancer,' said David. Years later, he was trimming a hedge when a smart sports car zipped by, then screeched to a halt and reversed up. It was Archie, still in his plasterer's dungarees and white from head to foot with the marks of his trade.

Like David Turner, Archie had probably realised that with the Depression looming, his office job was no longer secure, and he may have used this reasoning to persuade his father to take him into the family business as an apprentice plasterer. When his father reluctantly agreed to this, it was on the strict understanding that he would be treated exactly like any other apprentice, tea-making and dirty jobs included. Undeterred, Archie went on to complete a full trade apprenticeship, but in his final year he

71

decided to pursue another great ambition of his — to be a pilot.

Ever since boyhood, when he had read about the exploits of World War One aces like Mannock, Ball, McCudden, Billy Bishop and others, Archie had been determined that one day he would fly with 602 City of Glasgow Auxiliary Squadron.

On making discreet enquiries as to his suitability, he was told that his application was likely to be successful. Delighted, he asked his father for permission, only to be met by an outright rejection. 'Flying is far too dangerous an occupation, Archie,' John McKellar told his son. Bitterly disappointed, Archie then did something that was alien to his nature — he decided to go against his father's wishes, and to take flight instruction in secret with the Glasgow Flying Club at Renfrew, paying for the lessons from his own pocket.

He proved an apt pupil, if a little over-confident, and quickly gained his pilot's 'A' licence. To celebrate his success, he swooped low over his home in Bearsden, waggling the wings of the Tiger Moth, and at the same time, according to M. J. Elder, whose family lived close by, he dropped a box of chocolates to his mum as a birthday present!

A fellow pupil at the Glasgow Flying Club was Donald Jack, who described Archie as a natural flyer, who quickly became the club's star performer. It wasn't long before Archie's great skill and enthusiasm as a pilot was noticed by the then Commanding Officer of 602 Squadron, the Marquis of Clydesdale (later Duke of Hamilton), who promptly invited him to join 602.

On 8th November 1936, Donald Jack and Archie McKellar were commissioned together as Pilot Officers in the squadron. Later, Archie would gain his RAF 'wings' a few weeks before Donald, in the summer of 1937.

Like the others, he flew three weekends a month, plus two evenings a week in summer, and attended one evening a week in winter for ground training. According to Hector Maclean, Archie was always first to arrive at Abbotsinch on training days, and although he tended to push himself forward a bit, his enthusiasm was so infectious that none of the others seemed to mind.

Aside from work, the squadron had a fairly active social life, which Archie seemed to enjoy immensely. The winter dinner-dances were a great way of meeting new girls, and Archie took full advantage of this opportunity. John Fairley can recall Archie's mother showing him a large photograph of a stunning blonde

WAAF, whom she said was Archie's latest girl friend. 'She was an outstandingly beautiful girl,' said John. However, I was unable to confirm a reported engagement.

By May, 1938, Archie had become a Flying Officer, working up to operational standards on the Gloster Gauntlet. A year later, 602 Squadron was re-equipped with Spitfires, becoming the first Auxiliary squadron to have them. While learning to fly the Spitfire, Archie had a rather embarrassing moment. Not used to the retractable undercarriage, he simply forgot to lower the wheels and made a somewhat undignified belly-landing. Glen Niven, a former 602 pilot, remembers that day — and Archie — very well. Glen recalls him as a wee, ebullient, bouncing chap, always on the go and full of high spirits. After the incident, he arrived back at the crew-room with a huge grin on his face. 'Just put it on my mess bill as breakages,' he said.

When the war came, 602 Squadron was assigned to perform routine shipping escort duties in the Firth of Forth area, operating from Drem airfield in East Lothian. On 16th October 1939, however, they were alerted to intercept a force of German bombers heading for the Forth. As the Junkers 88s (JU88s) approached Rosyth dockyard, they were challenged by the Spitfires and Gladiators of 602 and 603 Squadrons.

Flight Lieutenant George Pinkerton and Flying Officer Archie McKellar latched on to one of the JU88s and chased it out over the Forth. Pinkerton fired first, and as the German fell towards the sea, Archie got in a second burst before it hit the water. It was the first enemy aircraft shot down in World War Two, and was credited to George Pinkerton.

Twelve days later, McKellar and others were investigating reports of enemy air activity in the Lothian region, when Archie caught sight of a Heinkel 111 (HE111) and immediately dived to attack it. His fire killed the rear gunner, and the stricken HE111 was then attacked by other Spitfires of 602 as it flew at low-level across the border countryside. It finally crashed six miles south of Haddington, becoming the first German aircraft brought down on British soil in World War Two. This victory was shared by several 602 pilots, and John Fairley still has a piece of the wreckage given to him by Archie.

Only a few weeks later Flying Officer McKellar was on patrol near Tranent when he spotted puffs of anti-aircraft fire in the distance, and immediately flew over to investigate. He found a

HE111, which he at once attacked, setting one engine on fire and killing the rear gunner. As the damaged HE111 attempted to land it was finished off by other pilots of 602 Squadron. Rightfully, though, the victory was given to Archie McKellar. It was his first full 'kill'.

This was to be his last taste of combat for more than eight months, and Archie found the lack of Germans irksome. 'We should be down in London,' he complained to his friend Hector Maclean, 'where the Huns will be coming in every hour.' Then he shook his head in frustration. 'It'll be all over by Christmas, and we won't get a look in.' Nevertheless, for Archie McKellar, the 'phoney war' period was a time to bring his great natural ability as a pilot to a point of near perfection. Frequent training in such things as mock attacks, interceptions, practice dogfights, all helped to sharpen the edge of his flying skills.

Archie's reputation as a crack pilot had been formed in his early days with 602, when fellow pilots dubbed him 'the little whirlwind' in recognition of his marvellous talent for quick thinking and inspired aerobatics. In Sandy Johnstone's opinion, no finer team-mate ever existed or ever will. 'Right way up or upside down, Archie was always there, flying alongside.'

Returning to Drem after a short detachment to Dyce, Aberdeen, the squadron found itself in company with 605 Squadron, newly arrived in Scotland after an arduous spell of duty during the Dunkirk battles. Though badly fatigued, the 605 pilots were now highly experienced air fighters, and 602 lost no time in learning about tactics and technique from them. Archie McKellar struck up a friendship with the 605 Squadron Commander, Walter Churchill, who was so impressed by the Glasgow man's enthusiasm and keenness, that when a vacancy came up on 605 he invited Archie to fill it. Archie accepted, and on 21st June 1940, he was posted to 605 Squadron as a Flight Commander, with the rank of Flight Lieutenant. Archie's arrival on 605 was like a breath of fresh air. 'He was such a bubbling, cheerful, effusive, happy-go-lucky guy,' said Chris Currant, a fellow pilot on 605. 'Always looking on the bright side, always ready for a laugh.' But when it came to flying, Archie was very serious indeed. His new squadron was equipped with Hurricanes, and to prove his complete mastery of this machine he gave a dazzling display of aerobatics over Drem airfield.

Then on 15th August, he was back in the war. Around 12 a.m.,

605 Squadron was scrambled to intercept a large formation of German aircraft approaching Newcastle from the south-east. Some time later, they spotted about one hundred 'bandits', consisting of HE111 bombers, with large numbers of Messerschmitt 110s (ME110s) acting as escort.

During this engagement, 605 Squadron accounted for eight HE111s, with three probables, Archie's personal score being three Heinkels down, with one probable. At the end of that month Flight Lieutenant McKellar was awarded the Distinguished Flying Cross.

This experience of combat on a large scale had only served to whet Archie's appetite for the 'real thing' down south. And when the move came, on 7th September, he was jubilant. After a brief refuelling stop at Abingdon, the squadron finally landed at Croydon around 6.30 p.m. Chris Currant remembers that night. 'They had set London ablaze, and it was a very unnerving experience to see the glow of the fires . . . and to hear the bombing going on. . . . I thought: "My God, we really are in the thick of it, we're really up against it."'

Next morning, after a sleepless night, the pilots of 605 Squadron were scrambled to intercept a huge formation of Dorniers, JU88s and ME109s in the Maidstone-Tunbridge Wells area. Archie McKellar, leading B Flight, carried out harrying attacks on the JU88s and the leading Dorniers. At the same time Chris Currant's flight made a port attack on the Dorniers. The tactics were successful, and the Germans turned for home without unloading their bombs. Although several Dorniers were damaged, no 'kills' were reported.

That night, Archie McKellar, with Pilot Officer Humphreys and Pilot Officer Forrester, 'borrowed' a Bedford truck and set out through the bomb-damaged streets of London for an evening's entertainment in the West End. Next morning, the Squadron Log reports: '. . . they returned in truculent mood, having found no consolation for lack of sleep, whereas we at Croydon slept soundly.' In less than 24 hours, Forrester would be dead and Humphreys seriously wounded.

Next day, 9th September, in the Maidstone area, Archie sighted a large formation of HE111s, escorted by some 50 ME109s, with about 20 ME110s guarding the bombers' flank. He decided to scatter the 109s first, shooting one down, before turning his attention to the bombers.

It was then that Squadron Leader Walter Churchill saw Archie turn up-sun and swing in to attack a tight formation of three Heinkels from behind. As he did so, the Heinkels also turned and headed straight for Archie. Closing at around 750 km (600 miles) an hour, Archie aimed a burst of fire at the leading Heinkel, which instantly blew up. The explosion knocked a wing off the machine on its port side, and both went down. At that moment the starboard Heinkel ran into Archie's hosing bullets, and with black smoke pouring from its engines, it appeared to rear up for a moment before it too plunged to the earth. With a single hail of bullets, Archie had destroyed three enemy bombers in as many seconds.

On 11th September, Archie McKellar and Pilot Officer Jones chased a Heinkel all the way to Beachy Head before shooting it down, the crew baling out. Earlier, McKellar had almost certainly put paid to another Heinkel. That night, despite several air-raids going on, Archie and his fellow pilots set off to enjoy a celebration dinner in the local Greyhound Hotel. Driving back, a bomb exploded only a short distance away, completely demolishing the local gas works. Shortly afterwards, four bombs fell quite close to a mess hut, but only one went off.

September 15th broke bright and clear, and by early morning it was evident that the Luftwaffe was planning a major assault. Just before 11.30 a.m., the Hurricanes of 605 Squadron were airborne, with orders to break up a pack of Dorniers, JU88s and HE111s heading for London. In the ensuing battles, Archie's 'bag' for the day was a Dornier 17 and two ME109s, one of the latter shot down near Croydon.

Later, in the early hours of 16th September, he made the squadron's first night 'kill' when he destroyed another Heinkel, after promising his controller a bottle of champagne if he could lead him to a German. The champagne was duly delivered.

Writing to Sandy Johnstone, he said that his night flying practice with 602 Squadron had been put to good use. 'I had the great luck to bag one of these Night Bastards,' he wrote.

The award of a Bar to his Distinguished Flying Cross came as no surprise. Already tagged 'Killer McKellar' by fellow pilots, the citation, to what amounted to his second DFC gained in less than a month, described him as being a particularly brilliant technician, displaying an excellent fighting spirit, who led his pilots with great skill and resource. It also mentioned his astonishing consistency:

eight planes destroyed in only eight days of fighting.

At the end of September, Walter Churchill left to take up a new command, and Archie was promoted to Squadron Commander with the rank of Acting Squadron Leader. On 9th October, the squadron was diverted to Westhampnet, where 602 Squadron was based. There, Archie had a brief but happy reunion with old friends like Sandy Johnstone, who recalls thinking how utterly weary Archie looked. Untypically, he complained that life at Croydon was hard going, with pilots flying up to four operational sorties a day, then being unable to sleep at night because of the bombing. According to Sandy, he was already showing signs of combat fatigue, but had refused to take leave while the battle was on.

Yet only a few days earlier he had scored one of his greatest triumphs. In only a few moments of savage fighting, Archie had disposed of four ME109s in quick succession, and later shot down a fifth.

On 12th October, one of his young Sergeant pilots was reported missing in the Romney Marsh area, and when no further word was forthcoming, his father and brother set out to search the area for themselves. They eventually found the crashed Hurricane, with the pilot's body still strapped in the cockpit. It would be Archie's duty as Squadron Commander to write to the family, expressing the Squadron's sympathy in their loss. Senior officers like Archie, often exhausted after a long day of air fighting, would sometimes sit up far into the night carefully composing such painful letters, at times trying without success to recall the face of the pilot they were writing about. This kind of strain, coupled with his daily task of leading the squadron into battle, was having its effect on Archie.

On 20th October, he downed one more Messerschmitt and damaged another. A few days later, 26th October, he repeated this success, and on 27th October, came his last official victory: a further ME109 shot down, believed to be his 21st victim.

Since his arrival at Croydon, less than seven weeks before, Archie had accounted for 17 enemy aircraft destroyed, and many others damaged, a feat rarely matched by any fighter pilot in any war. It established him clearly as an outstanding RAF ace in the Battle of Britain. Later, historians would award him a definite 16 destroyed, and place him at the top of the list of British pilots in the battle.

He seemed to lead a charmed life. Nothing ever went wrong for him. No matter how desperate the situation, he always came out on top, always triumphed against the odds. Yet, unknown to the others, for he would keep the knowledge to himself, the strain was becoming unbearable.

'We were weary beyond caring' recalled Peter Townsend. 'Our nerves were at breaking-point.' Archie knew this, and had at last agreed to take a short leave in Glasgow in early November. But it was not to be. November 1st was the last morning of his life. Chris Currant still remembers it vividly.

'I had just returned from a few days' rest, and was in the bathroom shaving when Archie came in. "Why are you up at this time, Bunny?" he asked. I said I was getting ready for ops that morning. "There's no need to, old lad," he replied. "It's all taken care of. I'm doing your turn this morning, so you can rest until the afternoon." He went out of the door', said Chris, 'and I never saw him again.'

Bob Foster recalls that it was a time when small groups of German aircraft would come over, more to harass the RAF than to achieve any specific objective. At 7.50 a.m. came a warning that such a nuisance raid was under way. 'Archie and I and others took off to intercept these chaps,' wrote Bob Foster, 'and we were somewhere down over the Kent side of the Thames estuary . . . and there was a general sort of dogfight. I didn't get anything, and I lost Archie, we all lost him, didn't know where he'd gone. When they found him he was further down towards the Kent coast, a long way down, so I think he was chasing something, and was probably jumped or bounced by others . . . and that was it . . . .'

So what happened? Some say Archie's vision was so poor that he may have accidentally rendezvoused with a group of 109s, mistaking them for his own Hurricanes. Certainly he took great care of his eyes, bathing them frequently, but this is not evidence of deterioration. After all, only three weeks before, he had shot down five ME109s in one day, hardly an indication of failing eyesight. Perhaps the explanation is simpler. Separated from his comrades, he broke the cardinal rule of air fighting and went 'hunting' on his own — paying the penalty with his life.

We shall never know exactly what happened. But shortly after 8 a.m. his Hurricane was seen to fall from high up, and eye witnesses said that it seemed to fly a crazy inverted circuit before crashing into the grounds of a mansion near Mayfield. There were reports that Archie had been killed by a single bullet. Whatever the truth, one of the greatest of all RAF aces was dead. Nearby, they found the wreck of an unclaimed ME109, thought to have been Archie's last victim.

'For days,' said Chris Currant, 'I just couldn't accept that he was dead. It seemed impossible.'

Shortly before he was killed, Archie had met the Secretary of State for Air, Sir Archibald Sinclair. 'Recently I met a young Scot,' said Sir Archibald later, 'who was proving himself a leader among leaders. His name was McKellar. It was quite apparent to me that he had the whole squadron with him. He was regarded with the greatest admiration and respect by his officers . . . I shall never forget meeting him . . . .'

Archie McKellar was one of Churchill's Few. A Scotsman, his contribution to victory in the Battle of Britain was extensive. The qualities nurtured in him by his Scottish upbringing, courage in adversity, steadfastness in the face of danger, regard and concern for his fellow man, all played their part in making him a valiant and skilful pilot, and a magnificent leader. Today, nearly half a century later, he is still remembered with great affection by surviving comrades of both 602 and 605 Squadrons. He was one of Scotland's bravest sons.

Archie was buried in New Eastwood Cemetery, Glasgow, on 6th November 1940. Among those attending were the Marquis of Clydesdale, and the Lord Provost of Glasgow, Pat Dollan. Several of his comrades from 602 Squadron were there, but for operational reasons, no member of 605 could be present. There were more than 100 wreaths, including one from his parents in the shape of a DFC and Bar. Others came from the girls in a Glasgow flower shop, and from the car park attendants at St. Enoch's station. There was also one from a lady calling herself 'The Knitter', who had apparently knitted many woollen garments for Archie. To this day, her identity remains a mystery.

In early November came the award of a DSO (Distinguished Service Order). Previously, on 31st October, Archie had been mentioned in dispatches by Fighter Command Chief Lord Dowding. The citation to his DSO stated that Squadron Leader McKellar's magnificent fighting spirit had proved an inspiration to his pilots, and that he led the squadron with outstanding courage and determination.

Early in 1941, John McKellar travelled to Buckingham Palace to receive from the hands of King George VI the high honours awarded to the son whom he had warned of the dangers of flying many years before. It was a very sad, yet very proud moment for him.

There is, however, a strange postscript to Archie's story. By a cruel irony, it had been decreed that the Battle of Britain should end officially at midnight on 31st October 1940. Since Archie was killed eight hours later, his name was not added to the battle Roll of Honour. Already, it seemed, Archie McKellar was becoming the forgotten ace.

AUTHOR

Jim Foley is retired from the Civil Aviation Authority and lives in Prestwick.

BIBLIOGRAPHY

L. Deighton, *Fighter*, Cape.
R. Wright, *Dowding and the Battle of Britain*, Macdonald.
A. Price, *Battle of Britain: The Hardest Day*, Granada.
V. Orange, *Sir Keith Park*, Methuen.
Cluett, Bogle, Learmonth, *Croydon Airport and the Battle for Britain*, London Borough of Sutton Libraries and Art Services.

ACKNOWLEDGEMENT

The author is indebted to Cluett, Bogle, Learmonth, and to the London Borough of Sutton Libraries and Art Services for permission to use copyright material.

CHAPTER 7

John Muir
A Protector of Nature
(1838 — 1914)

Marinell Ash

In 1867 a young Scottish immigrant to the United States set off on a walk that would change his life, and the lives of millions of other people in the years since. The man was John Muir, and although he had lived in the United States since he was 11, he had been born in Scotland in 1838. His Scottish childhood was crucial in shaping his life.

When I was a boy in Scotland I was fond of everything that was wild . . . . Fortunately around my native town of Dunbar by the stormy North Sea, there was no lack of wildness . . . . With red-blooded playmates as wild as myself I loved to wander in the fields to hear the birds sing, and along the seashore to gaze and wonder at the shells and seaweeds, eels and crabs in pools among the rocks when the tide was low; and best of all to watch the waves in awful storms thundering on the black headlands and craggy ruins of old Dunbar castle when the sea and the sky, the waves and the clouds, mingled together as one. (*The Story of My Boyhood and Youth*)

Muir never lost his awe at the power, beauty and complexity of nature, just as he never lost the influence of his Scottish upbringing: the ruined castle, the tales of Bruce and Wallace, the poetry of Burns and the language of the King James version of the Bible which his austere Calvinist father caused him to learn virtually by heart. Although later in life John Muir was not conventionally religious his attitude towards nature was deeply reverential, and his writing is permeated with the language of the Bible. From his religious father John Muir also gained a sense of his own destiny and righteousness, an intensity of belief that led him often to be seen (and to see himself) as a kind of prophet.

One evening in Scotland John Muir came home from school with his brother David to be told, 'Bairns, you needna learn your lessons the nicht, for we're gan to America the morn!' The Muir family arrived in Wisconsin and took up a homestead. Muir's father saw the land as a wilderness to be subdued at the cost of unremitting, backbreaking toil. John Muir was put behind a plough at the age of 12. In the summer he worked 17 or 18 hours a day but, in the midst of all this, he was able to observe nature closely — and contrast its lessons with the drudgery of the farm and the physical chastisement frequently meted out by his father.

This sudden plash into pure wilderness — baptism in Nature's warm heart — how utterly happy it made us! Nature streaming into us, wooingly teaching her wonderful glowing lessons. Here without knowing it we were still at school; every lesson a love lesson not whipped but charmed into us. Oh, that glorious Wisconsin wilderness! (*The Story of My Boyhood and Youth*)

Muir was also interested in mechanical things and while a teenager began making inventions, some of which were displayed at the Wisconsin State Fair. This led him eventually to the University of Wisconsin where he spent several happy years, although he left without taking a degree to study in 'the university of the wilderness'.

By now the American Civil War was raging. Muir did not wish to fight and spent the next few years wandering in Canada and the United States. Only two years after peace had been declared at Appomattox he set out on what he called his 'Thousand-Mile Walk to the Gulf of Mexico' right through the most devastated lands of the former Confederacy. On this journey John Muir travelled light; but his Scottish background went with him, for he carried a plantpress, comb, brush, towel, soap, change of underclothing along with a copy of Burns's poems and a *New Testament*.

When he reached the gulf on the west coast of Florida he crossed to Cuba, planning to go to South America, but he was unable to find a ship. Instead he decided to visit California for a year or two to study its flora and fauna and visit the Yosemite Valley. John Muir did not know it then, but he had finally set out upon the journey that would shape the rest of his life. When he arrived in San Francisco he asked a passer-by the way out of the city.

'But where do you want to go?' the man said.

'To any place that is wild.'

With a Cockney friend he crossed San Francisco Bay and walked south through a pass into the Great Central Valley. Muir recalled that the view over the valley to the Sierra Nevada mountain range beyond was 'the most beautiful I have ever beheld'. He was drawn, irresistibly, towards the distant mountain range. In *The Mountains of California*, Muir wrote, 'It seemed not clothed with light, but wholly composed of it, like the wall of some celestial city. Then it seemed to me that the Sierra should be called, not the Nevada or snowy range, but the Range of Light.' John Muir spent his first summer in the Sierra Nevada working with a shepherd, driving a flock from the foothills into the forests and valleys of the mountains. He continued his practice of keeping regular journals that are full of lyrical and glowing descriptions of what he found there. Already Muir was aware of the threat posed to wilderness by uncontrolled development. Even his flock of sheep he viewed in the light of a biblical plague in the pages of his journal.

10 July: On through the forest ever higher we go, a cloud of dust dimming the way, thousands of feet trampling leaves and flowers . . . [the sheep] cannot hurt trees, though some of the seedlings suffer, and should the woolly locusts be greatly multiplied,

as on account of dollar value they are likely to be, then the forests, too, may in time be destroyed. Only the sky will then be safe, though hid from view by dust and smoke, incense of a bad sacrifice (*My First Summer in the Sierra*)

At the end of the summer Muir returned to the Great Central Valley but already he had noted in his diary, 'For my part I should like to stay here all winter, or all my life, or even all eternity.' He returned to the Sierras as soon as the snows cleared the following year and took various jobs in the Yosemite Valley which allowed him freedom to explore the mountains and forests in long, demanding and solitary walks.

But John Muir was not cut off from the rest of the world, nor did he cut himself off. He had, like so many Scots, a good conceit of himself, and was not backward in putting himself and his ideas forward. His solitary explorations had led him to a theory about the formation of these mountains that involved him in one of the great scientific controversies of the 1870s. How had the great valleys of the Sierras been formed?

The California State geologist, Josiah Whitney, had written in the official guide book to Yosemite that the valley had been formed in some cataclysmic earthquake. From his first summer in the Sierras Muir had been convinced that the mountains and valleys had been shaped by the slow, relentless, grinding action of glaciers. As he said, 'the bottom never fell out of anything God made.' The only way to prove his theory was to find a glacier at work in the Sierras. In 1871 he succeeded, by following traces of a glacier's retreat in the striations of the rock face, and found the glacier itself. His discoveries were reported in the *New York Tribune* in 1871 and the young naturalist began to attract attention. In that same year the ageing transcendentalist philosopher, Ralph Waldo Emerson, one of the great heroes of Muir's life, visited him in Yosemite. It was a decisive visit for both. Ever afterwards, when asked who were the men who most influenced him, Emerson included John Muir.

In his journeys through the mountains Muir travelled light. He usually carried little more in his knapsack than tea and bread and — like generations of Scots on the move — oatmeal. In 1879, however, he made a different journey — by ship to Alaska to explore the forests, mountains and, above all, the glaciers, especially those emptying into the sea at a place named by the Indians, 'Big Ice-mountain Bay' (later called Glacier Bay). The huge Alaskan ice sheets were to become the second great passion of John Muir's life, so that when he was adopted into a local Indian tribe he was given the name 'Great Ice Chief'. Glaciers were at the forefront of his thoughts, therefore, when Muir returned on his only trip to Scotland in 1893.

> Edinburgh is, apart from its glorious historical associations, far the most beautiful town I ever saw. I cannot conceive how it could be more beautiful. In the very heart of it rises the great castle hill, glacier sculpted and wild, like a bit of Alaska in the midst of the most beautiful architecture to be found in the world. . . . From feeling lonely and a stranger in my own native town . . . I am a Scotchman and at home again. (*Private Letters*, 1893)

During the years he explored mountains and glaciers from California north to Canada and Alaska, John Muir stored up his experiences and impressions in his notebooks. These journals were later revised and published as articles beginning in the late 1870s, when John Muir's philosophy of nature first reached a wider audience. Man was not necessary to nature, but nature was necessary to man. He must not dominate or change it, but instead be open to the lessons it could teach and the experiences it brought.

Muir's feelings about wilderness were deeply religious, but conventional creeds had no place in the beauty and majesty of nature, which he saw as a higher spiritual reality. In one of his books John Muir tells a story against himself — and by implication against conventional religion — when he describes an encounter with a Douglas squirrel. It's a passage that represents Muir's nature writing at its best.

> The Douglas is the squirrel of squirrels, flashing from branch to branch of his favourite evergreens. . . . One never tires of this bright chip of nature — this brave little voice crying in the wilderness. . . . One calm, creamy Indian summer morning I was camped in the pine woods of the south fork of the San Joaquin where the squirrels seemed about as plentiful as ripe burrs. I whistled a tune — curious to see how (one squirrel) would be affected by it. The instant I began to whistle he darted up the tree nearest to him, and came out on a dead limb opposite me and composed himself to listen. . . . I sang or whistled 'Bonnie Doon', 'Lass o' Gowrie', 'O'er the water to Charlie', 'Bonnie woods of Craigie Lee', etc. all of which seemed to be listened to with bright interest, my Douglas sitting patiently through it all, with his telling eyes

fixed upon me until I ventured to give the 'Old Hundredth', when he screamed, turned tail and darted with ludicrous haste up the tree out of sight . . . as if he had said 'I'll be hanged if you get me to hear anything so solemn and unpiny.' (*The Mountains of California*)

Despite his lack of orthodox Christian beliefs Muir naturally resorted to the language of the Bible in his writing, especially when he was deeply moved, or dealing with things about which he felt strongly. His great love was trees. In the early 1870s he had begun to trace the extent of the Sequoia forests — the giant California redwoods. The effect of these trees on Muir was overwhelming. In one of his letters he writes, 'Do behold the King in his glory, King Sequoia! Behold! Behold! Seems all I can say. Some time ago I left all for Sequoia and have been and am, at his feet, fasting and praying for light, for is he not the greatest light in the woods in the world. I wish I were . . . descending from this divine wilderness like a John the Baptist . . . crying, "Repent for the kingdom of Sequoia is at Hand!" '

And that is exactly what John Muir did. He came down from the high places like a second prophet John to preach the gospel of nature and — on a more practical level — to fight for the protection of his beloved wilderness.

In the late 19th century the mountains and forests of California were seen by many as a resource to be exploited. Timber companies, for example, met immigrants off the boats in San Francisco, paid them to take out 160-acre homestead claims and sign them over to the company who then systematically stripped the land of its woods. In the Sequoia groves the giant trees were too big to be cut down, so they were dynamited from the earth. But for John Muir logging was not the biggest threat; sheep were.

In February 1876 the Sacramento *Record Union* newspaper carried an article: 'God's first temple: How shall we preserve our forests?' It was John Muir's opening shot in a long campaign to save the forests of America for future generations. His argument was an ecological one — a century before ecology became fashionable: the woods must be saved not just because they were beautiful, but because of their relation to climate, soil and water — and people.

John Muir had reached a turning point. Although he would continue to return to the Sierras he could no longer live there. The price of his new life was exile in San Francisco. Then in 1880 he married and settled down on a fruit ranch belonging to his father-in-law. His Scottish shrewdness made him a good businessman, but despite summers spent in the Sierras, he found the ranch work irksome. Nevertheless, his happy marriage and the success of the ranch gave him stability and, eventually, the financial security with which to continue to write and speak and campaign. From a small study at the top of the wooden, Victorian house overlooking his orchards at Martinez, California, a stream of articles flowed, destined for such well-known American journals as *The Century* and *Harper's Monthly*. In 1894 John Muir's first book, *The Mountains of California* appeared. He became the living symbol of the growing conservation movement in the United States.

In 1889 Muir had joined the influential editor of *The Century* magazine for a camping trip in the Sierras. Around a campfire in Tuolomne Meadows the two men discussed the possible setting aside of the Yosemite Valley as a National Park. The editor undertook to see that the proposal was brought before the Congressional Committee on Public Lands in Washington, D.C. In the following year Yosemite National Park was created. In 1891 the United States Congress established the first forest reserves which became the basis of the American National Forest system. In 1892 John Muir was instrumental in setting up the Sierra Club, which continues to be a major force in the American conservation movement.

Despite all this success, however, Muir often despaired of ultimate success. He recognised that laws alone could not protect nature; what was needed was a fundamental change in human attitudes. That this change has, in some measure, taken place over the ensuing century is largely due to the force and power of Muir's writings. Many of his books have remained in print virtually from the time they were published and sell today in ever greater numbers.

In 1901 John Muir found a new ally in Theodore Roosevelt who had just become President of the United States. The two men went for a short camping trip in the Sierras in 1903; a decisive four days in the history of the National Parks and Forests of the United States. Not much is known in detail about that weekend — beyond the fact that Roosevelt was thrilled to wake up one morning to find his blankets covered in four inches of snow. John Muir said, 'Camping with the President was a memorable experience. I fairly fell in love with him.' The feeling was mutual.

Roosevelt returned to Washington fired with a new enthusiasm. During the eight years he was American President, National Forest land increased from 46 million acres to three times that size. Yosemite Park was enlarged, by the inclusion of the Mariposa Grove of Sequoia trees. The number of National Parks was doubled — among the new parks was the Grand Canyon. As the President said: 'We are not building this country of ours for a day. It is to last through the ages.'

Ironically, however, it was about this same time that the city of San Francisco applied to the Federal Government for permission to dam one of the most beautiful of the Sierra valleys — Hetch Hetchy — to provide a fresh-water reservoir for the city. Muir was furious and, as usual, resorted to biblical imagery:

> These temple destroyers, devotees of raging commercialism, seem to have a perfect contempt for nature, and instead of lifting their eyes to the God of the Mountains, lift them to the Almighty Dollar.
>
> Dam Hetch Hetchy! As well dam for water tanks the people's cathedrals and churches, for no holier temple has ever been consecrated by the heart of man.

Nevertheless, in 1913 the bill to dam the Hetch Hetchy Valley was passed and construction began in the following year. It was the greatest defeat of John Muir's life and may have hastened his death from pneumonia in 1914. But the destruction of the Hetch Hetchy Valley had led Muir to see that the National Forests and Parks — if they were ever to be safe from such breaches — must be brought under unified control. A bill to create a National Parks Service was brought before Congress and was eventually passed in 1916.

Alistair Cooke has called the American National Parks system the greatest and most successful example of state socialism in the world — lands owned and administered by the state for the benefit and use of its citizens — and this model has been widely imitated and followed throughout the world in the 20th century. John Muir's legacy is now worldwide and he would be proud of this, for from the beginning he saw himself and his relation to wilderness as, in a real sense, cosmic. Inside the cover of one of his early journals he had written: 'John Muir, Earth-planet, universe'.

In his native country of Scotland there are no National Parks, although large areas have been set aside as nature reserves, including — in 1976 — the North Sea coast along which he used to play as a boy. 'The John Muir Country Park' features a wide variety of habitats from cliff and grassland to sand dune and saltmarsh and contains a nature trail, along with opportunities for sea fishing, horse riding, golf and walking. His birthplace in Dunbar has now become a small museum. In July 1987 the recently formed 'John Muir Trust' purchased a 3,000 acre site in Knoydart, as part of its aims 'to conserve and protect wild areas in Scotland'.

It is fair that Muir should be honoured in his own country for, as he foresaw, conservation has become a global issue; as one problem is solved others arise. In Muir's beloved California wilderness the problem now, ironically, is over-use. In some senses Muir's advocacy of wilderness has been too successful; too many people go to it and, in seeking its solitude and lessons, destroy what they seek. Also, much conservation thinking nowadays is as much concerned with management as preservation. This continuous change and development is something that Muir would have regarded as being as natural as the ceaseless flow and change of nature he recorded in his journals: 'from form to form, beauty to beauty, ever changing, never resting'.

On the other hand, the commercial (and energy) pressures upon the habitat have grown to sizes and complexities that John Muir could never have imagined. John Muir Country Park is now virtually in the shadow of the atomic electricity generating station at Torness.

Yet John Muir's message remains timeless. He knew that this would be so: 'A man in his books may be said to walk the earth long after he has gone.' The problem still is not just the protection of nature, but bringing people into a proper relationship with the world about them: 'Most people are *on* the world, not *in* it — have no consciousness, sympathy or relationship to anything about them — undiffused and separate and rigidly alone like marbles of polished stone, touching but separate . . . .'

Today John Muir's legacy can be found not just in his writings and ideas, but in the landscape itself. In his adopted state of California there are more places named for him than any other person. In his own lifetime a stand of coastal redwood trees north of San Francisco was set aside as John Muir National Monument (1908). The Pacific Coast Trail that traverses the coastal range from California to Canada is called the John Muir Trail. The High Sierras are marked by similar namings: Muir Meadows, Muir Pass, Muir Peak, Muir Crest, Muir Grove. Another name was added to the California map in 1966 when his ranch house at Martinez, California, was taken over by the National Park Service as the John Muir National Historic Site. In his childhood home of Wisconsin there is a Mount Muir, a John Muir Park on the campus of the University of Wisconsin and Muir Lake Scientific Area. In Glacier Bay National Monument in Alaska his explorations are commemorated at Muir Inlet and Muir Glacier. A college and several schools are named after him, as are a Sierra butterfly (*Thecla muiri*) and Sierra plant, 'the mousetail' (*Iversia muiri*).

John Muir lies buried under a plain headstone in a private graveyard near his ranch; he designed a simple image for the stone — a Scottish thistle. In a way this design is a symbol of the whole of Muir's life in America. Although he displayed many of the characteristics of the successful immigrant in America, he never became completely American. John Muir remained at heart a Scotsman. He was clannish towards his fellow countrymen (and distrustful of the Irish) and he prided himself in his Scottish speech, and the Scottish language, which he liked to claim had, 'an affluence and delicacy of fibre such as no other branch of the English language has yet attained. These qualities are most fully illustrated in expressing affections — the life of a pure love-illumined home.'

In Muir the essential Scottish characteristics — 'grit, skill and invincible determination and principle' — were leavened by the ambiguities of the Scottish conscience. He had grown up in a household where, as he later angrily recalled, 'we could never do what we most like to do but only what we like least.' It was only by breaking away from this childhood that the other, more positive qualities of the Scottish conscience could come into play. 'Scotch conscience' was a hard teacher; it both made him and scarred him.

Throughout his life John Muir was aware of himself as a Scot in America, standing at one remove from his adopted country. This meant he could speak and criticise with an added force due to his emotional distancing from the political and economic system of the country whose natural landscapes he loved. Being a Scot in such a mould did not make John Muir an easy character and he had many enemies amongst commercial interests and developers, and their friends in government. For this reason a proposal to name after him one of the National Parks in the California Sierras was abandoned; it became instead, 'King's Canyon'.

But the other side of his character meant that John Muir, for all his conscience-bred sense of righteousness and duty, had little personal vanity. How could he, in the face of his transcendent vision of the vast and unending continuity of nature, be vain? Even death itself was a part of this continuous process of change. Towards the end of his life John Muir returned in his thoughts to that first thousand-mile walk to the Gulf of Mexico. What he wrote about it could have been an epitaph for that simple stone gravestone at Martinez — and for the whole of his remarkable life.

'I only went out for a walk and finally concluded to stay out till sundown. For going out, I found, was really going in.'

AUTHOR

Marinell Ash is a Californian-born Scottish historian who lives and works in Edinburgh.

BIBLIOGRAPHY

Frederic Badè, *The Life and Letters of John Muir*, 2 volumes, Houghton Mifflin Co., Boston, 1924.

Stephen Fox, *John Muir and his Legacy: The American Conservation Movement*, Little Brown and Co., Boston, 1981.

Holway Jones, *John Muir and the Sierra Club: The Battle for Yosemite*, Sierra Club, San Francisco, 1965.

Tom Melham, *John Muir's Wild America*, National Geographic Society, Washington DC, 1976.

Herbert Franklin Smith, *John Muir*, Twayne's United States Authors Series, New York, 1965.

Edwin Way Teale (ed.), *The Wilderness World of John Muir*, Houghton Mifflin Co., Boston, 1954.

Frederick Turner, *Rediscovering America: John Muir in his Time and Ours*, Viking, New York, 1985; Sierra Club Books, paperback, 1985.

T. H. Watkins, *John Muir's America*, Graphic Arts, New York, 1981.

Linnie Marsh Wolfe, *John of the Mountains; The Unpublished Journals of John Muir*, Houghton Mifflin Co., Boston, 1938.

Linnie Marsh Wolfe, *Son of the Wilderness*, New York, 1945.

91

BOOKS BY JOHN MUIR

The Mountains of California, London and New York, 1894, and various subsequent editions including Anchor Natural History Library paperback, Garden City, New York, 1961.

My First Summer in the Sierra, Houghton Mifflin Co., Boston, 1911, and subsequent editions.

Our National Parks, Houghton Mifflin Co., Boston, 1901, and subsequent editions including University of Wisconsin Press paperback.

Stickeen, the Story of a Dog, Houghton Mifflin Co., Boston, 1909, and subsequent editions.

The Story of My Boyhood and Youth, Houghton Mifflin Co., Boston, 1913, and subsequent editions including University of Wisconsin paperback, Madison, 1965; Canongate, Edinburgh 1987.

A Thousand Mile Walk to the Gulf, Houghton Mifflin Co., Boston, 1916; paperback edition, 1981.

Travels in Alaska, Houghton Mifflin Co., Boston, 1915, and subsequent editions.

The Yosemite, 1912, and subsequent editions, including Anchor Natural History Library paperback, Garden City, New York, 1962.

CHAPTER 8

Sir William Collins
Philanthropic Publisher
(1817—1895)

Brian Fraser

To most Scots the name 'William Collins' will immediately bring to mind the famous and outstandingly successful Scottish publishing firm. There can be few Scots in the world today who have not read a Collins book or Fontana paperback, or, perhaps only a Collins Bible or Dictionary! Those who refuse to read for pleasure will, doubtless, have been subjected to Collins school books in their earlier years.

In this sketch of Sir William Collins we can see something of the rapid development of his firm in the late 19th century, but interest in the man goes far beyond his commercial fame. Sir William was not only a man of business, he was a significant public figure — a famous Lord Provost of Glasgow and friend of Gladstone; he was a Free Churchman of some influence in the religious life of late Victorian Scotland; and he was a quiet, but effective, promoter of charitable and educational work amongst the young and poor of Glasgow.

Sir William Collins was a man of his time and his story is that of a typical breed of Scot 100 years ago — the prosperous Victorian 'entrepreneur', devoting his time to civic and philanthropic work and bringing to this work a deeply held Liberal, non-conformist, evangelical outlook.

William was born in Glasgow on 12th October 1817. The country was recovering from the Napoleonic Wars and the city of Glasgow, in the midst of an industrial revolution which was to make it the second city of the Empire, was no longer 'that dear green place' admired by Daniel Defoe. Industrialisation and immigration had led to insanitary over-crowding where 'King Cholera' could reign without effective opposition.

William's father, like many others, was set on business expansion and, at the time of his son's birth, was in the throes of establishing a small printing and publishing business. William senior had come to the city from the village of Pollokshaws, south of Glasgow, with his wife, Jane Barclay, an amiable woman from Paisley, and had become involved in education before being attracted to the publishing world. He had opened a private school in Campbell Street in 1813 with successful day and evening classes. At this time Glasgow was becoming something of a literary centre, with the emphasis on religious publications. Collins was moving in the right circles and received fresh impetus in his ambitions when he was successful in his moves to bring the famous Dr. Thomas Chalmers from Fife to the Tron Church.

Chalmers was to remain a lifelong friend and when he became the founder of the Free Church of Scotland of 1843 at the 'Disruption' the Collins family followed him out of the Church of Scotland, initially to the new Free St. John's Church in Glasgow. Meanwhile, Collins set in motion his plans to enter the publishing world with the support of Chalmers who was becoming a prolific writer.

In 1819, William Collins opened a bookshop at 68 Wilson

Street, Glasgow and a small printing works nearby at 28 Candleriggs. Initial success led to the first Collins school book in 1821, on commercial arithmetic. The business expanded despite various financial setbacks and before long established another base in London.

It was into this world that William junior was born. With a younger brother and sister dying in infancy, William was destined to follow his father into the family business. He was educated in Glasgow to the necessary standard but was apprenticed into the firm as soon as possible. By the time he was 30 years old he had been made a partner and his marriage to Annabella Glen, followed by the birth of two sons, ensured continuity of the now nationally known firm of William Collins and Son.

William senior died in 1853 by which time he had made an impact, not only on the publishing world, but on the social and religious life of the city and the West of Scotland. This stemmed primarily from his support of the temperance movement which was growing with evangelical fervour and which was to absorb the interest of his son.

The Collins family became the first members of Britain's first Temperance Society, giving sterling support to Robert Kettle, the Methodist pioneer of the temperance movement. In 1830 (a year in which almost 9,000 Glaswegians were charged with being drunk and disorderly!), William exhorted the citizens of Edinburgh to 'arrest the progress of that plague' so that 'Scotland would again rise in the right of her moral grandeur, a glory among the nations'. For the next few decades, as William junior was taking his place in Glasgow society, the situation showed no improvement. Intemperance was so rife that the committal rate in 1853 for drunkenness and disorderly conduct in Glasgow was one for every 22 of the population! The proliferation of drinking dens and the public spectacle of hordes of drunken wretches being rounded up by the local police as they staggered into the city centre streets made a long and lasting impression on William.

William junior continued where his father had left off and gave much time and effort to the campaign for total abstinence. Temperance was, of course, much supported by many including Thomas Chalmers who, when Minister of the Free Church in 1824, apparently had 44 bottles of whisky in his cellar, together with an array of wines and spirits! However, *total abstinence* was another matter. In all his later civic and philanthropic work, William was always eager to practice his firm temperance views — leading to the unfortunate nickname of 'Water Willie'.

After his father's death, William continued as sole partner until 1865 when his two assistants joined him on the Board. Three years later his two elder sons became partners and the business expanded at an even greater rate. By 1880 a limited company had been formed with the shares all held by the family. The firm was now the largest of its kind outside London and, by William's death in 1895, was employing over 2,000 people. However, William Collins's influence on the world was no longer confined to business and temperance.

In 1868 William entered local politics as a member of the City Council for the fifth ward. He was to be returned without opposition on four successive occasions. In 1873 he became a magistrate and a member of the Licensing Court! It is said that he acted here with strict impartiality, to the extent that he offended temperance members by voting new licences to people who had lost their previous premises through no fault of their own. In 1877 he was elected Lord Provost of his native city.

What kind of public figure was William Collins? In appearance he was a gaunt, ungainly man without his father's gift of oratory. Contemporary sources paint a rather forbidding picture of him, but with probably some exaggerated journalistic malice. The *Bailie,* a kind of Victorian *Private Eye,* emphasises his basic principles of 'retrenchment and reform' while another journal of the same ilk, *Fairplay*, states that: 'In his uncompromising opinions he is as stern as an old Puritan, and, about as lovable.' However, we must look beyond this jibing at a public figure, to which we are not unaccustomed, to estimate William Collins's real contribution to the community.

His period of office, as a councillor and later as Lord Provost, is marked, not by an exhibitionist promotion of popular policies, but by meticulous scrutiny of issues and determined implementation of improvement schemes.

There was certainly much scope for improvement in the social fabric of later Victorian Scotland. Nowhere was this more so than in the densely packed, commercially vibrant city of Glasgow. When William Collins assumed the mantle of 'first citizen' in 1877, Glasgow and its suburbs contained almost three quarters of a million people, far outstripping any provincial city in the United

Kingdom. Although great strides forward had been made in the previous two decades as far as public health and communications were concerned the city's industrial and commercial progress had not been matched by housing improvements. The old city centre around the Gallowgate and Saltmarket continued to be a congested and disease-ridden warren of some 50,000 people occupying 90 acres. Little wonder that Dr. Chalmers's successor at the Tron Kirk described the area as: 'The wretchedest, foulest immoralest corner of Scotland . . . one mass of moral and physical filth, the worst under the canopy of heaven, a seething sea of sin and devilry and bestiality. . . . '

The powerful City Council headed by William Collins continued the move towards greater parkland and new housing which was to be a feature of the city to the present day but the continual waves of immigration from Ireland and the Scottish Highlands left the housing problem critical. The damaging effect of overcrowding and poor sanitation were to lead William Collins into much philanthropic work with the many 'improvement' agencies in the city both during his term as Lord Provost and in later years.

William's official Council work concentrated on finance as might be expected from his own commercial success. Although he was potentially an 'advanced' Liberal, his attitude to public finance was positively conservative. He took a 'Thatcherite' approach to local authority expenditure, attempting to ensure value for money for the ratepayer. It is said that no financial vote in the Council or its Committee was allowed to proceed without his closest scrutiny. He even involved himself in all official appointments to avoid any possibility of excess manpower. His crusade for effective public expenditure appears to have cooled somewhat as his term of office proceeded. Perhaps he realised that the problems of the city required considerable investment by a Council which was hardly spendthrift. One of his notable achievements was the unspectactular but nonetheless useful consolidation of the accounts of all the various municipal trusts.

There was one revolutionary, if not exactly popular, way in which William Collins saved public money. For the first (and possibly the last) time the temperance ideal was applied to all civic functions. No drinks! During his term of office the City of Glasgow used iced water for refreshments at civic functions.

The magazine *Fairplay* exclaimed: 'Oh those awful dinners: Three years of them made many a worthy Bailie almost forswear public service forever.'

Perhaps this policy explains why the Prince of Wales (not noted for his moderation) stopped at Hamilton Palace in January 1878 to be entertained by the Lord Provost of Glasgow. This does not, of course, infer that William Collins was a killjoy. Indeed he pioneered a novel series of civic functions designed to bring together and acknowledge various sections of the city's population. These functions took the form of a 'soiree' or 'conversazione' with large groups being entertained with music at buffet suppers in the Municipal Chambers or the magnificent St. Andrew's Halls. For example, in the first year of William's term of office he acted as host at the following:

December 1877	—	musical and scientific festival for 1,600 leading citizens.
January 1878	—	entertainment for 1,500 of the city's poor on New Year's Day at the City Hall.
February 1878	—	conversazione for 1,600 of the city's Christian workers.
March 1878	—	conversazione for 1,400 of the city's professional classes (including a personal address on temperance!).

This period in the city's history, of course, was not without its economic as well as social problems. Although unexcelled in shipbuilding, textiles and heavy engineering, the city suffered from nationwide commercial depression of the late seventies and eighties. A feature of this was the disastrous collapse of the city of Glasgow Bank in October 1878 with the ruin of most shareholders and the sentencing of the manager and directors in the High Court. William Collins, undoubtedly shocked to the core at such commercial catastrophe, immediately set about organising a relief fund for the unfortunate account holders. The first substantial contribution was from his own pocket.

Although an avowed Liberal, Collins decided not to take his political career further when he completed his term as Lord Provost. With excellent credentials he could, one imagines, have entered Parliament. As a friend of Gladstone, supporting him strongly in his famous 1884 Midlothian campaign and acting as his right-hand man when he was installed as Lord Rector of Glasgow University in December 1879, he would have had the opportunity, but decided against.

Perhaps the most significant contribution of William Collins to the community comes neither from his public office or business position but from his encouragement and tangible support of religious and social groups in their work with the young and poor of the city.

To call William Collins a man of his time is to see him as a public figure engaged in the social philanthropy of the Victorian period. There were a great many successful industrialists and professionals in Victorian Scotland who considered it their religious and social duty to provide for the less fortunate. To some this was a formal acknowledgement of their own place in society but to William Collins it was more than a gesture or formality. He was to involve himself in a great variety of organisations which came into being to protect the masses from the worst effects of Victorian 'laissez faire' attitudes.

The need for missionary work amongst the young and poor in late 19th-century Scotland was nowhere more evident than in William's own city of Glasgow. His influence in the city's public affairs as first citizen was later continued in social and religious affairs. William was an elder (a member of the ruling Kirk Session) in the city's College Free Church. The influential composition of this particular Church can be gauged from the fact that a meeting of its Kirk Session would constitute a quorum of the Glasgow Chamber of Commerce! Situated in the West End beside the training college and headquarters of the Free Church (later Trinity College), William was a driving force in the Church's evangelical outreach to the working classes who were spreading west from the old city. Inspired by Moody and Sankey's American evangelical campaigns in the 1870s, William brought his substantial experience (and financial resources) to bear on the 'improvement' agencies hard at work in the city.

One of these agencies was the Association for Promoting the Religious and Social Improvement of the city which was concerned with both the social problems of the poorest classes and their non-attendance at any kind of public worship. It identified a total of 138,000 such persons in 1871. The fact that the poorest of the working classes had no interest in church attendance reflected a common enough situation throughout the country. However, William Collins set himself to put this right, as far as it was within his power. The formation of evangelical groups to seek out the 'lapsed masses' across the city had his blessing and support.

At the same time, William supported the growing Working Men's Evangelistic Association which had been formed in 1869 to bring about 'the religious and moral improvement of the working classes'. Working mainly in the East End of the city, this organisation carried out house visitations and provided free suppers and Christmas treats as well as Sabbath meetings and Bible classes. In the summer, evening services were held in a marquee on Glasgow Green (hence the origin of the 'Tent Hall' evangelical meetings which continue to the present day).

These groups of social reformers were noted for their evangelical fervour of the more radical Protestant type, which was reflected also in the temperance movements and Band of Hope Union. All these accorded with William Collins's outlook on life; the need for moderation, high moral values and social control. He was not, however, a mere onlooker, making the necessary contributions to charitable funds. Although still heavily involved in his booming publishing business he took part in the day-to-day affairs of these organisations. He was a director of the United Evangelistic Association and a leading light in its finance committee. Not content with this, he involved himself in the Association's missionary activity encouraging Dr. William Sommerville and his son on their overseas work. Dr. Sommerville was to return to Glasgow to later form the 'Girls Guildry' at the Free Anderston Church — the beginning of female uniformed youth organisations.

William Collins took a particular interest in the various organisations for young people in which Scotland, and especially Glasgow, was leading the world. He encouraged the growth of the Boys' Brigade whose founder, William Smith, was a member of Collins's own Church, and began his first Company in the College Free Church's mission hall in North Woodside Road. Collins was one of the principal subscribers to the fund which allowed William Smith to give up his business and become the full-time leader of the world's first uniformed youth organisation. William was also a supporter of the Glasgow Young Men's Society and helped to liquidate its debt in 1877 when it combined with the Glasgow YMCA. He became honorary Vice-President of the

Glasgow United YMCA until his death, leaving it a legacy. The publishing firm continued William's subscription to the YMCA after his death.

William Collins was at the peak of his activity when the country saw the introduction of its compulsory education system in 1872. Scotland had been the envy of the world with the widespread post-Reformation system of parish schools and its four ancient universities (twice as many as England!) for the 'lad o' pairts'. Now, however, the universal state provision of schooling required a proper system of organisation and accountability. The new School Boards faced a tremendous task, particularly in a city like Glasgow with a large number of school-age children. The Glasgow School Board would require substantial expertise in implementing its statutory obligations and who better to be one of its leading members than William Collins?

The first Glasgow School Board contained 15 seats and William Collins was one of the six Free Church and United Presbyterian Church members. They set to work with a flourish, ensuring that, before the end of the decade, elementary education would be available for those between five and 13. Ten schools were opened by 1874 with a further 20 added each year throughout the 1870s. William Collins, as a representative of both the Church and the ratepayers, took particular concern to avoid extravagance but he was enthusiastic about the spread of educational provision. At every turn, of course, he took the opportunity to promote temperance teaching in the school curriculum!

Despite all his activity for the people of Glasgow, William continued to expand his business and it cannot be said that William Collins and Sons had suffered from their Chairman's involvement in civic affairs. But how did the man relax? Did he never re-charge his batteries? Well, as so often happens with busy public figures, little is known of William's social or leisure life — perhaps because there would have been so little of it. He did manage in later years to get away from it all for short spells, with a house in the country and a steam yacht to afford him his great recreational pursuit of sailing. A leading member of the Royal Northern Yacht Club, he was often observed sailing among the Western Isles, when not attending to his business or the affairs of the people of Glasgow. His advocacy of open spaces spilled over into his official work and, as a member of the Glasgow Improvement Trust, he was instrumental in the creation of the open square at the Royal Infirmary and Glasgow Cathedral.

By this time William was a Justice of the Peace and Deputy Lord Lieutenant of the County of Lanark and the City of Glasgow. He had been knighted in 1881 for his public service. In 1893 Lady Collins, his second wife, died, and from this time Sir William's health began to fail. However, he continued to attend to the affairs of his business with as much rigour as possible. In 1895 he moved temporarily to a house at 6 Melville Street, Edinburgh, while his Glasgow home underwent extensive repairs. While out walking in Edinburgh he contracted a chill which developed into influenza. Before long pneumonia had set in and, at the age of 78, Sir William Collins slipped peacefully out of what had been a hectic life. He was brought back to his native city and buried in the necropolis, close to the cathedral and his own printing works in Cathedral Street. Fittingly his grave, close to that of his father, is overlooked by the huge statue of John Knox.

Sir William Collins handed on a thriving business to his son, the third William Collins. The company continued its development and expansion with a wide range of children's books, and the famous Collins Pocket Classics. Sir William had already overseen the impressive success of the Collins diaries and bibles which are 'best sellers' to this day. In the 20th century the company's impact on the world of books has been no less spectacular. The third William Collins was succeeded by his nephew, William A. Collins IV, who presided as Chairman, over a remarkable expansion overseas. His brother, Godfrey, emulated his great-uncle by entering public life — at national, rather than local level. He is well remembered in Scotland as Member of Parliament for Greenock for 26 years and as Liberal Chief Whip in the 1920s. A Cabinet Minister in the early 1930s, he went on to become Secretary of State for Scotland. Knighted, like his great-uncle before him, Sir Godfrey Collins took the family name again to the forefront of public affairs. After the Second World War, the business continued to expand and moved from its premises in Cathedral Street, Glasgow, to its new, spacious accommodation at Bishopbriggs.

The William Collins Group are today publishers and printers of international distinction with a current turnover approaching £150 million. Expansion continues apace and Sir William would have been delighted to see in 1988 the re-establishment of the firm as a major force in North America, taking a 50 per cent stake in the prestigious American publishing house, Harper and Row. As the largest stationery and book manufacturing business in the Commonwealth, the company owes much of its pre-eminent position to the repeated success of its leaders. In Sir William Collins, a standard was set in both commercial and public affairs which might have been difficult to follow but was indeed followed.

Sir William stays in our mind, not as a warm, hearty Glaswegian, but as a scrupulous, caring citizen whose severe demeanour, like many of his Victorian contemporaries, hid a wide range of activity for his fellow men. His own workforce held him in high regard and in 1887 were given by Sir William the 'Collins Institute' built and equipped for educational, social and recreational purposes. The water-fountain erected on Glasgow Green, appropriately enough by Sir William's temperance colleagues, to his memory pinpoints only one of his areas of activity. A comprehensive memorial to the work of Sir William Collins cannot be erected in stonework. How could one depict a lifetime of service to business; to education; to social reform; to Christian mission; and to the civic affairs of a great city?

The life of William Collins is both extraordinary and yet typical of a breed of Scotsman — dour, hard-working and innovative. His achievements in business and public life are still obvious today. Behind these 'official' achievements, however, we can see the other typical Scot — compassionate, concerned for his fellow men and determined to channel his success for their good.

AUTHOR

Brian Fraser, who lives in Eaglesham, Scotland, is Director of Personnel at the University of Glasgow and also lectures in Modern History.

BIBLIOGRAPHY

D. Keir, *House of Collins*, Glasgow & London, 1952.
C. Brogan, *The Glasgow Story*, London, 1952.
C. A. Oakley, *The Second City*, Glasgow, 1967.
J. M. Roxburgh, *The School Board of Glasgow 1873—1919*, London, 1971.

The Bailie, Nos. 1—108 1872—1976, Mitchell Library, Glasgow.
Fairplay, Nos. 33—221 1899—1966, Mitchell Library, Glasgow.
Glasgow Scrapbook, vol. 2, Mitchell Library, Glasgow.

CHAPTER 9

Chief Ronald (right) with his cousin Keith.

Ronald MacLennan
The Stormy Petrel
(1925—   )

Colin Crisswell

It would be hard to imagine anyone less like a professional killer than Ronald MacLennan of MacLennan, the 34th Chief of the Clan MacLennan. He appears at first sight to be a typical Highland gentleman, kindly, courteous and good humoured, his conversation punctuated by rumbles of laughter from deep in his throat. Ronnie does not quite fit the picture of a proud and arrogant clan chief but he would certainly pass as a benign family doctor or a slightly eccentric professor. At the same time it soon becomes clear that he has some exceptional qualities. Like all Highlanders, he is a great story-teller and enjoys talking late into the night. As he speaks of his visions of the future, of his plans for his clan and his belief that he has an, as yet undefined, role to play in bringing about world peace, the listener is caught up in the magic of his words and convinced by the force of his enthusiasm. It is only later that practical difficulties come to mind. Ronnie would have been a great preacher, as, indeed, were some of his ancestors.

As a young man, Ronnie never professed any interest in following in their footsteps and indeed any chance that he might follow a conventional career was shattered by the onset of the Second World War. The exigencies of war were to decree that Ronnie would become a trained assassin operating behind enemy lines, known to friend and foe as 'The Stormy Petrel'.

Ronnie was born in Edinburgh in 1925. He spent much of his early life in the Highlands and it was from his grandfather that he learned the melancholy history of his clan. The MacLennans have one of the oldest authentic pedigrees in the western world, for the clan can be traced back at least to AD 565 to Finan, the tutor of St. Columba, who came to Scotland in that year. Sometime around the sixth century, the MacLennans, together with other Gaelic clans, settled along the west coast of Scotland, displacing the native Picts. The principal seat of the MacLennans was in the vicinity of Kintail. However, although the MacLennans were of ancient royal Celtic descent and claimed both renowned warriors and ecclesiastics among their ranks, they were never a numerous clan. Not surprisingly, in view of its history of desperate struggles against more powerful clans, it is disastrous defeats that feature most prominently in clan memories. One of these was the Battle of Drumderfit in 1372. A party of marauding MacLennans was laying waste to the lands around Inverness. However, the Provost of Inverness was a wily man and he sent them barrels of whisky as a peace offering, with the result that most of them were in no state to resist a counter-attack in which many clansmen, including Chief Gilligorm MacLennan, were killed. The ruin of the clan was completed at the battle of Auldearn in 1645. The MacLennans were bearing the standard of Lord Seaforth fighting in opposition of the Marquis of Montrose. The tide of battle turned in favour of Montrose but unfortunately a runner sent to the MacLennans with the order to retreat was killed before he could deliver his message. The MacLennans stood firm around the standard but were cut down one by one by Montrose's cavalry until only Ruairidh was left. He spurned an offer of honourable surrender and was then shot dead. The loss of the chief and 18 of his captains was a serious blow to a small clan and James Boswell, writing of his travels in Scotland with Dr. Johnson, noted that the clan widows, like the Scythian ladies of old, married their servants, the MacRaes, who thus won dominance in Kintail. Although Ruairidh had a young son, who later became a general in the Swedish army, the demoralized survivors never proclaimed him chief. The decimated clan played little part in the Risings of 1715 and 1745 and in later years many remaining MacLennans emigrated to Canada and Australia.

This was the story told to Ronnie by his grandfather who impressed upon the boy that he was the direct descendant of Chief Ruairidh. He gave his grandson, born to a family without wealth, member of a clan without lands or a chief, an extraordinary commission — to claim the chiefship, now lapsed for over 300 years, re-unite the clan, and realize the ancient prophesy of the Brahan Seer by restoring the clan to its rightful home in Kintail. Ronnie was no ordinary boy and he accepted his grandfather's commission. But the realization of this dream was to be delayed by the outbreak of the war.

Ronnie suffered a serious head injury in the later stages of the war and his recall of the stirring events in which he took part is fitful and uncertain. There is also a reluctance to attempt to bring back to the surface memories so painful that, in order to retain his sanity, Ronnie had to bury them deep in his subconscious. Official records are not much help. The British authorities then and now have never been willing to admit that they trained men specifically as assassins. That they did so is certain. The 'official' history of British military intelligence* refers briefly to Operation Ratweek, a European-wide operation in February 1944 aimed at assassinating Gestapo officers, but the details are still confidential and may never be revealed. A reconstruction of Ronnie's experiences is like trying to put together the remains of a shattered vase from which many of the pieces are missing.

When the war began Ronnie was still attending Boroughmuir Secondary School in Edinburgh. His school holidays were spent

* F. H. Hinsley, *History of British Military Intelligence in the Second World War*, H.M.S.O., 1979.

with relatives in Ullapool and it was here in 1941 that he met and fell in love with Greta, the daughter of the captain of a Norwegian fishing boat engaged, like the *Shetland Bus,* in the highly dangerous business of running an escape route from Norway to the north of Scotland. At the height of the war, when the future seemed at best highly uncertain and at worst disastrous, people acted impulsively without thought of the consequences. The young lovers decided to marry but Greta insisted that they should return to Norway on her father's boat *Nuri* just long enough for a traditional exchange of vows in the village church. After their arrival in Norway, word of this crazy venture leaked out, and the entire wedding party was arrested by the Gestapo as they left the church. Ronnie never saw Greta or her father again and he learnt that they died in the hands of the Gestapo. He himself was questioned and tortured but after several weeks he was able to escape in the confusion caused by a British bombing raid. Ronnie is uncertain of where precisely he was imprisoned but RAF records reveal that, in the summer of 1942, a night raid by four squadrons of Halifaxes was made on the *Aasen Fiord* near Trondheim, with the German pocket battleship *Tirpitz* as the target.

After his escape from the hands of the Gestapo, Ronnie, who could speak some Norwegian, was picked up by the Norwegian Resistance. He was smuggled down to Helsingbor in Sweden on a timber boat and from there, with help from the Danish Resistance, he was taken on the escape route back to Britain. Ronnie was still only 18 but his experiences in the previous months had aged him beyond his years. Superbly fit, familiar with Resistance operations, with some knowledge of Norwegian and Danish, and burning with a desire for revenge, the young volunteer made an ideal recruit for SOE (Special Operations Executive). He was trained in demolition work and in the techniques of guerrilla warfare becoming, in his own words, 'a killing machine'.

Early in 1944 he was dropped by parachute near Flensburg on the German-Danish border with instructions to co-operate with a Danish Resistance group known as the *Tre Makere* (the Three Partners), headed by Chris Christiansen, in an operation in connection with Operation Ratweek. The group successfully ambushed and killed a high-ranking Gestapo officer, Ronnie escaping by a hair's breadth from his pursuers through thick forest. With the aid of the Danish Resistance, Ronnie returned to base a few weeks later. D-Day was at hand and Ronnie's next mission was to Belgium where, under the code name 'Stormy Petrel', working closely with members of the SAS, he carried out demolition work behind enemy lines. He was caught up in the Ardennes offensive in the winter of 1944. Although he sustained head injuries in the fighting, he succeeded in leading a small party of encircled Allied troops to safety. This exploit earned him the *Croix de Guerre* from both Belgium and France and the highest Polish award, the *Virtuti Militare,* belatedly awarded to him in 1982 by Count Nowine-Sokolinicki, the Polish President in exile, together with a commission granting him the rank of Brigadier General in the Polish Armed Forces.

Ronnie's injuries, which caused a spell of temporary blindness, led him to be withdrawn from operations in Europe. He was by now well-known to the Gestapo and, as a security precaution, he was given the identity of a MacLennan from Australia who had recently been killed and to whom he bore a close resemblance. However the war in Europe was drawing to an end and Ronnie's services were not needed there again. His desire for revenge was still not burned out and he volunteered to go to Burma but arrived in the East too late for active service.

The war was finished and trained killers were not only unemployable but also a potential embarrassment. Ronnie, still not 21 and now holding the rank of staff sergeant, was summoned to the War Office where he was told that the 'Stormy Petrel' was dead and that his exploits would never be recognized by the British authorities. Officially he was classified as a 'parachute instructor'. All that could be done for him was to offer him a new life. Ronnie was given three choices: he could return to Scotland, go to the university of his choice anywhere in Europe, or he could go to Australia. Unsettled by his experiences, Ronnie had no desire at this time to return to Scotland. He decided to enrol for a physical education course at the University of Copenhagen where he would be among friends from the Danish Resistance.

Ronnie completed his course at Copenhagen in 1949, and in that year represented Denmark in the Lingiad Gymnastic Games at Stockholm. In vacations his gymnastic ability enabled him to earn some extra money by performing in a circus. He was still uncertain what to do with the rest of his life, feeling that he had some mission to perform, impatient to begin it, but unsure of what it was. However, the call of his homeland was strong and so

Ronnie returned to Scotland where he obtained a teaching post at the Royal High School, Edinburgh. His holidays were spent walking in the Highlands, where he was much attracted to the remote village of Shieldaig on Loch Torridon. He obtained permission to build with his own hands a small wooden house in a deserted hamlet on a small bay, a mile or so from Shieldaig. Here, planting and tending his small but exotic garden, he felt at peace with the world for the first time for 10 years. As a small boy Ronnie had been inspired by the words of his grandfather and now, in this peaceful bay, he recalled these words again. After years of uncertainty the road ahead was clear; he must fulfil his grandfather's mission 'to go out into the world, do good and unite the clan'. Ronnie discovered that in the sixth century one of his forebears, St Maelrubha, had a cell practically on the same site as his house and it is to this that he attributes the spiritual guidance that he experienced there.

In an interview with the Lord Lyon King of Arms, Ronnie learned that in order to have any chance of bringing the title of Chief of the Clan MacLennan out of abeyance after 300 years, he would have to undertake research into the history of the clan that was likely to take over ten years. With the singlemindedness that had characterised his career as an undercover agent, Ronnie set to work on this daunting task. By his efforts, undertaken in his spare time at his own expense, he was not only able to lay claim to the chiefship but he also completely revised and considerably extended the history of the clan, which hitherto had only existed in the form of short and largely erroneous accounts in standard works of reference. An important stage was reached in 1968 when he was granted matriculation of arms by the Lord Lyon's Court. However, before he could be recognized as chief, it would be necessary for him to win the support of an established clan parliament. With this in mind Ronnie, aided by an ever-growing band of kinsfolk, set about to form the Clan MacLennan Association.

Meanwhile Ronnie had continued with his career as a teacher and lecturer in physical education and physiotherapy both in Scotland and Denmark. Somehow he found time to work for good causes. Before the 'Outward Bound' concept became widely known, he took groups of underprivileged adolescents on climbing expeditions in the Highlands. One notable fund-raising feat which he performed was to take a kayak through 50 miles (80 km) of dangerous open sea from Ullapool to Stornaway. He was also a widely known performer and teacher of the art of Scottish dancing. It was while performing for a party of German tourists aboard a cruise ship at Ullapool that he realized that all his wartime hatreds had gone. That phase of his life had completely finished. His mission now was first to work for the clan and then for the broader cause of better international understanding.

The energy, enthusiasm and high spirits of Ronnie Mor, or Big Ronnie as he was known in Gaelic, were irresistible. MacLennans around the world responded to his lead and by the early 1970s over 15,000 MacLennans and bearers of sept names from Britain, Canada, the U.S.A., Australia, Holland and South Africa had joined the clan association. The first clan gathering for 330 years was held in 1975 and three years later Ronnie matriculated arms as the Principal Chief of the clan. The value of his historical research was acknowledged by other scholars and in 1969 he was invited to become a fellow of the Society of Antiquarians and in the following year he became a fellow of the Royal Historical Society. His long awaited book on the history of the clan appeared in 1978 and in 1982 he was awarded an honorary doctorate in acknowledgement of the original research he had undertaken. Of the three charges given to him by his grandfather two had been carried out; he had successfully revived the chiefship, and had united the clan. The third, to bring about a return of the clan to Kintail, seemed an impossibility but Ronnie was determined to make at least a symbolic gesture. In 1975 a plot of land in Kintail was acquired and permission was obtained for the construction on it of a clan museum. The museum was ceremonially opened at the triennial clan gathering of 1983. After the ceremony clan members attended the local fete day and fittingly a team of MacLennans defeated a team largely composed of their ancient rivals, the MacRaes, in a tug-of-war.

During these exciting years, while the hopes of generations of MacLennans were at last being realized, Ronnie found personal happiness. In 1970 he married Margaret, daughter of Donald John MacLennan of Dores and now has two daughters, Kirsteen and Lorna, as well as an heir to the chiefship Ruairidh, born in 1977. Sometimes accompanied by Margaret, sometimes alone, Ronnie has made numerous official visits to the U.S.A., Canada and Australia. The love of the Scots for their homeland seems to increase in proportion to the miles that they are distant from it

111

and Ronnie received an enthusiastic welcome wherever he went. He has been made an Honorary Citizen of Texas, an Honorary Colonel of the Oregon National Guard, and, through his interest in the culture of the Red Indians, an Honorary Chief of the Cherokee and Navaho nations. Other honours have been showered upon him, compensating to some extent for the veil of secrecy drawn across his wartime exploits: member of the Standing Council of Scottish Chiefs, Knight Grand Officer of the Order of St Lazarus of Jerusalem, Knight of the Noble Company of the Rose and Knight Grand Cross of the Knights of Malta, to name only a few.

A shadow fell over these years of success, when, in the early 1980s, Ronnie's increasing physical weakness was diagnosed as leukaemia and his doctors gave him, at most, four years to live. His professional career as an educationalist came to a premature end. He was forced to move from his home in Ullapool to a house at Dores, on the banks of Loch Ness, where he could be near the medical facilities of Inverness. Money was short, for Ronnie's duties as Chief involved considerable expense, and he had only a reduced pension to live on but Margaret, with her usual cheerful pragmatism, took on the job of postmistress of Dores, converting part of their home into a post office. It is a pleasant house with a magnificent view of the loch but is far removed from the turreted castles inhabited by more favoured chiefs. Its only distinguishing feature is the flagpole on the lawn from which the banner of the MacLennans proudly flies.

Ronnie refused to accept the doctor's verdict and with characteristic will power and obstinacy he has managed to regain his health. In 1986 he flew to the United States to be guest of honour at the Williamsburg Scottish Festival in Virginia and proudly watched the representative of the clan he had revived lead the march-past. The following year, three years beyond the span allotted to him by medical opinion, he presided over the triennial clan gathering in Inverness which was attended by hundreds of kinsfolk from many parts of the world. The vigour of the clan overseas is illustrated by the fact that Ronnie has appointed seven Lieutenants in Canada and the U.S.A., one in Europe and one in Australia. There are over 20 overseas branches, all of them established since Ronnie matriculated arms as clan chief. Three days after the gathering ended, Ronnie flew off for a gruelling two week tour of Canada. Ronnie now devotes all his working time to the clan. His belief that his mission is still incomplete prevents him from even contemplating the idea of giving up. With good reason, the motto on his coat of arms is '*Dum Spiro Spero*' — 'While there's life there's hope'.

AUTHOR

Colin Crisswell is Chief Ronald's first cousin and is a teacher and writer based in Hong Kong.

SOURCES

Ronald MacLennan, *History of the MacLennans*, 1978.
Conversations with members of the MacLennan clan.

CHAPTER 10

Andrew Fisher
The Pit-boy Premier
(1862—1928)

John Malkin

Among the legions of ordinary people who have laboured and suffered without thought of self to establish the socialism which is flowering in Australia today, none occupies a higher place than an immigrant Scottish collier named Andrew Fisher.

Born in 1862 in the mining village of Crosshouse 3.22 km (two miles) from Kilmarnock where the first edition of the poems of Robert Burns was printed, Andrew Fisher worked as a union organiser in the local pits before family circumstances, unemployment and victimisation forced him to emigrate to Queensland in 1885. In the next 30 years, as trade unionist, Labour member of the State Parliament, Labour member of the Federal Parliament, and, finally, as Labour Prime Minister in three separate governments, he made a massive and radical contribution towards the betterment of life for the ordinary people of Australia.

Politically, Fisher was a man ahead of his time. The 1939-45 war was to run its course before European politicians were compelled by popular pressure to concede the reforms bestowed upon Australians by Fisher's Labour Party 25 to 30 years earlier.

The cruelty and hardship of life, not just in the mining community of Crosshouse, but the depressed and exploited masses the world over, played upon Fisher's natural sympathy for the victim and made of him a political crusader bent upon emancipation of his class under the banner of socialism.

'From pit boy to Prime Minister' — a phrase with a fairy-tale ring about it which has often been used in describing the career of Andrew Fisher. In reality, there was nothing of the fairy-tale about the world he knew.

Fisher was undoubtedly a man with a purposeful determination to reach the heights of political influence. He had to get to the top of the political ladder because he knew from experience that only from this supreme vantage point would he be able to advocate the principles he stood for with any hope of seeing them put into practice.

It is said of Andrew Fisher that he was not a brilliant man, that many in Australian politics in his day could outshine him. Be that as it may, Fisher's record as Prime Minister of Australia is irrefutable proof that he had qualities of mind and judgement which, allied to personal integrity, made him if not a brilliant man, at least one whose contribution to his fellows shone with dazzling brilliance.

Crosshouse, when Fisher was born in 1862, was almost exclusively a mining community. Scarcely a dozen years earlier, women had joined their menfolk in the backbreaking toil of winning the coal. Though female labour was no longer permitted, the employment of children in the pits was still tolerated. Fisher himself was only 10 years of age when he started work.

In those days — the years from Fisher's birth in 1862 until he emigrated to Australia in 1885 at the age of 23 — Crosshouse people depended on the pits for a living, and most of them also depended on the owners for shelter. Miners were accommodated in rows of houses built by their employers, but-and-bens, most of them with stone or earthen floors, lit by oil lamps and served by outside privies, middens and washhouses. Water for cooking and drinking was drawn from street pumps supplied from an underground reservoir. Water for washing clothes was drawn from the Carmel Water and carried in pails slung on shoulder harnesses. Coal was used to fire the washhouse boilers, and treading in barefeet supplemented hand-scrubbing in the removal of dirt from clothes. It was not uncommon for families of six, seven, eight and more to exist under one roof.

When miners returned home on conclusion of their shift, they washed the coal dust from their bodies in a hip bath in front of the kitchen fire. It was the duty of the womenfolk to dry their 'pit claes' in front of the fire, ready for the start of the next shift.

A miner's day was long, sometimes lasting 12 hours. His working week lasted at least from Monday to Saturday. At the latter end of the year, miners often went to work in the dark and returned in the dark, never seeing daylight from Sunday to Sunday. It was unremitting toil for most. Men were frequently crippled by falls, explosions and lung disease. To lose your job often meant losing your house as well, and consequent penury for the whole family. Small wonder, then, that unrest was rife.

These were the social conditions in which the Fisher family lived — Robert Fisher, his wife Jane, whom he married in 1859, their sons, John, Andrew, Robert, James, David and William and their daughter, Janet. In spite of the harshness of life, Robert Fisher and his family, with a strength inherited from generations back, wasted no time in rancour. Their very industry and tolerance formed a shield against contamination.

One of the great formative influences in young Andrew's life was the local Cooperative Society or 'The Store', as it was popularly named. The Store was, in fact, the mainstay of village life, feeding and cladding the community, providing library and reading room where members could read and study.

Robert Fisher played an active part in founding Crosshouse Cooperative in March 1863. Initially, the Society sought only to function as a retail grocery which would improve the material standards of living for its members. In spite of opposition from some local farmers and merchants (they insisted on cash for any goods supplied to order), the Society prospered. Between 1872 and the mid-1890s, a new store and bakehouse was opened in Crosshouse and branches were set up in neighbouring villages. Growing in experience and confidence, the Society readily helped in setting up the great Cooperative supply unit, the Scottish Cooperative Wholesale Society. The first manager was James Borrowman, one of the local men who had joined Robert Fisher and others in founding the local Society. Like Robert Fisher, Borrowman was a collier.

Some of the harshness of life, therefore, was being alleviated by the local Cooperative Store by the time Andrew Fisher was going to school. The moral and political standards set by his parents made Andrew the radical he was always to be. The formal education which he obtained at elementary school and night school was supplemented by book reading in his spare time. He visited the local minister to discuss the problems of life, and to borrow books and magazines. The Cooperative reading room and library provided people like Fisher with an opportunity for quiet study of the newspapers and magazines of the day and gave them access to the literary works of the world.

Like all who get involved in the affairs of the world, Fisher liked discussion, debate and argument. He was never afraid of opinions which differed from his own. Fisher saw differences, not as divisive, but as constructive, believing that the oftener people exchanged views, and the more who did so, the more likely were they to reach some acceptable solution of their difficulties. Fisher was a prominent participant in the discussions which were regularly engaged in at the bridge over the Carmel or at the Bakehouse Corner. It was here in Crosshouse that world problems were tackled and passionately argued, here that Fisher began to take form, not as a great orator, but as a man of integrity, sincerity and honesty of purpose. He learned in Crosshouse that, among the highest attainments of life is unselfish service to others. He looked around, saw that all was not well with his people, and determined to devote himself to their welfare.

Handsome and athletic in appearance, always well groomed, Andrew Fisher was of a serious turn of mind. He was usually happy without ever being light-hearted, a trait which may have been responsible in later political life for the charge that he had little sense of humour. Becoming increasingly aware of the harshness of life for the miners, he sought refuge and strength more and more in books, especially those propounding philosophies which helped him to solve problems and face up to situations. Emerson and Carlyle were avidly read. He was a fervent admirer of Robert Burns, believing with the bard that, while 'man was made to mourn' he was, nevertheless, moving irresistibly towards the day when, 'for a' that, he would brothers be the warld o'er'. Keir Hardie's advocacy of the miners' fight for better conditions strengthened his own militant support.

Andrew Fisher had an unshakeable belief that good people far out-numbered the bad, and that society could save itself from perdition simply by establishing a benevolent and beneficent control. He regarded victory as inevitable though not imminent.

Everything that Andrew Fisher did had purpose about it; much of his effort was directed towards acquiring the education which he saw as a liberating force. When his work finished at the pit, he found respite exploring the countryside around Crosshouse in the company of his father and his brother, John. Walking was one of his pleasures, and he was to indulge it all his life. Fresh air and the openness of nature freed him from his pit cage and nurtured his independence of mind. He loved fishing, for he found that it concentrated his mind and, at the same time, gave him a chance to fill his stomach.

Andrew Fisher reacted with civilised compassion and controlled anger to the great social injustice which was all around him. Aware of the negative consequences of bitterness, justifiable though this kind of reaction might be, he was able to project his opposition in a manner which was moderate but, at the same time, firm, determined and positive.

The year 1879 had great personal significance for Fisher. Though only 17, he was already actively engaged in the fight to force the colliery owners to improve the miners' working and housing conditions, their safety underground, and their wages. Not surprisingly, the colliers of Crosshouse did not allow Fisher's youthfulness to dissuade them from recognising his commitment and contribution to their welfare. There was no resistance to his appointment as Crosshouse District Secretary of the Ayrshire Branch of the recently-formed Miners Union.

Fisher's Union appointment in 1879 coincided with an outbreak of strikes in the coalfields of Lanarkshire and north England.

When the strikes spread to Ayrshire in 1881, Fisher fought to make the strike bite by organising resistance and seeing that the miners and their families suffered as little as possible.

Bad organisation, caused principally by the inexperience of the young Miners Union, and the intolerable suffering which the strike caused in the mining communities, brought resistance to an end after no more than 10 weeks. To the credit of the employers, they gave the miners an increase in wages a month after they returned to work. But the strike had eaten so deeply into Union funds that much of the miners' enthusiasm for trade unionism evaporated. Along with others as far-sighted as himself, Fisher campaigned inside the Union and in public to strengthen the conviction of his workmates that their only hope of a better future for themselves and their families lay in cooperating one with the other in a trade union. Though the Union was eventually regenerated in Britain, it was an event which Fisher was to witness from abroad.

Blacklisted and sacked for his part in the 1881 strike, Fisher received the same punishment for supporting a second strike in 1885. The events were to lead almost at once to Fisher's departure for Australia. For some time past, James and he had been thinking of making a new life abroad. Family loyalty had prevented them making the break. John, the eldest of the family, had joined the Liverpool police force, and Robert had embarked upon a course in colliery management with Andrew as financial backer.

The unemployment forced upon Andrew, the departure of John, the need to support Robert, the growing decline in their father's health which seriously reduced his earning power, finally brought a decision in favour of emigration. Perusal of Australian Government literature decided Andrew and James to go to Queensland to follow their trade as miners.

In June 1885, the Fisher brothers made their way into Kilmarnock to board the train for London. They arrived in Brisbane, Queensland, in August 1885. Andrew's experience in Scottish pits brought him quick promotion. Within two months of starting work at Torbanelea Pit, he supervised the sinking of a new shaft and was made mine manager. Disappointed when rejected for an even better post, Andrew left Torbanelea and his brother James, and went to work in Gympie Goldfield 80 miles to the south.

Andrew Fisher's arrival in the Gympie Goldfield was to herald a brilliant political and union career. Obtaining work at North Phoenix in April 1888, he settled down for about three years. Though abstemious habits as a teetotaller and anti-gambler tended to isolate him socially from his mates, Fisher shared their political sympathies and the dangers of work and this made him a 'digger' no less than did the traditional garb of moleskin trousers, flannel shirt and calico cap.

Blacklisted for a third time, again for supporting a strike, Fisher put his unemployment to use by studying for an engine driver's certificate. Having secured the certificate, he found employers willing to forget his union record to get the benefit of his broad experience in the mines. He was taken on as an engine driver with the South Great Eastern Extended Railway Company in 1891 and worked until the company folded up the following year.

The period 1888 to 1893 saw Fisher change from union to political activist. When he wasn't working in the mines, he was preparing himself for politics and the struggle which he knew could only be won from the top. His education continued apace, particularly his study of political philosophy. He taught himself shorthand so that he could the better note arguments and points which he wanted to resist or adopt.

Formation of the Australian Labour Federation in 1889 was followed by campaigns within the unions for and against affiliation. Knowing the value of numbers, Fisher supported affiliation as secretary and treasurer of the Gympie District Branch of the Australian Miners Association.

With an eye on the state elections due in 1893, Fisher showed thoroughness and expediency by getting himself widely known. He joined the Oddfellows, a local Presbyterian church, Gympie Cooperative Society, and Gympie Chess Club. In 1893, he was elected on a Labour ticket to the State Parliament of Queensland as representative for Gympie. Immediately, he was made vice president of the Parliamentary Labour Party.

Losing his seat at the state elections in 1896, Fisher as usual used the setback constructively. A look at the Gympie political scene convinced him that the animosity of the press had been behind Labour's defeat. In partnership with Henry Boote, a Brisbane compositor with journalistic experience, he started a Labour newspaper, *Gympie Truth*. Boote fulfilled the duties of editor and Fisher of printer. In their hands, *Truth* persuaded the electorate to restore Fisher to the Queensland State Parliament in 1899.

Well-known and trusted by now, Fisher was invited to take the portfolios of Minister of Railways and Minister of Works in the Dawson Lib-lab Government. Executive duty in Government, however, was delayed, for the Government fell in a few days, its unity destroyed by political differences within the coalition.

Andrew Fisher, like Labour Leader John Watson, was an advocate of federation. He wanted an end to the colonial subservience of the states to London and to see them bonded together under a federal parliament. In the Queensland legislature, Fisher worked persuasively within the Labour Party with the purpose of convincing members of the benefits of federation. Australians showed their support of federation in a referendum.

Opening of the first Federal Parliament of Australia took place on New Year's Day 1901. Fisher was one of the Labour members, a popular choice with the electorate of Gympie. Later in the year, he married Margaret Irvine, daughter of Mr and Mrs Henry Irvine, whose house in Maori Lane had been home to him since his arrival in Gympie.

In 1907, the Fishers moved to Melbourne, seat of the Federal Parliament. Here, in a house which Fisher built for £50 in Dinsdale Street, they brought up a family of five sons and one daughter. The sons made a success of careers in banking, journalism, engineering and chemicals. Two are still living — Henry, an engineer, in the United States, and James, an industrial chemist, in Surrey. Their sister, Miss Margaret Fisher, lives on in the family house in Dinsdale Street.

Though Fisher's political duties prevented him from spending as much time with his family as he would have liked, the close bond which he had with his wife reflected itself in security and happiness within the home. A passionate believer in 'Christian socialism', Fisher made no attempt to 'brainwash' his family. John, who earned his living as a freelance left-wing journalist, was the only member of the family to take an active interest in politics. Not one of the six was baptised. James confesses that knowledge of his father's political life was mostly learned from others. Nevertheless, he has a vivid and respectful memory of his father as 'this tall, stern man, fair and generous to a fault, especially with children. Though never well off, small change never lasted long in his pocket.'

The maturity which Fisher had gained from 25 years in the Labour and trade union movements persuaded Labour Leader John Watson to appoint him Deputy in 1905. Together, they gave the Party the reliability which was to make it acceptable as Government.

Fisher had his first taste of executive power in the Federal Parliament in 1904 when he was appointed Minister for Trade and Customs in Watson's Labour Government. The job lasted no longer than the five months which it took the Opposition parties to join together and bring the Government down. For the next few years, Government was in the hands of the Liberals under Alfred Deakin.

In November 1908, Fisher, who had just succeeded Watson as Labour Leader, headed his first Labour Government. Though the Opposition soon brought him down, Fisher was finally put securely in office when the 1910 election gave Labour comfortable majorities in the House of Representatives and the Senate.

Under Andrew Fisher, Labour settled down to a period of secure power which added immeasurably to the quality of life in Australia and served as an example abroad. In all, the Government of 1910-1913, Fisher's second, put 113 Acts of Parliament on the Statute Book.

Fisher's commitment to 'federation' made him realise that physical communication between the states had to be improved and that a new method of financing development was needed. The Trans-Australian Railway was started, development of the Northern Territory, Australia's outback, was speeded up, the Commonwealth Bank was instituted with the intention of destroying the political power of the private banks, and a new paper monetary system, with backing from the Commonwealth Bank, was created. Correspondence within the Empire was made cheap for Australians by the introduction of the Penny Post.

Fisher's liking for compromise, a result perhaps of the privations suffered by Crosshouse miners and their families in the 1881 strike, could have been behind the improvements which the Labour Government made in the Conciliation and Arbitration Act, instituted to ease the settlement of industrial disputes. And, having earlier had much to do with giving legal force to measures for improving safety in the mines, Fisher put through an Act providing compensation for victims of industrial accident or disease. Maternity and invalid allowances were introduced, and the pension age for women was reduced from 65 to 60. Significant increases were made in retirement pensions and in money paid to beneficiaries.

Development of the big estates was forced upon owners by a land tax. Sheep farming gave way to crop cultivation. The Royal Australian Navy, destined to play an important part in the coming war of 1914-1918, was brought into being for defence of the Commonwealth. Labour's defence policy also included compulsory military training for land forces, expenditure being borne entirely from revenue to encourage Australians to decide whether or not they wanted it.

It was the Fisher Government of 1910-1913 which negotiated the purchase of land from New South Wales on which they built a new federal capital. Rejecting, with undisguised affront, a suggestion from his cabinet that the capital should be called after him, Fisher showed his sympathies for the 'first Australians' by giving it the Aboriginal name, Canberra — Meeting of the Ways. In 1927, Canberra had progressed enough to take over as federal capital.

Fisher's opposition to the employment of low-paid Polynesians in Australian sugar plantations further illustrated his resolute opposition to injustice and exploitation whether perpetrated on the white or the coloured man. It offended Fisher to see the Polynesians, or Kanakas, as they were called, treated no better than the black slaves of America. Racism was not unknown in Australia, but, fortunately, most Australians agreed with men like Fisher and soon brought an end to the exploitation of the Kanakas.

In spite of the popularity of the second Fisher Government, it lost power to the Liberals in 1913 by the narrowest of majorities, one seat.

The Liberals' tenure of office lasted little more than a year. By September 1914, soon after the outbreak of the 1914—1918 war, the Australian people showed their continuing trust in Fisher by electing him Prime Minister for the third time. It was during the hustings leading up to the election that Fisher made his famous declaration that Australia would support Britain 'to the last man and the last shilling'. Scarce two years later, his words were being used out of context by supporters of the demand for conscription which he had always opposed.

Fisher saw no advantage to Australia in the war; concepts of martial glory were no part of his character. Nevertheless, in line with his duties as wartime Prime Minister, he placed the Australian Navy at the service of the Admiralty and despatched two divisions of Australian soldiers to Egypt under British command. Subsequent transfer of the Australians to the deathtrap of Gallipoli was unknown to him at the time. He was to learn of it only after the landing. The impact made upon his sensitive mind by the sight of wounded compatriots returning home must have been traumatic. His immediate decree that the soldiers should be given preference for jobs in the public service would hardly relieve him of a deep unease about the carnage.

The heavy burden of wartime duties, the sturt and strife of politics, the harshness of life which he had known from childhood, ill health and the growing demand for conscription — all these influences came together and finally forced Fisher to give up the Prime Ministership to his pro-conscription deputy, William Morris Hughes. As he anticipated, the Labour Party united behind Hughes, giving Fisher at least the satisfaction of knowing that his sacrifice of office had ensured the unity of the Labour Party so dear to his heart. He was later to refuse a request from Hughes to sign a public declaration of support for conscription. In recognition of Australia's contribution to the war and his own work in the Dardanelles Commission, France bestowed upon him membership of the Legion d'Honneur. True to himself, Fisher declined to accept.

And so, Andrew Fisher, the miner who had risen from pit-boy in the Ayrshire village of Crosshouse to become Prime Minister of Australia, bowed out of the tough arena of Australian politics and chose exile in the salubrious formality of the diplomatic corps as Australian High Commissioner in London. Like every other role he had played in his life, Fisher played diplomat to the best of his ability. But, he was too informal, too much himself, Andy Fisher, to be comfortable in the role. It had always come naturally to him to put a point of view with passionate zest, a little clumsily at times but no less sincerely for that, and he found it impossible to cultivate the prepared oratory of the after-dinner speaker. He was never more at home than among his ain folk, and he showed the bond was indestructible by visiting his native village of Crosshouse in 1911, and, for the last time, in 1927.

In the latter years of his life, Andrew Fisher refused a

knighthood and withdrew from public view. In 1921, he gave up the post of High Commissioner and died in London on 22nd October 1928, at the age of 66. He was buried in Hampstead Cemetery.

Popular tributes to Fisher continued after his death. Australians living in London erected a memorial over his grave. 'Andrew Fisher's life was a great life, a wonderful life,' said Ramsay MacDonald, Britain's first Labour Prime Minister, when unveiling this memorial. In Crosshouse, on the site of the house where the Fishers lived, a cairn has been erected in Fisher's memory by the people of Crosshouse, Kilmarnock, and Strathclyde, the Government of Australia, and the miners of Ayrshire. It was unveiled in 1978, by the then High Commissioner of Australia in London, Sir Gordon Freeth, to mark the 50th anniversary of Fisher's death.

Gympie pays tribute to Fisher with a museum featuring the reconstructed house in Maori Lane where he and his wife, Margaret, began their married life. It has been furnished in the style fashionable in Fisher's day. In the grounds of the museum is a steam winding engine similar to the kind worked by Fisher in the Gympie mines.

Perhaps the best testament to Fisher is the story often told by his wife, Margaret. It seems that, having spent the day steering his Government through legislation dealing with oil rights and concessions, Fisher arrived home in Melbourne to find a handsome new oil lamp burning in the sitting room. 'Where did that come from?' he asked his wife. 'It's a present to you from an oil company,' said Mrs. Fisher. 'It was delivered by a charming gentleman . . . ' 'Would you ruin me, woman!' said Fisher, interrupting. 'What do you think the Opposition would do to me if they found me accepting a gift from a shopkeeper?'

Picking up the lamp, Fisher carried it outside and left it burning in the street. No doubt the neighbours learned why it was there and gave their approval.

Essentially a practical man, Andrew Fisher was also a political visionary. He could see beyond the bombs and the violence, beyond the hysterical and manufactured hatred which nation has for nation, class for class, creed for creed, colour for colour. Self-interest, arrogance, conceit and pomposity could not obscure his view ahead, only slur it. Away in the distance, he could see green and fertile fields where men willingly laboured for the common good. Today, 60 years after Fisher's death, mankind is still striving towards the 'socialist Canaan' he dreamed of.

AUTHOR

John Malkin is a Kilmarnock-based writer who in a period of over 40 years has been involved in journalism, script writing and editorship of magazines, newspapers and guides.

SOURCES

Various newspapers and journals: *The Australian Worker, Brisbane Courier, Gympie Times.*

CHAPTER 11

Norman McLeod
A Calvinist Ayatollah
(1780—1866)

Margaret McBride

There are many remarkable stories in the long history of Scottish emigration, but surely none so unusual and intriguing as that of Reverend Norman McLeod, who led his followers firstly from Sutherland to Nova Scotia, Canada, by way of Melbourne, and finally to Waipu in New Zealand.

Today, in each of these Commonwealth countries, there exist hardy God-fearing communities, who cherish the values and follow the ways of the Normanites — even to the holding of annual Highland Games, regular ceilidhs and the speaking of Gaelic.

Norman McLeod has been called a 'Calvinist Ayatollah', 'an embodiment of the mighty spirits of Israel', 'a tyrannical Presbyterian' and 'more of a Cromwell than a Moses' — strong descriptions indeed, of a character who was undoubtedly no ordinary man of the cloth.

Born on 17th September 1780 in the village of Stoir Point in the parish of Assynt, Norman McLeod grew up in a traditional fishing and farming community. McLeods had lived here for generations in the tough but fiercely close-knit, traditional clan system — groups of kinsmen led by a chief, who settled on land which was usually, but not always, owned by the chief.

Norman was the son of pious parents and well connected. He attended the local parish primary school, and later joined his father as a fisherman working in the harsh environment of the North Atlantic. He is described in *Lion of Scotland* by Neil Robinson as a 'clever, irreverent, forward youth'.

Norman grew up in a period of great social change. Following the unsuccessful Jacobite risings of 1715 and 1745 and the ultimate defeat at Culloden in 1746, the power of the clan chiefs was broken and the clans themselves were fragmented and in disarray.

The notorious Highland Clearances, in which thousands of families were moved by military intervention from the more fertile regions to the drab coastal areas in order to make sheltered land available for sheep grazing, was a time of great turmoil. Clansmen were forcibly evicted from their meagre homes which were then burned behind them. The county of Sutherland suffered particularly, and its population was dispossessed, dispirited and disintegrating.

A description of Sutherland by Revd. Donald Sage says:

Summonses of ejectment were issued and despatched all over the district. These must have amounted to upwards of 1,000. The summonses were delivered with the utmost preciseness. They were handed in at every house and hovel alike. The middle of the week brought on the day of the Strathnaver clearances. At an early hour of the day Mr Seller, accompanied by the Fiscal and escorted by a strong body of Constables, Sheriff, Officers and others, commenced work at Gunmore. Their plan of operations was to clear the cottage of its inmates, giving them about half an hour to pack up and carry off their furniture, and then set fire to their cottage. To this plan they ruthlessly adhered. Nothing could more vividly represent the horrors of grinding oppression. (*Lion of Scotland*.)

Clansmen were allocated tiny strips of land not large enough to afford a family a living. Farming, fishing, weaving and spinning, as well as occasional work, were undertaken to supplement income from produce and the harvesting of kelp (fossilised seaweed). Famine was commonplace and ever-increasing rents the norm.

Many clansmen joined the newly-formed Highland regiments. Between 1793 and 1815, over 37,600 men enlisted to fight in North America, India and Europe. Emigration was increasing steadily, as promising reports of life in the New Countries where soldiers and traders had settled, began to filter back home. Crowded migrant ships set sail for Novia Scotia, the nearest place to their homeland.

Dr. Johnson wrote that in 1773 'there seems now, whatever be the cause, to be through a great part of the Highlands, a general discontent . . . and he that cannot live as he desires at home listens to the tale of fortunate islands and happy regions where every man may have land of his own, and eat the product of his labour without a superior.'

Samuel Boswell, Dr. Johnson's travelling companion, illustrates the move to find better circumstances overseas: 'The new management and high rents took the tenants by surprise. They were indignant at the treatment they received, and selling off their stock they emigrated to America. In the 20 years from 1772 to 1792, 16 vessels with emigrants sailed from the western shores of Inverness-shire, the Hebrides and Ross-shire, containing 6,400 persons.'

Local migration was growing too, as young men left home to seek work in the newly emerging lowland towns of the Industrial Revolution, Glasgow in particular.

The Church of Scotland had been affected, too, by the changing social upheaval undermining the previously strict moral standards of many of its members. Norman McLeod's parish minister at Assynt from 1768-1816, the Revd. William McKenzie, was weak and lacking in spiritual leadership through being addicted to the demon drink, and was hardly a good example for an impressionable youth.

However, religion, education and a strong family background, the traditional Scottish values, certainly played a major part in Norman McLeod's formative years. Simple piety and a regard for truth and honesty, fostered a strong and robust character. Respite from the harsh living environment was found in the neighbourly get-togethers known as ceilidhs, when families would gather to tell stories, recount legends and sing ballads.

However, a parish assistant appointed in 1806, Revd. John Kennedy, brought a new lease of religious life to the parish. Revd. Kennedy was a fervent evangelist. His mission was to awaken, regenerate and save sinners and Norman McLeod was impressed. He turned to religion, to the fundamental principles of John Knox, from which the contemporary Church of Scotland had strayed.

Through the Bible, McLeod found all the answers to his questions on morals, codes of behaviour and standards for dress and daily living. Aged 27, he decided to enter the ministry and left for Aberdeen University. He graduated with a Master of Arts degree in 1812, having received a gold medal for his studies in moral philosophy. He married Mary McLeod, also from Assynt, and entered Edinburgh University to study theology.

Norman was dismayed, however, with what he saw as the lax standards of discipline and lack of energy prevailing in Edinburgh, both in kirk and university. His rigid beliefs and conduct were unyielding and, after a series of stormy meetings with the professors, he quit after two terms, feeling he could never adhere to the established Church of Scotland.

Returning to Sutherland, McLeod began to teach, and to preach in Ullapool, not far from his birthplace. He soon won many followers through his uncompromising heaven or hell stance, his outstanding powers of oratory, and his equally imposing physical stature. At over six feet tall, powerfully built and with strong features, he was a commanding figure. 'A giant, physically, mentally and spiritually,' was how one of his flock described him in a letter to the *New Zealand Listener*.

Such a singular character, who was attracting a growing flock while still an unlicensed preacher, McLeod could not help but antagonise the local Church of Scotland's easy-going minister, Dr. Ross, who refused to baptise Norman's first-born son John Luther. Following many subsequent arguments, Norman's livelihood was cut off when his salary as a school teacher was stopped by the parish.

There was only one recourse, to seek a new life elsewhere, where he and his followers could maintain their beliefs and live their lives in harmony. McLeod, and many of his flock, left on the barque *Frances Ann* from Lochbroom in July 1817, for Pictou, Nova Scotia. His wife Mary and three children joined them the following year.

The 10-week voyage was not without incident. Strong Atlantic winds and rough seas made for arduous sea journeys with scarce creature comforts. In mid-voyage, the *Frances Ann* suffered a terrible battering from stormy westerly winds and, following an equally stormy meeting of crew and passengers, the captain decided to return home. All but Norman McLeod agreed. Claiming he had seen a vision, McLeod, a spellbinding orator, said: 'If we turn back, we are lost.' McLeod convinced his fellow passengers that they were nearer to Nova Scotia than to Ireland. After threatening to clap him in irons, the captain eventually followed McLeod's advice and the *Frances Ann* did reach Pictou, where there was a large Scottish settlement already established.

For three years Norman McLeod and his Normanites lived in Pictou which in many ways, both scenically and in terms of way of life, was typical of their Scottish homeland. Life for the new arrivals was not easy, as all the best land had already been taken by the early men of Sutherland 30 years before.

During 1817, McLeod visited the United States and was ordained a minister of the Presbyterian Church in Geneva, in New York State. This was followed by a short period ministering to a Scots colony settled in Ohio, where for a while, he was tempted to stay permanently. Deciding, however, he could not abandon his original flock, he returned to Pictou.

In Pictou, he was 'loved and honoured. The people will go much farther to hear him preach than any other minister in Pictou. McLeod's influence was so great that it extended to all parts of the country, and by his followers he was regarded with unbounded devotion,' is one description of McLeod in 1817 recorded in *Idyll of the Shipbuilders*. But, equally, a man of such singlemindedness aroused controversy.

'Those who have heard him at this time describe his preaching as consisting of torrents of abuse against all religious bodies and even against individuals, the like of which they had never heard, and which was perfectly indescribable,' is one contemporary verdict found in *Lion of Scotland*. As is : 'His preaching was so austere that a majority of the inhabitants were not well disposed towards him.'

There is no doubt that he produced strong feelings in whomever he encountered.

Following an urgent call from a Highland settlement, Norman considered returning to Ohio — but this time with all his followers, who numbered over 500 persons. To transport them, the Normanites built a ship using all the skills and craftsmanship learned not too long ago in Scotland. The 20 ton vessel was named, somewhat ominously, *The Ark*.

The Ark set sail with 50 or so passengers in September 1819, bound for Ohio by way of the Atlantic Ocean, the Gulf of New Mexico and then up the Mississippi. However, an early encounter with wild weather in the Atlantic forced *The Ark* back to land. The passengers took shelter in St Ann's, on the coast of Cape Breton Island.

Here was a welcome haven indeed! The land was fertile, tall trees plentiful and the surrounding waters teemed with fish. The survivors of *The Ark* decided to go no further, and so it was that 'they resolved to make homes for themselves on the shores of St Ann's. This constituted the first Presbyterian congregation that ever gathered for the worship of God on the Island of Cape Breton,' according to correspondence from the Revd. John Murray to Geo. O. Macdougall, in October 22nd 1931, from *The History of the Presbyterian Church in Cape Breton.*

Norman McLeod set up his log-built church on land at South Gut, having negotiated the purchase of a two-square-mile area from the Government. He and his followers thrived physically, as well as spiritually, secure in the knowledge that they were creating a simple world according to God's will. McLeod worked as a schoolmaster, refusing any salary in order to preserve his independence — he existed on gifts from his parishioners. The women of the district would help with domestic tasks and the men cleared the land and put up his house.

The new and struggling community looked to McLeod as a spiritual leader, but more so, afforded him the respect and reverence of a clan chief. He offered them advice and opinion on all matters: from 'the pitiful and degenerate . . . Church of Scotland' to 'extravagance in dress', on which he elaborates in his book *The Present Church of Scotland and a Tint of Normanism*. He looked with suspicion on the new ministers who came to St

Ann's as the population swelled, following the arrival of further immigrants from the Highlands.

Revival meetings by their sheer exuberance were specially scorned by McLeod. He described the congregation at such an occasion thus: 'some are screeching and screaming — others peeping and tooting — or snuffling and snorting — far beyond their pulmonary power; others falling down prostrate, monkey-like, spring with surprising agility. Another sort sit still, statue-like, in a wild and vacant gaze.'

Women, particularly, seemed regularly to offend the minister, and he would chastise them from the pulpit for wearing too bright a dress, or too gaudy a hat — his own wife included! Such haranguing frequently turned people away from religion.

The community prospered and a new church seating 1,200 was built in 1821. The McLeod family increased to eight children and lived a modest life in harmony with their fellow Highlanders. Among the recorded family names of the original settlers of Cape Breton are: McLeod, Ross, Fraser, McDonald, McKenzie, Munro, McInnes, McKay, McAskill — the latter well known in folklore for the huge seven-foot nine-inch Giant McAskill. There were French families also, and one Fraser married a Red Indian princess.

Daily life consisted of farming, fishing, wood-cutting, spinning and weaving, in the tradition of the Highlands; shipbuilding and exporting timber were later developed during the 30 years that McLeod and his original followers dwelled in Cape Breton. Children were taught in Gaelic by John Munro, a man well-respected in the community, who was elected in 1852 to represent Victoria County in the Nova Scotian Legislative Assembly.

'Games, gossip and church' were the order of the day. As spiritual leader, teacher and magistrate, Norman McLeod had a pre-eminent position in the community and his guidance set the tone for generations to come. His own austerity was followed by his parishioners — no alcohol was allowed at any time for any reason; work of any kind was forbidden totally on the Sabbath; so much so, that potatoes or other vegetables for Sunday dinner had to be prepared on Saturday. In a letter of the time, the residents of St Ann's are described as 'the most intelligent, moral and the strictest Sabbath observers that ever came to the country.'

In all his 30 years' preaching in St Ann's, Revd. McLeod never dispensed Communion or administered Baptism. This was not due to any disapproval of these rituals, or to lack of regard for their spiritual value. On the contrary, he did have a high opinion of these rites — it was just that he felt no-one in his parish had reached the degree of holiness required for such spiritual undertakings. (A good example of McLeod's over-zealous fundamentalist approach to religion.)

In 1848, the pattern of rural simplicity at St Ann's began to deteriorate. Devastating potato blight was rife, the wheat harvest was under threat from adverse weather, and the likelihood of famine was present. Norman's long-suffering wife, Mary, was continually in poor health, too. A letter arrived out of the blue from their second son, Donald, from South Australia where he was employed as a newspaper editor.

He told his family in very positive terms of the new colony, of its excellent climate, good land and its great potential for settlers. This letter caused quite a stir in the community, coming as it did at such a depressing time. People became interested in the seemingly brighter prospect of Australia, and there was much talk of further migration.

Norman was now aged 68 and hesitant of making such a drastic move. However, he felt that Divine Providence would guide him, and wrote to Donald for more details. Acknowledging there were 'sinners still among us', he began considering the idea of a new start in the vast unpopulated territory of Australia, where he could leave behind after his death a prosperous, settled community which would live in harmony according to his strict religious principles. He prayed and meditated frequently.

McLeod's own family were keen to see their brother and, through their coaxing and the strong desire of the community, plans were laid to undertake the voyage to Australia. Under the minister's guidance and with regular daily worship, shipbuilders, mariners, farmers and merchants set about their various tasks.

The intriguing aspect of the venture was that it was an established, settled community which was planning to up and leave, and not because of the results of war or because of harsh circumstances (excluding the recent poor harvest in 1848). An inherited spirit of adventure, coupled with the utmost loyalty to their spiritual leader, combined to provide a powerful impetus for men seeking further horizons.

This migration of an entire community (over half the population of St Ann's) was not only led by its minister, but also included several schoolmasters and men and women versed in every likely trade and craft. Even their own member of parliament was with them — John Munro, who was later to sit in the New Zealand House of Representatives.

The ships to carry them were entirely built by skilled artisans from St Ann's, and officers and crew were supplied from the community too. Families gathered their own provisions for the entire journey. Neil Robinson describes in *Lion of Scotland* how 'potatoes, shredded and evaporated were packed in birch-bark wrappers. Codfish was dried, boned and packed in the same way. So that, with the addition of water, palatable food could be quickly prepared. For the first time, "dehydrated" food had been exported from Canada.'

A six-month voyage by families over 12,000 miles of rough sea on an unfamiliar route to an unknown land was an exceptional undertaking for those times. Rigorous preparations were made, because this was a practical and far-sighted community who would leave nothing to chance. The McGregor brothers, master shipbuilders, laid the keels for the first two ships, and the brothers McKenzie, Murdo and Duncan, administered the other considerable tasks.

The first two ships involved in the mission were the *Highland Lass* and the *Margaret,* named after Norman McLeod's youngest daughter. In the ensuing eight years, from 1852-60, the *Gertrude, Spray, Breadalbane* and *Ellen Lewis* set sail. These were vessels around 200 tons or so, apart from the last ship, *Ellen Lewis,* which weighed 336 tons.

The day of the *Margaret's* departure for the promised land was a momentous occasion, marked by a fiery and eloquent speech from the 71-year-old minister which made everyone present feel they wanted to go with him. There was an emotional farewell from the assembled community as the 136 passengers and crew of the *Margaret* left St Ann's on 28th October 1851. McLeod assigned his church to the Free Church of Nova Scotia prior to his leaving.

The 164-day voyage, under the command of Captain Watson, was fairly uneventful, although a young nephew of the minister died at sea. The *Margaret* sailed her course steadily over the Pacific, calling at St Jago, Cape Verde Islands and at the Cape of Good Hope, to take in supplies of fresh water, vegetables and fruit.

This voyage to new horizons in the classical and biblical sense, must have seemed strange to those who witnessed its passing. Morning and evening worship was held daily, with hymn-singing in Gaelic. There was no ranking system among those on board, as captain, minister, officers, crew and passengers ate at the same table and occupied the same quarters. Songs, games, bagpipe music and story-telling were encouraged, as Norman McLeod was a past-master in all that concerned the welfare of the mind.

Days passed on the eastward journey in regular fashion. The weather was good and warm, the *Margaret*'s passengers in fine health and spirits. Children went to school daily and adults went about their particular trade or task on the ship.

Revd McLeod, as well as leading his followers in the spiritual sense, took an active part in the *Margaret*'s navigation. He took daily readings of the sun in order to check the officers' calculations, and his were found to be totally accurate.

Australia was sighted as early as March, 1852, and the *Margaret* laid anchor in Adelaide on 10th April. As soon as the anchor was fast, Norman set up an altar and all assembled gave thanks to God for a safe journey, finishing with the sung version of the 23rd Psalm in Gaelic — 'The Lord's my shepherd, I shall not want.'

Donald McLeod, the minister's journalist son, had already moved from the area and left word he had headed on to Melbourne. This was a disappointment to all, which was augmented by the appearance of Adelaide: a mere collection of scattered buildings and only a handful of dwellings and new settlers. The 'promised land' fell far short of expectations.

The *Margaret* docked in Melbourne in early June to find a bewildering, disorganised squatter town in the grip of gold fever. What a contrast to the fond aspirations of the Nova Scotians. Home was now a tent in the middle of a swelling canvas town whose population was growing at an alarming rate — from 23,000 in 1851 to a staggering 191,000 ten years later.

The *Margaret* was sold — the last tangible link with Nova Scotia — and many of the young men headed enthusiastically for the gold fields. Such a 'get rich quick' environment was in total contrast to the peace and quiet of Nova Scotia, and brought with it much of the unsavoury side of life. Thieves, murderers, insanitary conditions and disease were all around. Sadly, McLeod's three sons — Alexander, Samuel and Edward — died of typhoid within the short space of six weeks. Norman was devastated, and had to struggle long and hard with his faith.

The minister was taken captive by a band of marauders one day when he was lost in the bush. In characteristic fashion he led them all in prayer and scolded them on their evil way of life. This eloquent sermonising impressed the raiders so much that they gave him a horse and sent him home the following day unharmed.

The way of life in Australia was not to the liking of the Normanites, although several men who followed the gold trail became quite rich. A few decided to make their life in Melbourne, but the majority felt as strangers in a strange land. Norman spent much time in prayer. Finally, he felt his prayers were answered when the Governor of New Zealand, Sir George Grey, agreed to his request to form a settlement there early in 1853.

The arrival of the *Highland Lass* in October of 1852 had delighted the first Normanites who were pleased to have their support and determination to move on to New Zealand, away from Melbourne's den of iniquity.

The first Normanites arrived in New Zealand on 17th September 1853, and settled in Auckland, where Norman McLeod preached in St. Andrew's Presbyterian Church. The Government granted them a huge parcel of land obtained from the Maoris in 1854 — this was Waipu in the North Island of New Zealand. The final migration was over.

On 30,000 acres of fertile land, the Normanites set to, turning it into a thriving rural farming community. There were hills, there was sea, there was forest — and the weather was pleasantly warm. Here, indeed, was the 'promised land'. During the following two years, there were new arrivals from Nova Scotia, bringing the total number of the community to over 800 men, women and children.

Norman McLeod lived a vigorous and active life, riding long distances on horseback to preach in both English and Gaelic. He died aged 86 years on 14th March 1866, his wife having preceded him by nine years. As in Cape Breton, there exist today followers of Revd. McLeod who practise the old ways and faith of this 'born leader, a man of indomitable spirit, and, above all, a crusading knight'.

Descendants of the Highlanders have contributed in no small measure to the prosperity of both present-day Cape Breton and Waipu. Allan J. MacEachan, Deputy Prime Minister of Canada, and Prime Minister Malcolm Fraser of Australia, can both trace their ancestors to the original settlers of Nova Scotia.

Fine granite monuments have been erected in memory of Norman McLeod in both Cape Breton and Waipu, but perhaps the most telling legacy yet remaining of the formidable preacher is the absence to this day in Waipu of a licensed public house.

AUTHOR

Margaret McBride — wife, mother, editor and native Glaswegian — has lived 12 years in Hong Kong. She plans to retire to Sutherland after 1997.

BIBLIOGRAPHY

J. D. Mackie, *A History of Scotland*, Penguin, 1982.

N. R. McKenzie, *A Gael Fares North*, Whitcombe and Tombes, NZ, 1935.

The Bible Society, *Idyll of the Shipbuilders*, Clarke and Matheson Ltd, Auckland, 1929.

Neil Robinson, *Lion of Scotland*, Hodder & Stoughton, 1974.

Flora McPherson, *Watchman Against the World*, Whitcombe and Tombes, NZ, 1962.

CHAPTER 12

Ethel Baxter
Woman of Taste
(1883—1963)

Marian Pallister

The women of Scotland's uncompromising north-east are accustomed to backing their men in their chosen work. The unceasing efforts to make the land or sea yield a living created this tradition. But at the turn of the 20th century it was still not acceptable for a wife to be seen doing more than support her husband. Ethel Baxter flouted that convention to create one of Scotland's most successful business partnerships — and almost as a sideline she created the dynasty which still rules not only in

Scotland but everywhere in the world where good food is savoured.

When Ethel joined the Baxter family in 1914, she was joining a family already experienced in purveying fine foods. But this handsome, independent young woman wanted to be more than just part of a flourishing village grocery business. She urged her new husband to borrow cash and together they crossed the river from Fochabers, the little Morayshire village some 105 km (65 miles) north of Aberdeen where her in-laws had created their grocery business, to build a tiny factory on the banks of the River Spey. Baxters of Speyside had been born.

Life for Ethel had first been breathed in the crystal clear air where a glittering grey North Sea meets rich agricultural earth. Her father, Andrew Adam, managed a farm called Meadow-hillock on the estate of Roseisle owned by Alexander Gordon. He married twice — not uncommon in those hard days when the round of childbearing and heavy farm work carried off many a first wife and left tots motherless. Etheldreda — she never heard the name given her at the christening from the lips of her family — was the lusty daughter of Andrew's second wife Elizabeth. She arrived in 1883 to swell the ranks of a family which eventually numbered four girls and four boys.

Meadowhillock was a good place to grow up in. From the brae looking west across the rich estate lands, little Ethel could see the distant majestic purple skyline of the Cairngorms. The bracing air from the Moray Firth flowing into the cruel sea which ruled the lives of their fisher folk neighbours mingled with the softer winds of sheltered farm lands.

Weekdays saw her father harnessing the sturdy plough horses or tending cattle. On Sundays, this devout Presbyterian family put on its Sabbath best and listened to the sermons at the local kirk. Ethel's mother was a quiet, loving woman who was firm with her children, and her father was known as a man of considerable strength of character whose simple, honest philosophies came from those Sunday kirk sessions.

It was in this caring Christian home that Ethel watched her first seasons passing — the cereals pushing through in summer, the woodlands below the steading offering a kaleidoscope of reds and golds in autumn, the unyielding stormy winters. But this healthy playground had to be left behind for school days, and Ethel went off to Keam School at Duffus, near Gordonstoun.

It was not simply her loss of freedom which was to make Ethel hate school, however. The schoolmaster was a man named Corrigal. Mr. Corrigal's temper was vile and pupils who tried his patience would be on the receiving end of a violently-flung missile. It was the era of chalk and slate, not jotter and pencil. To the end of her days, Ethel bore a scar on her breastbone where a slate hurled by Mr. Corrigal had painfully struck her. Her crime? She had got her sums wrong. But as time went by, she got them right, and gained sufficiently good reports to go on to train at Aberdeen Royal Infirmary as a nurse. This was one of the few socially acceptable jobs a woman could undertake in those days.

Ethel specialised in midwifery and became a member of the Central Midwives Board. She left the hospital to take up private nursing in those pre-welfare-state days, which meant that her patients were those who could best afford it. The north-east was a favourite area of the aristocracy. There were many wealthy estates, and plenty of professional people in the prim but prosperous little towns.

She saw a life far removed from that of Meadowhillock. Ethel would be called upon to stay for quite lengthy periods at the grand houses to nurse her patients back to health. Food at home had always been plentiful but plain and wholesome, manners honest and countryfied. Now she experienced the fine foods and sophisticated lifestyles of 'the toffs'. She was young and impressionable, but her solid Presbyterian background meant her head was never turned.

She absorbed this new scene, and added to her own inbred qualities of warmth and practicality, that of taste. She was at home in the houses of lords and ladies, lawyers and professors.

One of her patients was the mother of Sir John Reith, later Lord Reith, the first director general of the British Broadcasting Corporation. Another was Willie Baxter. Willie had first seen this tall, handsome young woman when she came to the village of Fochabers to nurse a young boy who had been impaled on the shafts of a pony trap. Later, when Willie Baxter was in need of a nurse, Ethel Adam was again called to Fochabers. He was one of two sons of George Baxter, the local high-class grocer.

George had worked on the estate of the Duke of Richmond and Gordon as a gardener when he was a lad. But when he was just 23 years old, the doctor told him he had only a few months to live. He was suffering from 'consumption' — tuberculosis. Devastated, he left his job in the grounds which lead from the end of the village's main street. But he decided to make the most of his 'death sentence' and borrowed £10 from an uncle to set up a grocery shop in the village in 1868. The business flourished, and so did George's health.

At first, a lot of bartering went on. The handsome young George appealed to the local women, who would bring in their strawberries, blackcurrants and gooseberries and wheedle him into taking them for their grocery orders. Maybe they thought they were doing a good deal with their home-grown fruits. George did a better one. He began to make jams in the back shop, and judging from the tastes of the aristocratic visitors to the Richmond and Gordon Estate, they were good jams.

With his young wife Margaret, he created the first high quality Baxter jams, and soon his customers were high quality customers. The gleaming wood counters were polished with the passing of fine foods. Tin boxes painted with the exotic scenes of their contents' origins lined the walls, and shining brass scales weighed measures for the villagers and their landlords.

Two sons arrived — George junior and William — but sadly Margaret died in 1881, leaving the infants motherless. Willie grew to be a young man of indifferent health but high spirits. He loved to dance, to sing the latest tunes, to dress in style.

Willie also loved the look of this tall, quiet nurse with her own distinctive sense of style. Theirs was a classic patient-nurse romance. Willie lost a large part of his intestine following a duodenal ulcer, but he gained a wife when Ethel came to nurse him back to health.

Willie Baxter and Ethel Adam were married in 1914 as the nation went to war. His health would not allow him to fight, and the young couple moved into Ford Cottage in Fochabers to join the family firm. Ethel saw immediately that there were too many people trying to live off the grocer's shop, however successful it may have been.

She wanted independence and she wasn't afraid to let Willie know it. She urged him to set up on his own, leaving his father, brother and the rest of the family to carry on at the shop. So, like his father before him, Willie borrowed money from relatives and from the bank to set up a new business.

He and Ethel moved across the salmon-plenty Spey and built a tiny factory on the bank opposite Fochabers. It was jam, of course, which they decided to make in that first little canning shed. And Ethel, a woman of enormous determination, insisted on being involved from the outset.

Willie was a natural salesman, Ethel a woman of foresight, energy, practicality — and taste. He went out to seek orders for their products, she stayed home and ran the factory.

With men away in the Great War, maintenance could have been a problem for a more average woman of the times. But not for Ethel. She would hitch her skirts and climb to the rafters. There she would oil the wheels which ran the pulleys that operated the belts of the first primitive canning machines.

As the war came to an end, the Baxter family began to grow. The couple's first child was born on 8th February 1918, the second on 20th June 1920. Two days before the birth of son Gordon, destined to become chairman of the company, Ethel stood in the factory and made three tonnes of blackcurrant jam.

But the golden days in the north-east were dimming. After the tragedies of the war came the poverty of the Depression. Local merchants found it hard to pay their bills. Their own customers were on the breadline and the invoices the Baxters sent out often had to go by the board.

The young mother wanted the best for her boys, and this wasn't the way of getting it. So Ethel decided that Willie should take his order books south to seek trade where the Depression had not bitten so deeply. Ethel's days in the grand houses of north-eastern Scotland had taught her the power of Harrods, the world-renowned quality shop in the English capital. She persuaded Willie to pack his bags and his samples and seek an audience with the grocery buyer of the top London store. So top-drawer was the shop that 'seeking an audience' was not a misused phrase.

Perhaps it was the fact that Willie arrived on a Saturday morning which got him off on the wrong footing. Mr. James Stirling, the grocery buyer, was a grand gentleman who played golf on Saturday mornings. He had an appointment on the golf course that particular Saturday, and he told the uniformed flunky to send Willie Baxter away. Like Bruce and the spider, Willie had three tries at getting in to see Mr. Stirling, and like the spider, his patience and determination paid off.

With a very ungentlemanly greeting of: 'Mr. Baxter, what the hell do you mean by this, interrupting my Saturday morning?' James Stirling admitted Willie to the inner sanctum. Willie explained he had come some 1,130 km (700 miles) to show him some extra-special products. He opened his case, and withdrew from within the folds of his neatly-packed pyjamas tissue-wrapped jars of Ethel's jam. There were jams, jellies and marmalade.

Mr. Stirling stuck out a pinkie and nibbled delicately a taste from each jar. He was impressed. This stuff had taste in every sense of the word. But what impressed him most and brought out his skills in well-bred wheeling and dealing was Ethel's wild strawberry jam, made from fruit from the Cairngorms. Only one other supplier in Britain could let him have jam like this. They were Wilkins of Tiptree, a firm which specialised in supplying grand houses directly. As something of a favour, they would let Mr. Stirling have a case or so each year to display on Harrods' shelves. 'How much do you have?' he quizzed Willie. 'A gie lot,' said Willie giving little away.

Mr. Stirling kept his golf appointment, though history does not record if his concentration suffered after his encounter with Willie and the wild strawberry jam. What we do know is that on the Monday morning he kept another appointment — this time with Willie Baxter, who went home with the first-ever orders from the mighty Harrods.

Those orders have never ceased, and over the years it was the Saturday morning task of Willie and Ethel's boys to open the Harrods envelope. And of course, what Ethel knew was that the world's wealthy shoppers all passed through Harrods' portals at some time or another. When they went home, they demanded of their own quality stores the products they saw and liked in Harrods.

The trip that she encouraged Willie to make in the depths of the Depression bore fruit beyond their wildest dreams. The orders began to come from Macys in New York, from Marshall Field in Chicago, from H. J. Thrupps in Johannesburg — from every top shop where good food was sold.

Willie continued to travel the country while Ethel ran the factory and their home. He would send his orders by train each night, tipping the station attendant half-a-crown on a dimly lit platform to make sure Ethel would receive them.

She would start work in the factory at 8 a.m. and never finish before 8 p.m. Often she wouldn't get back to the grey sandstone house across from the canning-sheds until midnight. The boys were looked after by a nanny, but they regarded Ethel as a wonderful, loving mother who strove to give them the best in life.

That's not to say that Ethel was perfect. She may have been compassionate and understanding with both her sons and the girls in the factory, who saw her as something of a mother hen but she would scream her displeasure at anyone who didn't meet her high standards in every sphere and she and Willie had some spectacular battles over the years. They were, however, a couple who complemented each other. His outgoing nature was a good foil for her more reserved character. His ideas were matched by her practical abilities.

Life became more comfortable as the years went on, but it remained a struggle, and they combated that struggle together as a team. Though she had that strict Presbyterian upbringing, her years with Willie gave her tolerance and humour. But she never stopped working hard, and her endeavours continued to increase the firm's stature.

Her discerning tastes influenced a new generation as convenience foods took over from traditional cooking. In 1929, she put the Baxters in the soup. Literally. Willie had stumbled across the carcass of a deer on the platform of Aviemore station as he sent off his nightly dispatches to Ethel. His enquiries uncovered the fact that the 'toffs' shipped off some of the fruits of their shoots on the Highland moors, but most of the dead beasts were buried on the hillsides because there was no market for them.

Back home, Willie asked Ethel what she could do with venison. Could they use it in the business? She uncovered an old traditional recipe for game soup, and together with Marian McNeill, the doyenne of traditional Scottish cuisine who had roots in Fochabers, she concocted what became the best-selling quality soup in the world. Millions of cans of Royal Game soup are now made to that first, additive-free recipe and marketed around the world.

Such imaginative gambles are landmarks on the Baxter path to success. There was pickled beetroot, for instance. Today, Ethel's son Ian supplies many of the vegetables for the soups and other products. But in the 1930s, there was no pickled beetroot in the catalogue.

Willie had happened to call in at an Italian warehouse in Banff. The warehouseman was a friend of Willie's and he wasn't a happy

146

man. He took Willie through to the back of the building where he showed him a royal purple ceiling. Upstairs in a storeroom, jars of pickled beetroot were hitting the roof. The beets had fermented and the jars were exploding wildly. 'Can't you make pickled beetroot, Willie?' asked the warehouseman.

More, one suspects, because the beet had been bottled by a rival firm from Glasgow than any other reason, Willie took the explosive problem home to Ethel. She pondered over the situation and ordered half a tonne of beetroot from Oakbank Reformatory School in Aberdeen, where recalcitrant lads kept out of trouble raising vegetables. She cooked the beets and put them into the strongest malt vinegar available, numbered 24. The beets certainly didn't ferment. But nor could anyone eat them. The vinegar was the equivalent of trying to drink 100 per cent proof Scotch whisky. It cut your throat.

Back to the drawing board, and Ethel eventually succeeded in diluting the vinegar until the product was so highly palatable that it, too, became a best-seller and today 50 tonnes of beetroot are prepared daily to meet the demand. They followed up that success with another pre-war favourite, beetroot in wine vinegar.

Ethel used the rapidly-developing new technology to best advantage. Always before her time, she put haggis in a can before the last war, and popped poussins — whole baby chickens — into glass jars with jelly.

But life didn't simply revolve around the ever-expanding Speyside factory complex. Ethel, five feet nine inches tall and strongly built, was well known as a sportswoman. One of her brothers was a cricketer who came home to Speyside with gossip of the great cricketing names. Ethel ensured that her sons played the game and played it well. She had tennis courts built at the back of the house beside the factory, and there the whole family enjoyed the sport when it encouraged finer qualities than perhaps it does today. She wanted her boys out in the fresh air. She wanted them to be scholars. She barred them from the factory and insisted they spend their summers studying in the garden. And at home, she began what has become a Baxter tradition of entertaining clients as guests — using her taste and culinary skills to charm them over the long dining table.

As time went by, she also became embroiled in raising funds to save the Fochabers Scottish Episcopal Church. Episcopal Church? This daughter of canny kirk-goers? She became a member of the

Scottish Episcopal Church when she married Willie. The Baxters, too, had been staunch Presbyterians. But business got between George and finer feelings.

The local minister in Fochabers had some difficulty in paying his grocery bills, so Willie's father simply stepped across the street from the kirk to the family chapel of the Dukes of Richmond and Gordon and became an Episcopalian. It turned out to be a good move as far as the Episcopal congregation of later years would be concerned. The chapel was used to station soldiers in the war and was ill-used. Then came the news that the run-down building was to be turned into a cinema. Ethel Baxter would hear none of it. With the dean of an Episcopal-run children's home, she tirelessly raised cash until the church was not only saved from housing a silver screen but became the gem in the crown of the diocese. Neo-classical windows were restored, the building was refurbished, and the members of the tiny congregation still remember her in their prayers.

Ethel never forgot her original profession, either. Always proud of her midwifery qualifications, she became a fund-raiser for a variety of nursing and midwifery bodies, too.

She has inspired in subsequent Baxter women a determination to live up to her multi-faceted talents. And the loyalty she and Willie engendered has led to the family closing ranks against all attempts by multi-national companies to take over the firm. At the last count, there have been almost 150 take-over bids, each disdainfully turned down. Ethel and Willie founded that dynasty. There is no doubt that Ethel's taste and skills created the original interest in the food firm with the classy products.

In 1952, Ena Baxter joined the team when she married Ethel's son Gordon, today's chairman. An art teacher, she suddenly found she was making soups for Baxters. On a trip to America she picked up some recipes, including one for chicken gumbo soup. Knowing how much husband Gordon adored soup, she gave it a whirl, but had problems when she came to okra in the list of ingredients. It was something she was unfamiliar with, and Fochabers was hardly the place to find it. So she stepped out into the garden, picked some green beans and improvised. Gordon was delighted, and Ena has been improvising with recipes for soups and sauces and gourmet dishes ever since. Cream of Pheasant, Game Consomme and Salmon Bisque are just some of her creations. Trial and error perfected her de luxe tomato soup. Now she is producing soups for the Japanese market. Just as the Depression hit Ethel and Willie, the business had to be put back on its feet after the last war, and Gordon has inherited his father's selling skills while Ena has proved herself a Baxter woman in Ethel's mould.

Ethel's imaginative, driving, creative role in the Baxter company enabled it to become a world leader in high-quality canned and bottled food, laying the basis on which her sons could expand in a fiercely competitive post-war market.

Her emphasis on quality founded the reputation which husband Willie could sell to the world's top retailers. Instilling the importance of that quality into her sons allowed them to rebuild Baxters of Speyside after war-time setbacks into the much-sought-after company it is today, with its £20-million-plus annual turnover, £1-million-plus annual profits and 500-strong labour force. The firm is classed by the Scottish Development Agency as one of the top 50 in Scotland.

There have been around 150 take-over bids for Baxters, including one from rival canning giants, Heinz. All have been turned down, because Ethel also instilled into her sons the intense family pride which keeps them independent and quality conscious.

Willie Baxter sold to Harrods and Macys; his son Gordon has added prestige contracts with Hilton Hotels, Trusthouse Forte and top airlines, and Heinz recently brought out a new up-market range to challenge the Baxter grip on the quality market.

Gordon and Ena's daughter Audrey has now joined brother Andrew and Michael in the family firm. So fierce is her family loyalty that when she marries she will retain her maiden name — although she admits this has caused arguments reminiscent of Ethel's ding-dong battles with Willie!

Audrey is a merchant banker and as the company continues to grow — it sells around £25 million worth of soups, jams, sauces and gourmet items around the world — she is to plan its progress.

Ethel Baxter died after a colostomy operation in 1963, and Willie lived for another decade. For all Ethel had learned of fine manners in grand houses, she never became the grande dame even when she and Willie achieved their own fame and fortune. She tempered her Christian principles instilled in childhood with a compassion learned in the sickroom and got a dash of salty humour from Willie to round out her character.

It was Ethel who told the factory girls not to tangle with the

149

servicemen stationed in the area. And Ethel who told them what precautions to take if they did!

It is accepted that today's women like Audrey Baxter will take a career and continue it after marriage. Ethel Adam Baxter wasn't just a pioneer in becoming a working woman — she was prepared to take massive risks with her future when most women were rocking cradles.

She is buried in a hillside kirkyard on the way from the factory to Speymouth where the glittering grey North Sea meets rich agricultural land — land she helped make famous around the world by her own unceasing efforts.

AUTHOR

Marian Pallister is a journalist working with the *Evening Times* newspaper in Glasgow. She was Scottish Journalist of the Year in 1985.

SOURCES

Family and company background information supplied by Gordon Baxter, Baxters of Speyside chairman, and his daughter Audrey.

CHAPTER 13

Patrick Manson
Oriental Dairy Farmer
(1844—1922)

Nigel Cameron

Patrick Manson, like many another 19th-century pioneer in that era of opportunity and opportunists, was born in unremarkable circumstances. He was the second son of a typically 19th-century family of nine children, in the parish of Oldmeldrum, Aberdeenshire. When he was grown, Patrick sometimes referred to their Orkney ancestors as 'Norwegian pirates'.

His father was laird of an estate named Fingask, lying just outside Aberdeen, and he also managed one of the local banks. His mother, a woman of some distinction, was credited with both beauty and good spirits, and with 'artistic talents and great power of resource'. And to judge by Patrick Manson's later attainments in life it seems likely that he inherited much of his character from her. He grew up in Cromlet Hill, a comfortable square stone-built house of modest proportions in which he had been born. The house still stands.

The boy showed an early fascination with subjects that were then considered to mark him as a dull child. Frogs and insects seemed to interest him more than the usual childish things. When he was 13 the family moved into Aberdeen town for the sake of the children's education. Patrick attended a good school there and proved a studious but not particularly brilliant pupil. He had a fondness for cricket, something quite unusual in those days in northern Scotland, but he also liked 'tickling trout'. He was quite a good shot and, having killed a stray cat on his father's farm, he went on to dissect it, using the roof as his laboratory and discovering to his surprise that it had a tapeworm.

When he reached 15 his parents, oddly enough for people who appear to have taken trouble with his education, apprenticed their son to an iron works belonging to a member of the family. With his apparent interest in natural history this was surely a strange choice. And perhaps it was a sense of deep revolt against the work there that led to Patrick's developing a curvature of the spine with a related sluggishness of the right arm that was to remain with him for the rest of his days. On medical advice he was put flat on his back in bed, allowed up for only two hours each day.

His waking time was occupied with studying natural history, the more so when he discovered that this could count toward a medical curriculum. It was by this time obvious that he had made up his mind to become a doctor.

In 1861 the young Manson passed the entrance examination for Aberdeen University, and during his time there supplemented his studies with work at Edinburgh University during summer recesses. At the tender age of 20 he passed the final examination — too young for even the most brilliant student to be granted a degree. Filling in the following year with more study, he graduated in 1865.

His first job was in Durham Lunatic Asylum where he seems to have concentrated on post mortem dissection, and where he had in his own words 'ample opportunity of finding out how crassly ignorant I was and how terribly inadequate was the medical training of those days'.

Manson wrote his MD thesis on a subject he had researched in the course of those many post mortems, achieving the degree in 1866. The adventurous spirit in him was already marked, as was the ardent desire for knowledge that he had shown since childhood — and he was scarcely likely to be happy for long with the routine of the Durham or any other Lunatic Asylum. Another young Manson was already in Shanghai. Patrick wrote to him, seeking a post in the East.

At that time, under the terms of a treaty imposed on the Chinese by Britain, the Chinese Maritime Customs was headed by Sir Robert Hart who recruited most of his officers from Scotland — that pool of the century's empire-builders. It has to be admitted by even the most patriotic Scot that Scotland in mid-Victorian times was hardly the most lively place in the world. For a bright young doctor or an aspiring engineer in that age of steam and steel the furthest reaches of an expanding empire offered opportunities and the sort of promise hardly to be discovered at home. However idyllic Queen Victoria considered the Highlands to be — the area surrounding Balmoral Castle which included Patrick Manson's home — the permanent inhabitants of the region could well be forgiven for taking a somewhat less romantic view. Much as Manson delighted in his native heath, returning to it with pleasure in later years, the adventure of life beckoned more urgently in his youth.

By June 1867, Manson was disembarking at Takao in Taiwan, joining the service of the Chinese Maritime Customs and a society of 16 Europeans resident there. This was to be his home for the next several years, his official duties including the inspection of ships calling at the port and treating the ailments of their crews. With his by now developing drive, it was not long before Manson had set up a private practice among Westerners and Chinese, had involved himself in the local mission hospital, and was making journeys up-country to investigate the endemic diseases — leprosy and elephantiasis. He wrote that he managed even to make contact with the 'aborigines' of the highlands.

In three years he was able to repay his father the £750 spent on his medical training. After five, when he was about 27, political events of a local nature forced the British consul in Taiwan to advise his departure.

153

Early in 1871 Manson set sail for the China mainland, settling in Amoy, another of the Treaty Ports wrested from China at the end of the first Opium War. There his routine continued much on the lines of that in Taiwan with researches both practical and theoretical into what had by this time become his main interest — tropical diseases. By 1875 Manson was on leave in Scotland where he married. Then it was back in Amoy with a quickly growing family. Another home leave in Aberdeenshire in 1882 was spent shooting and fishing. 'It is good to picture him,' his two stilted biographers write of this period, 'the complete Scottish edition of the British hunting squire. . . . It is good to picture him unscathed in mind and body by ardent but little appreciated work in a trying climate, forgetting his labour . . . forgetting *filaria* and gout. . . .' The direct, unpretentious Manson would have been very uncomfortable in this sea of sententiousness. 'Early in the summer of 1883 he was "owre the sea" again and back in the Amoy harness, once more at work on *filaria* (a parasitic worm), on that confirmation of its metamorphosis within the mosquito. . . .'

The still young Manson was within an inch of discovering the way in which the *filaria* is transmitted from mosquito to human beings in the act of its piercing the skin. The discovery was made by others and published in *The Veterinarian* of March 1883. But, communications being what they were then, Manson did not see the report.

Now a man of almost 40, Dr. Manson began to consider the responsibilities which his growing family laid upon him, and he decided to move to Hong Kong which probably appeared at that time very much more dynamic and challenging than the infinite backwaters of Amoy. He moved to the colony in 1883 and set up there in private practice.

On his arrival Manson was met by (among other members of the profession) Dr Phineas Ayres, the colonial surgeon. And it was from this encounter, with all it implied in the realisation of the health conditions in Hong Kong, that stemmed the great compulsion in Manson to begin what were to be his own lasting memorials as well as his great contribution to his new place of abode. The characteristics of the pioneer — the essentially Scottish seeker after the new and the better in society — were at this point afforded their chance. Manson did not hesitate.

It came about in this way: Dr Ayres had been appointed in

1873, one of his duties being to write an annual report on the state of public health in the colony. These were to be forwarded to the governor whose duty it was to send them on to the Colonial Office in London. Dr Ayres's first report, revealing as it did the preposterous and potentially disastrous state of all forms of sanitation, and by implication the total inattention to duty by everyone concerned, from the governor himself downward in the civil hierarchy, which had permitted this state of affairs to exist and to persist, was suppressed by the governor. The two following reports also failed to reach London.

A few sentences from these reports suffice to reveal the squalor, and the threat of disaster to the public inherent in the situation.

> However much on the surface the town of Victoria [on Hong Kong island] may appear cleaner than most Eastern towns, beneath the surface it would be difficult to find a filthier condition of things. My first series of inspections revealed that pigs were kept all over the town by hundreds, and that pigsties were to be found under the beds and in the kitchens of first, second and third floors. . . . Either from convenience or from ignorance of a late Inspector of Markets, whose duty it was to see that pigs were kept in proper places, many of these people had Government licences to keep their pigs there. Imagine houses whose upper floors are constructed of thin boards . . . and whose lower floors are inhabited, and the state they would be under these circumstances, the pigs' urine, etc., dropping through from floor to floor.

Ayres described how cows were driven into basements as calves, and kept there during their whole milk-yielding lives — these being the 'dairies' which supplied milk to the European households situated 50 metres (45 yards) uphill from them on the then fashionable Caine Road. Down the hill in the pullulating Taipingshan district of Chinese dwellings and 'dairies', milking and everything else was carried on by lamplight, and when a cow had to be removed, it had to be dismembered on the premises since its bulk prevented the carcass from exit through the narrow door. In one place, wrote Dr Ayres, 'I found a quarter of beef hanging over the bed of a man who was in the last stages of smallpox.'

When such reports were eventually forced out of the hands of a reluctant administration, London sent out an energetic man with powers to remedy matters. But by the time of Manson's arrival he had been able to make only a minimal impression on the problem.

Here, then, was a state of affairs threatening dire calamity for the whole community of the colony. Plague in epidemic proportions could break out at almost any moment. Manson, the tropical disease specialist, the spirited Scots doctor, reacted in two ways. Involved as he was with a busy practice and also in research into the malarial parasite, he 'came to the front', in his biographers' words, with his 'first public venture in the forming of a local medical society'.

His presidential address to its first meeting in 1886 was a farsighted one. He enthused on the vast field for medical research in China, remarked on how imperfect was medical knowledge of even the commonest fevers. He underlined the weakness of Hong Kong's medical profession in its lack of a local publication that would report experience and encourage the exchange of knowledge and ideas; and he voiced a plea, novel in those times, for proper medical care of the large class of *Eurasians,* as well as for Europeans.

The Medical Society duly set up, Manson turned his energies to establishing a college of medicine, setting up in embryo just such an institution within the newly built Alice Memorial Hospital. For funds he badgered the western community, even succeeding in co-opting Li Hung-chang, the illustrious and most forward-looking of officials in the Imperial Government of China. Ironically, the first and brightest graduate of the college was Dr Sun Yat-sen, founder of the revolutionary Kuomintang party whose activities led, eventually, to the Communist revolution. Li Hung-chang would scarcely have approved.

Manson was joined in Hong Kong by a fellow Scot, Dr James Cantlie, who came from Banff and had qualified at Aberdeen. The two were soon to be involved in various schemes, and they maintained a curious friendship despite their very different temperaments.

Manson had always been a reserved character, verging on the stern: Cantlie was an outgoing enthusiast, filled with new ideas, even slightly eccentric. Possibly the bond between them was recognition of a similar driving force, however differently expressed in their actions. Its springs were rooted, as in so many Scots who made their mark on the world, in that peculiarly Scottish form of Calvinism in whose orbit they were raised. The principle that work and striving, especially if the effort involved the betterment of clan or family and, in a wider application, the 'improvement of society', are good in themselves is one deeply embedded in the Scots character. Its corollary, that pleasure is necessarily accompanied by a sense of guilt merely reinforced the need for that special thrust in the make-up of such men – especially in the 19th century.

Cantlie was to be drawn into the second of Manson's responses to the health situation in Hong Kong. This enterprise developed out of interest in the role played by nutrition in tropical climates in the general pattern of health. And doubtless in Manson's case the continuing need to buttress his resources in respect of providing for his family in the future was seldom far from his thoughts. Human actions are seldom inspired by a single motive. Manson decided to set up a dairy farm. He could not have known it at the time but this was the single most far-reaching decision of his life.

His initial memorandum on the subject is lengthy but succinct.

From a hygienic point of view the milk supply of a community [he meant the western community — Chinese did not then use dairy products] is second only in importance to its water supply. . . . Unfortunately, in consequence of the epidemic among cows from which the very inadequate, unreliable and exceedingly expensive milk supply [is derived] it seems likely to give out altogether . . . this is a serious matter, serious enough for the general public, but especially so for young children and the sick, with whom milk is the principal and often the only food. . . . It is felt . . . that the present is a good opportunity to establish, by means of a Public Company with an adequate capital, a Dairy Farm.

The farm would not only provide a good return on invested capital but also a reliably pure, bacteria-free, and adequate quantity of milk 'at such a price that what has hitherto been a luxury of the rich may become, what milk ought to be, one of the principal elements in the food of the poor in all communities.'

Manson had done his research into the feasibility of rearing cows in a subtropical climate such as that of Hong Kong. He had seen cows kept by Europeans in Amoy, and he now calculated the probable milk yield. 'What is accomplished there ought to be quite possible here.'

157

The memorandum is really the basis of a company prospectus complete with ways and means, costs and financial rewards, and goes into great detail about all aspects of the proposed farm.

Several daunting factors appeared. First, the hilly nature of Hong Kong terrain where hardly a piece of flat land occurs naturally. Second was the fact that in the subtropics the cow is an exotic animal requiring special care. It is not feasible to keep it outside during the roughly nine months of hot weather. Third, a large part of the fodder would have to be imported from the New Territories or from the mainland, the remainder specially grown on the farm. Ordinary grass does not readily grow in Hong Kong, and the solution to this problem – an eventual rather than an immediate one – came largely at the suggestion of Dr Cantlie to grow Guinea (sometimes called Elephant) grass.

But the most difficult obstacle of all to be overcome was finding a suitable site. Exploring far and wide, Manson came to the conclusion that the precipitous slopes of the southwest aspect of Hong Kong island where, it was alleged, there blew a cooler breeze in hot summer months, were the best location.

'Gentlemen desirous of forwarding the above scheme,' concluded the memorandum, 'are requested to subscribe their names.' Gentlemen did. And Manson, canny as ever, roped in some of the most solid businessmen and brightest brains of the colony. The Dairy Farm Company Limited was formed in the spring of 1886. Dr Manson had been a mere three years in Hong Kong. Already he had made a perceptible mark on his surroundings.

As chairman of the company his board consisted of Mr (later Sir) Paul Chater, an Armenian Christian businessman and one of the colony's leading figures; Mr Phineas Ryrie, another businessman whose wealth permitted him many charitable acts, and whose sole eccentricity was letting imported rabbits loose on a neighbouring island so that he could indulge a fancy for shooting them; Mr W. H. Ray, a leading figure in insurance; and Mr James Coughtrie, another insurance man and amateur artist. Dr Cantlie joined later.

The company formed, the farm started up in 1886, special cowsheds having been constructed according to an American design which was doubtless imported along with the first 80 head of cattle from the United States. But the results of the first working years were disappointing. The initial herd turned out to be poor stock, and the directors lacked experience in farming. They had also calculated without allowance for the fluctuating market price of fodder.

Manson need not take all the blame for this. His instructions on management were beyond reproach, far ahead of the times. The cowboys (the picturesque title given to the illiterate Chinese farm-hands and milkers) were given written instructions hung up in every cowshed (and doubtless communicated orally to them). These contained rules for sterilization of everything connected with the cows, the sheds, and the milking. The cowboys were to wash their hands, change into white coats provided, cleanse the cows' udders and let the first squirts of milk go, before milking proper began. Such detailed instructions − and there were many more − were not invariably carried out in farms in Britain even well into the 20th century. Any Chinese employee on the farm who had ever been employed in the Chinese dairies must have found the notices quite bizarre and probably put it all down to the curious ways of the 'red-haired barbarians'.

The first year's farming showed a loss of £13,000 − on a total capitalisation of £30,000. But the directors were 'encouraged to persevere,' as one early historical note on the company records, 'by the measure of public support afforded' their efforts. The second and third years were better, and the demand for milk developed steadily. In 1889 the company's capital was increased to £100,000 in order to finance construction of more cowsheds and fodder storage facilities.

At an extraordinary meeting in July that year it was also proposed to ask Dr Manson (who had by then relinquished chairmanship) to obtain in England an assistant manager − the post until then having been held by the chairman. More land was acquired, a central milk distribution depot was proposed; measures were taken to check the spread of cattle disease. And it was noted that the 'Government Analyst and also the Colonial Surgeon have expressed a very favourable opinion of its [the milk's] high-class qualities, classing it with that produced . . . by the Aylesbury Dairy Company of England.'

The struggle to produce virtually sterile milk in Hong Kong appeared to have been won. The feat was all the more remarkable in that no such thing could be said at comparable times of the milk supply in London. In fact, not many years before, samples of milk supplied in London could still be discovered which contained blood or pus. So Hong Kong's achievement was all the more remarkable.

Manson had now been in the colony since 1883, and seems to have felt in a position to retire from farming. He left with his family that year, seen off by representatives of all sections of the community. Despite his reserved character he had proved a popular doctor, and was certainly a much respected man. His several far-sighted public services, and the unstinting manner, once he had formulated what he wanted to do, in which he went ahead and achieved his goal, had singled him out as an important figure in the life of the colony.

He had been in China for a total of 23 years and, to quote once more his fulsome biographers, 'had not spared himself whether at the call of his profession or in his efforts to increase and diffuse professional knowledge; he was opulent in varied scientific experience, and he had also acquired reasonable wealth; so he decided to drop the responsibilities of medical practice.'

In March 1889 he sailed for home. While still in Hong Kong he had been appointed medical adviser to the Colonial Office in London, and on reaching Britain he set about reorganising the colonial medical service − with important effect.

Manson's contributions to humanity's health and welfare were not yet by any means ended. He was to found the London School of Hygiene and Tropical Medicine, an institution very much alive and at work on his lines today. He was to become a Fellow of the Royal Society and of the Royal College of Physicians in London. His home town, Aberdeen, honoured him with the degree of Doctor of Laws. Oxford University added to that its honorary Doctorate in Science. The old Queen Victoria made him a Companion of the Order of St Michael and St George in 1900, and in 1908 Edward VII made him a Knight of that Order, while George V in 1912 elevated him to its Grand Cross, the highest rank of the Order.

Manson lived on until 1922. His greatness lies in his direct, sincere, persevering application to his profession, and in compassion for the human race. Not content with an impeccably conducted medical practice, he sought continually to extend the scope of the healing arts into realms of scientific discipline at that time only beginning to be explored. In Hong Kong he saw the scourge of tropical disease and at once set about improving the quality of medical aid by initiating the movement to bring professional knowledge together and to form a medical college. He recognised the dangers inherent in the poverty of the public health measures, and he reacted swiftly by laying the foundations for a supply of affordable, clean, and safe dairy products. In the field of public health in a tropical place Patrick Manson can credibly be seen as the harbinger of 20th-century approaches to some of its more crucial problems.

The Dairy Farm gradually increased its herds and its activities under a line of Scots managers and mostly Scots personnel at executive level — something that remained a dominant factor in the company until well after the Second World War. With fluctuations in its fortunes but an overall progress, on the hilly terrain chosen by Manson, the company prospered and grew enormously. What Manson had founded with a few thousand pounds and a lot of determination in 1886 branched out to become the giant organization it is today. The farm itself lasted for exactly 100 years, when the gradual erosion of its steep acres in favour of housing estates for the population made it impracticable to continue: and milk is now supplied from the mainland where a much larger dairy farm is maintained. In its centenary year The Dairy Farm Company reported sales in excess of HK$10,000 million (£6,333 million).

The revolution in dietary habits of the nearly six million Chinese inhabitants of Hong Kong, which in the long past did not include dairy products, now accommodate the drinking of cow's milk, as indeed does that of most contemporary Southeast Asian peoples. Not all of this change is directly attributable to the work of Manson. But certainly he was the pioneer, the man on whose vision and achievement others later built.

AUTHOR

Nigel Cameron is an historian and art critic resident in Hong Kong for 27 years.

BIBLIOGRAPHY

Philip H. Manson-Bahr and A. Alcock, *The Life and Work of Sir Patrick Manson*, Cassell & Co., 1927.
Sir Philip Manson-Bahr, *History of the School of Tropical Medicine in London* (1899—1949), H. K. Lewis & Co., 1956.

CHAPTER 14

Sir William Alexander Smith
Founder of the Boys' Brigade
(1854—1914)

Brian Fraser

On the evening of Thursday, 4th October 1883, a young Glasgow Sunday School teacher stood in his Free Church Mission Hall awaiting the response to his new idea for the Christian development of teenage boys. At 8 o'clock, as the doors opened, 59 boys from the North Woodside area of the city surged into the hall. They were a disorderly group, between 12 and 16 years of age. Some were bent on mischief and some had little else to do. A few left but most stayed and the Boys' Brigade — the first uniformed youth organisation came into being. The young Scot was called William Smith, and his ideas pioneered the evolution of modern youth work and the growth of uniformed youth organisations throughout the world.

William Alexander Smith was born on 27th October 1854 some 300 miles from Glasgow at 'Pennyland House' on the outskirts of Thurso. His home overlooks Dunnet Head, the most northerly point on the British mainland. Until he was 14 years old, he lived and was educated in Thurso, a small Caithness town of 3,000 or so population. Not surprisingly, in an area where the army provided one of the few alternatives to crofting, the family followed a tradition of military service with Smith's father, David, having been an ensign in the 7th Dragoon Guards during the Kaffir War of 1849-50 before returning to Caithness where he joined the Volunteer Artillery Corps, reaching the rank of Major. William's grandfather, also William, had been commissioned to the 78th Highland Regiment of Foot (formerly the 'Rosshire Buffs'). The impact of the family's military history on William was considerable and provided him with many of the methods he was later to use in his work with teenage boys.

Although compulsory education was still some way off, William Smith attended a traditional Scottish parish school, the Miller Institution, later to be known as Thurso Academy. Little is known of his academic record, but his contemporaries speak of his love of outdoor activities, in particular the game of shinty.

In 1868 the pattern of life changed abruptly for William when his father, a Director of the Labuan Coal Company, died on 8th January, at Swatow in China. The widowed Harriet Smith moved with her family into the town of Thurso and accepted the offer of her brother, Alexander Fraser, a Glasgow merchant, to have William taken into his home and business in Glasgow. Alex. Fraser, an evangelical Free Church man, was a wholesale dealer in clothing and shawls, dealing principally with the South American market. Living with his three sisters on the edge of the prosperous west-end burgh of Hillhead, Fraser operated a successful business with premises in Princess Square, off fashionable Buchanan Street, and a summer home at Callander near the Trossachs. William and his family spent the summer of 1868 in Callander then, in November, when his mother, brothers and sister returned to Thurso, he remained behind in Glasgow with his uncle and aunts.

It is sometimes wondered why the world's first voluntary youth organisation began, not only in Scotland, but in the Victorian city of Glasgow. In a way, however, the man and his environment came together at the right time. By the late 19th century, Glasgow had grown to be the second city of the Empire with a population outstripping that of any other provincial city in the United Kingdom. Politically it was a Liberal city, with MPs from the middle-class Protestant group of radical free traders whose commercial and manufacturing progress had taken the city to its pre-eminent position. With a dependence on textiles, iron and heavy engineering, the city was the centre of industry and commerce in the West of Scotland. The growth in importance of the Clyde and its shipbuilding, combined with the success of the traditional industries to give Glasgow entrepreneurs a vibrant confidence dented only by rare setbacks such as the collapse of the City of Glasgow Bank in 1878. The city was held to be one of the most aggressively efficient in the Europe of this period and the all-pervading Liberal, Nonconformist influence gave support to the social philanthropy of the merchants and manufacturers which was to make itself felt in the new area of youth work. The same evangelical influence permeated the local corridors of power.

Although Glasgow could boast of an unequalled layout of parks and recreational grounds, and an excellent transport system, it suffered critical housing problems. The densely populated city had expanded rapidly, but remained compact with little or no suburban sprawl. Overcrowded housing had its consequential health problems, highlighted in the age group from which the Boys' Brigade was to recruit. By the late 19th century, the segregation trend in many British cities during the Victorian period was evident with the factories and workforce of Glasgow being concentrated, by and large, in the central and east end and the middle classes and their businesses edging westwards. As the city expanded, new artisan housing areas were located in close proximity to middle and upper class areas making missionary work simpler. The growth of the west end, where the Boys' Brigade was initially to establish itself, took an irregular shape about two miles in length from east to west and varying in width from 400 yards to one mile. This resulted in a residential area such as Hillhead (where William Smith and many of his Boys' Brigade colleagues lived) being sandwiched between the working-class suburbs of Partick and Maryhill. Domestic mission work could be carried out at only a short distance from the parent congregation. The need and scope for such mission work was becoming more apparent with the increasing number of young people — 10% of the male population in 1883 were between 10 and 14 years old. Prominent industrialists and philanthropists such as Sir William Collins, the publisher, and Michael Connal, the shipbuilder, were leading the way in this work and were to be strong supporters of the Boys' Brigade. Evangelical groups such as the 'Association for Promoting the Religious and Social Improvement of the City' had men like these in its membership — one of whom was William Smith's uncle, Alexander Fraser.

During his early years in Glasgow, William worked solidly in his uncle's warehouse, and took various classes to improve himself. He settled down to the routine of middle-class business life in the city, attending Y.M.C.A. lectures, sailing trips and soirées, but a growing estrangement from his uncle, accounted for his leaving Alex. Fraser and Company in 1878 to establish the firm of Smith, Smith and Company with his brother Donald, who had arrived in Glasgow in 1873. William's mother arrived from Thurso to look after her son's new home in nearby Kersland Terrace until his marriage six years later. In 1881, James G. Findlay, a friend and colleague, entered into partnership with him to form the firm Smith, Findlay and Company, dealing in a variety of shawls, plaids and tartans for export.

One of William's major disagreements with his uncle was over his involvement with the local Volunteer Forces. Alex. Fraser disapproved of his nephew's enlistment in the 1st Lanark Volunteers which ran counter to Fraser's more pacifist views. The influence of the volunteer movement on William and on the foundation and early development of the Boys' Brigade was, however, to prove considerable.

The Volunteer Force had been formed in 1859 with the military objective of providing some form of defence in the event of invasion at a time of British weakness. The likely perpetrators of such an offence were regarded as the French under Napoleon III. Men, however, enlisted for social as well as military reasons and, in some ways, it might be regarded as the military expression of the Victorian spirit of self-help. Apart from the contribution to the nation's defence, the movement offered opportunities for middle class and working class alike, providing for the former a pleasant and gratifying way of occupying increased leisure time, and for the latter, social and recreational activities otherwise denied them. For the nation it might provide a method of instilling into the younger generation the values of discipline, obedience and *esprit de corps* which were to be later extended to the teenage members of the Boys' Brigade movement.

The Volunteer movement was particularly strong in Scotland. Glasgow reflected the Scottish situation and most regiments consisted of companies formed by businesses and professions, led by a strong upper-middle-class group such as existed in the city. With the 1st Lanark Rifle Volunteers drawing from the prosperous west-end business population and with William Smith's family tradition of Volunteering in Caithness, it was perhaps inevitable that the young businessman now living in Hillhead should enlist. The 1st Lanark Rifle Volunteers included companies originally established for procurators and lawyers; accountants, stockbrokers and actuaries; bankers and clerks; as well as for particular businesses such as Messrs. Wylie and Lochhead, Buchanan Street, and J. & W. Campbell and Company, Ingram Street, and the leading shipping companies. The Regiment could later boast of a number of national figures, including two future Prime Ministers — Campbell-Bannerman and Bonar Law — and Jimmy Maxton, future Chairman of the Independent Labour Party. Volunteering was an enthusiastic business.

At the same time as he was pursuing his love of the military, William Smith was involving himself in the religious life of the city. This was to be even more important in his later work. Living in Alexander Fraser's household, he would have become familiar with the ideas of the Glasgow churchmen and philanthropists — work which was gaining in momentum and which was to be a major factor in the formation of the Boys' Brigade.

The religious complexion of late 19th-century Glasgow provides the canvas on which the emergence of the Boys' Brigade can be sketched and helps to explain the initial success of the movement. The new organisation was to be inter-denominational and its origins do not lie solely, or even mainly, within the established Church of Scotland. The first ten Companies were formed in association with the nonconformist congregations and, indeed, after five years of existence there were more Companies connected with Dissenting congregations than with the established Churches of Scotland and England.

166

The 'Disruption' in the Scottish Church in 1843, following a century of secessions and unions brought into being the Free Church as a rival denomination to the Church of Scotland. In Glasgow, a city with 31 religious denominations meeting in 331 churches and halls, the strength of feeling was reflected! The three principal Protestant denominations (Church of Scotland, Free Church and United Presbyterian Church) were fairly evenly represented in the city in the 1880s and the period is marked by an increase in church building and mission work. As the city expanded westwards, impressive buildings were constructed in the newly populated areas from where missions could be sent and youth work organised.

Both the geographical structure of Glasgow and the competitive outreach of the major religious denominations facilitated the extension of missionary work. By the 1860s this effort was being supplemented by the charitable and social reform work of evangelical associations such as the Glasgow City Mission and the Grove Street Home Mission (which has produced notable Scots such as Sir David McNee, former Commissioner of the London Metropolitan Police and a B.B. office-bearer). The Temperance movement which had originated in the Maryhill district of the city in 1829 under Robert Kettle, cotton manufacturer and friend of Thomas Chalmers, the Free Church leader, evolved into the Scottish Temperance League in 1844. The Glasgow Abstainers Union was active and the Band of Hope had 650 juvenile societies in Scotland by 1870.

As the century progressed there was an increasing awareness of the need to channel part of this social and religious missionary effort towards the teenage population. This assisted the new agencies leading the way in work with young people — the age group who were in a large measure lost to the Church. One major agency was the Glasgow YMCA which, by the 1880s, had developed from a relatively small organisation with a spiritual objective to an extensive flourishing association with 180 branches and over 7,000 members. The YMCA emblem, a triangle, denotes fitness of body, mind and spirit, and the wider spectrum of activity (which included evening classes, athletic clubs and a range of 'extra-mural' activities) was in evidence when William Smith and his colleagues were leading their own congregational Young Men's Societies and Sunday Schools. He himself joined the Glasgow YMCA in the autumn of 1872.

167

By the time the Boys' Brigade had been formed, further specialised work and organisations for the adolescent were in evidence. William Quarrier, an evangelical Baptist better known for his orphans' homes, had formed Working Boys' Brigades in the 1860s — Shoeblack Brigade, News Brigade and Parcels Brigade — with distinctive uniforms and access to residential accommodation and educational or recreational facilities. Quarrier was supported again by the same families of Liberal Dissenters later to be associated with William Smith — J. Campbell White (later Lord Overtoun), chemical manufacturer; William A. Campbell, warehouse owner (later Campbells, Stewart and MacDonald), Robert Binnie, builder; W. S. Blackie, publisher, and the Coats family of cotton thread manufacturing fame in Paisley.

The influence of the local movements was important in creating the environment within which William Smith was to work. One particular organisation influenced William and his contemporaries but it is not well known, even to Scots — The Glasgow Foundry Boys' Religious Society.

During the formative years of the Boys' Brigade, the Glasgow Foundry Boys' Religious Society was at its peak and many of the early Brigade leaders were associated with it. The origins of the Society lie not in the missionary zeal of the middle- and upper-class philanthropists of 19th-century Glasgow, but in the compassion of a working-class girl, Mary Ann Clough. As the Industrial Revolution reached its zenith, a large number of iron foundries were sited on the banks of the Forth and Clyde Canal, in the north of Glasgow. To assist the moulders, many boys were employed from age 10 to 12, and, thrown in among the rough and ready foundry workers at an impressionable age, they would quickly assume the habits and manners of their adult colleagues. It was fear of this which motivated the young factory girl to obtain the use of a room where she was employed to hold Sunday afternoon meetings for around 50 boys. When she emigrated to New Zealand in 1862 it seemed that this small pocket of missionary effort would disappear. However, in 1865 the work was taken up by four Glasgow businessmen — William Hunter, William Martin, James Hunter and Alexander MacKeith — and the Glasgow Foundry Boys' Religious Society was officially launched. The organisation, supported by familiar city figures, experienced a rapid growth, reaching a peak of membership in 1886 with over 16,000 boys (and girls) and almost 2,000 leaders.

Thereafter its strength slowly declined until World War I, after which a sharper decline was suffered, although it remains active in a few areas of the city today.

The Foundry Boys' Religious Society which had spread throughout Scotland was concerned with the same age range as that with which The Boys' Brigade was about to deal and it organised itself in four areas — religious, educational, social reform and provident. The formation of evening classes, savings banks and excursions followed the increasingly familiar pattern, but of greater relevance, and influence, for William Smith, was the introduction of drill. By obtaining the services of local Volunteers (from 1st Lanark Artillery) the methods of the Society were later used by the Boys' Brigade. The influence of the Society on later uniformed youth organisations has not generally been recognised. As the Boys' Brigade established itself, however, many aspects of the Foundry Boys' work and philosophy can be discerned. The similar age grouping, use of drill, religious basis, encouragement of temperance and development of outdoor activities, provided a link which was strengthened by the welcome given by the Society to William Smith's great idea in 1883.

The influence of this atmosphere on the teenage William Smith must have been considerable. In 1874, when he was 20 years old, his religious beliefs were further deepened. This was the year of Moody and Sankey's evangelical revivalist campaign and their work made a great impression on William. Moody and Sankey's Scottish campaign in 1873-74 had a considerable impact on Scottish religious life, and nowhere was this impact stronger than in Glasgow where the glass-built Crystal Palace was packed to a capacity of 5,000 time and again. This evangelical revival initially affected the middle classes and provided a strong stimulus to the social and philanthropic work already begun in the city. The missionary agencies were infused with fresh religious spirit as a result of the significant success of the evangelists. Young upper- and middle-class business and professional men, such as Henry Drummond and Campbell-White, who were later to be associated with the Boys' Brigade, communicated directly with Moody and followed him in his campaigns, enthusiastically taking the revivalist message back to their particular Church congregations.

As well as strengthening and directing William Smith's religious convictions, the Moody and Sankey campaign provided further support for the establishment of the Boys' Brigade by stimulating

169

the social and missionary outreach of the city's Churches. One of Moody's most devoted followers was the Rev. George Reith (father of Lord Reith, first Director General of the BBC), the young minister of the College Free Church where Alexander Fraser and his family were members.

After attending Moody and Sankey's meetings, William Smith joined the College Free Church on 12th April 1874, thus switching from the Church of Scotland denomination within which he had been raised to his uncle's Free Church denomination. In September 1874 he proposed to the Rev. George Reith that a Young Men's Society be formed as the Woodside Morning Branch of the YMCA. Smith was joined in the leadership of the Society by two brothers, James and John Hill, who were to be officers in the 1st Glasgow Company, and James Moffat, whose later translation of the Old and New Testaments was to become world famous. Smith remained a member of the Society, becoming President of its evening meetings, until the North Woodside Boys' Brigade Bible Class was formed. It is unlikely that William himself would maintain that he had had an actual 'conversion' during the campaign of Moody and Sankey, as he in later years consistently doubted the value of spontaneous pledges and never encouraged the boys in his charge to risk the subsequent dangers of disillusionment. The feeling engendered, however, led directly to his involvement in the Young Men's Society and to Sunday School work at the College Free Church, before later moving to the North Woodside Mission Sunday School as a teacher and then Secretary. Smith was held in high regard in his Church congregation as an able and conscientious young man. This, no doubt, led to his being directed towards North Woodside. The Mission there promoted an extensive programme of religious, club and charitable activities throughout the week for the benefit of the surrounding population. It was into this busy programme that The Boys' Brigade was inserted after 1883, initially each Thursday evening at 8 p.m.

The mission activity which led directly to the establishment of the Boys' Brigade was that of the Sunday Schools. The maintenance of class order was in many instances extremely difficult and was not proving any more manageable now that compulsory elementary education was taking over much of the *raison d'être* of the Sunday School movement. Allied to this difficulty of fulfilling the object of the Sunday School was the

170

failure to retain the older children. Smith, at the North Woodside Mission, came face to face with the problem. In his direct involvement with it he was also grappling with the week-by-week difficulties of controlling Sunday School boys, and in 1883 he vigorously sought a solution. It was never imagined that the solution would have such far-reaching consequences.

In the summer of 1883 William Smith put the idea to the Rev. George Smith and his office bearers at the College Free Church, that Sunday School boys aged 12 and over should be formed into a Brigade. Although the proposal to introduce week-night activities within a framework of military discipline caused anxiety in some minds, Smith and his colleagues, the Hill brothers, were allowed to proceed and on the 4th October of that year held the first meeting of an organisation whose remarkable development could scarcely have been envisaged. In preparation for the inauguration of the movement, the initial format and regulations had been carefully planned. Having decided on the title 'The Boys' Brigade', the organisation's object was defined as: 'The advancement of Christ's Kingdom among boys and the promotion of habits of Reverence, Discipline, Self-respect and all that tends towards a true Christian manliness.'

The text of this object has remained the same for a century with the addition of the word 'obedience' in 1893. The design for a crest was agreed as the now familiar anchor, on which was enscribed the motto 'Sure and Stedfast' (taken from Hebrews, chapter 6 verse 19 — 'Hope we have as an anchor of the soul, both sure and stedfast'). The biblical spelling of 'stedfast' has been retained. Initially 59 boys joined, probably for a variety of reasons, not least of which would be the likelihood of further amusement at the expense of the Sunday School leaders. However, the application of strict discipline (no-one was allowed to 'fall in' if even a minute late) brought some surprising results and confirmed Smith's view that boys liked strictness and discipline as long as it was fair. At first all the boys were connected with the Mission but soon other Sunday School lads in the area were attracted.

At the beginning of the second session, 1884/85, The Boys' Brigade, as yet, consisted of just one company. However, by January 1885 the first indications that it might extend further were evident from the other Glasgow Churches. The 2nd Glasgow Company was formed in connection with the Berkeley Street

United Presbyterian Church Mission in North Street, near Charing Cross, Glasgow, an area not dissimilar to North Woodside. J. B. Couper, later to become M.P. for the Maryhill district of Glasgow, was the instigator, despite some initial reservations on the part of the parent Church. Couper was a recruit in the 1st Lanark Rifle Volunteers, and a leader of the Glasgow Foundry Boys' Religious Society in the Anderston area. When he called on Smith to collect a Volunteer prize for shooting, the two men spoke of their common interests and the experiment at North Woodside. It was in such a way that Smith's ideas percolated through the west-end area of Glasgow where many of the early Glasgow companies were to be located.

As Smith realised the potential of the movement he had begun, he called a meeting of those involved in the two existing companies together with other interested youth workers. On 26th January 1885 the meeting agreed to designate itself as the Council of the Boys' Brigade. A constitution was drawn up and it was confirmed that a company requesting registration required to be connected to a Church or other religious body. Thereafter, the Brigade advanced dramatically and by the time the newly formed Council had held its first annual meeting on 12th October 1885, 15 companies had been enrolled, 12 in Glasgow and 3 in Edinburgh. In Glasgow, the success of Smith's ideas led to the establishment of companies in all denominations, with the Nonconformists predominant.

When the Council met in October 1885, the potential of the new movement had already been recognised. The success of the 1st Glasgow Company had been consolidated and Smith could report that, of 55 boys on the roll the previous session, 51 remained and movement from the Brigade into YMCA or Church Young Men's societies had begun. The Council elected J. Carfrae Alston, Captain of the 5th Glasgow Company, as the first President of the Boys' Brigade. Alston was an influential tobacco merchant, a founder Volunteer and a leading member of the Renfield Free Church congregation. It is a reflection on the character of William Smith that he preferred to take the less illustrious, but infinitely more difficult office of Secretary. Three distinct administrative units of the organisation were established — (1) The Company, (2) The Battalion and (3) The Brigade. A further unit – the District – was interposed between (2) and (3) in 1913 to assist the more isolated companies and co-ordinate activities over a wider area. The estimated cost of establishing a company of 50 boys was calculated by Brigade Headquarters in the 1880s as being £3. 15. 5d, net. (£3.77) taking into account the sale of uniform items and an annual subscription of 1/- (5p).

William Smith's Boys' Brigade, now firmly established in Glasgow, was reaching the ears of others, not only in Scotland, but across the nation. Companies sprang up rapidly, both in the major cities and in small towns and rural areas. By 1890 there were 15,000 boys in membership, and on the tenth anniversary of the movement this figure stood at 26,000. Further promotion and expansion gave a total home and overseas membership of 75,000 at the turn of the century. The explanation for this dramatic progress lies in the social and historical conditions already described and in the attraction to boys, leaders and churches of Smith's ideas on boyhood. His observant study of adolescent nature, its 'gang' instincts and its potential when given, in his own phrase, an *esprit de corps*, predates the voluminous theories of later behavioural scientists. Smith appealed to the military and to the spiritual mind and to the many early leaders who would lay claim to both. The fusion of the ideals of the public school, the Volunteer regiment and Christian boyhood gave many philanthropists and mission members a tangible way of reaching those they were trying to help. Smith's crystallisation of the adolescent problem made many look in his direction.

But what were all the boys actually doing? What made William Smith's ideas so attractive to teenagers across the country — and, shortly, across the world?

Although based on Christian education and drill the Boys' Brigade was to give boys a far wider spectrum of activity, as it still does. The Sunday Bible Class and weekly Parade Night remained the central focus, but soon new and exciting activities emerged. Bands — pipe, bugle, flute — proved highly popular and enduring. Athletics and gymnastics were supplemented by competitive sport — a great outlet for Victorian teenagers (and no less an outlet for the teenagers of today). The Boys' Brigade pioneered organised youth sport on a competitive basis — football, cricket, basketball, swimming were in vogue from the early years, now added to by later 20th-century sports such as volleyball, badminton and table-tennis. It is perhaps football which has always attracted most boys. William Smith encouraged its development within the Brigade with strict rules of conduct – for both players and spectators! It is interesting to observe that many notable footballing Scots began their playing career in the Boys' Brigade — including some recent World Cup stars such as Kenny Dalgliesh and Gordon Strachan. Scotland's last team manager, Alex Ferguson, is himself an ex-Boys' Brigade player and great enthusiast of the movement.

In the educational sphere William Smith encouraged 'extra-mural' type classes as part of his Brigade scheme. To round off a boy's development he at the same time organised 'adventure' type activities. Perhaps the most significant of these is camping.

William Smith pioneered camping as a recreational activity and many Scots today will have fond memories of Boys' Brigade camps which, themselves, were the forerunner of modern family camping, school camping and the like.

Long before the turn of the century, William Smith had organised his personal life in such a way that he could devote himself fully to the implementation of his ideas. In 1889 he became full-time Secretary of the Boys' Brigade. In the initial years, lack of funding had precluded such a possibility, but by 1887 the development of the organisation had demonstrated the need for a full-time appointment. Smith voiced his concern to Carfrae Alston the Brigade President, which resulted in an appeal. Such was the response that in April 1888 a trust was formed to administer funds donated by prominent Scottish businessmen, giving a salary of £350 per annum to Smith 'as long as he holds office as Secretary'. The principal subscribers were, in fact, many of those philanthropists already mentioned for their work in the Glasgow area — John Templeton, James Stevenson, J. Campbell-White, William and James Campbell, Sir William Collins, Carfrae Alston, J. G. A. Baird, and the Coats family. There were 38 other contributors making a single payment. Again they consisted of well-known Scots, including Sir John Neilson Cuthbertson, Chairman of the Glasgow School Board; John Stephen, shipbuilder; David McBrayne, shipowner; Henry Drummond; and Henry Campbell-Bannerman, the future Prime Minister. The support of these men enabled William Smith to withdraw from his business and devote himself full-time to the Boys' Brigade. We cannot estimate the sacrifice this would have involved. Although no records of his firm survive, contemporary opinion indicated a business capacity which Smith's competence and effectiveness in Brigade affairs would lead us to assume. It is unlikely that he was improving his financial prospects by accepting £350 per annum.

On 5th March 1884 William had married Amelia Pearson Sutherland, daughter of a former Presbyterian Chaplain to the Army in Gibraltar. They had first met in 1872 and had entered into a lengthy engagement, primarily at the request of Amelia's parents. Setting up home at 4 Ann Street (now Southpark Avenue) Hillhead, close to Glasgow University, Amelia Smith, called 'Pearcie' by her husband, readily supported her husband's activities at the North Woodside Mission. A particular feature of her work for the Company was the extensive entertaining carried out for the boys. Mrs Smith's drawing-room tea parties with lavish home baking for each company squad in turn made quite an impression. This reversal of normal mission and fellowship work — whereby the homes of the poor were visited — was something of an innovation but it was highly successful and, by all accounts, highly appreciated. In 1889 the Smiths' first son, George Stanley, was born, and in 1891 their second son, Douglas Pearson. Amelia Smith's sympathy with and involvement in her husband's life's work was a source of great strength both to him and the movement. We can presume a ready acquiescence on her part when Smith later gave up his business interests. Tragedy struck, however, in 1898 when Amelia died, aged 42. The Smith household was thereafter managed by Kate Smith, William's sister, and the family moved round the corner to 12 Hillsborough Terrace (now Bower Street) Hillhead.

In the early years of the 20th century William Smith saw his ideas spread across the world, with the formation of Boys' Brigade companies in the U.S.A., Canada, Australia, New Zealand and South Africa. Rapid development was to take the organisation into all continents. Today it is to be found in over 60 countries.

At the same time, other people were picking up William Smith's new ideas and forming their own uniformed youth organisations — The Church Lads' Brigade (linked to the Anglican Church), the Jewish Lads' Brigade, the Catholic Boys' Brigade and most significantly the Boy Scouts.

Many people fail to realise that the Scouts owe their origins to William Smith and the Boys' Brigade. Baden Powell began his youth work as a Boys' Brigade instructor organising the Boys' Brigade Scouts as just one activity in the Brigade movement. When scouting proved to be so popular Baden Powell worked hard to entice William Smith into an amalgamation of the organisations but William stood firm in his insistence that the Boys' Brigade with its strong Christian foundation, remain a separate movement, albeit in close and friendly co-operation with its 'rival'.

One testing event for William Smith came in 1910 when the Liberal Government tried to absorb the uniformed youth organisations into the War Office's 'second line' of national defence. William had no intention of foresaking the religious aims of the movement in order to forge links (and gain benefits) with the military machine. His courageous stand was successful and dispelled any lingering criticisms of militarism which might be made against the Boys' Brigade.

By this time William Smith's personal life had taken several twists bringing both joy and grief. In 1906 William had married Hannah Ranken Campbell a cousin of the Prime Minister, Campbell-Bannerman, whose family he had known for many years. The household moved to more spacious accommodation at 13 Belmont Crescent in Glasgow's West End. Hannah and William visited the U.S.A. the following year in a successful tour of Boys' Brigade companies and local communities. However, tragedy struck after only a year when William was widowed for a second time. The catastrophe happened at Tighnabruaich on the West coast of Scotland where the 1st Glasgow Boys' Brigade Company was camping. William and his sons were at the camp while Hannah was living in a nearby cottage. She had been suffering from a nervous ailment and was found dead on the morning of the 27th July, having taken carbolic acid. It was thought that she had mistaken bottles in the medicine cabinet and death was pronounced as accidental. However, the mystery remains.

Two years later, at the same camp, William Smith dashed off to London to receive a much deserved knighthood at Buckingham Palace. He wanted, in his usual style, to be away from his Company camp for the shortest possible time.

The years leading up to World War I were ones of expansion and development for the Boys' Brigade, to William Smith's great satisfaction. By 1914 there were almost as many Boys' Brigade boys overseas as in the U.K. and over 120,000 in total. His sons, Stanley and Douglas, became leaders in the movement and were to devote their lives to it. In 1914, however, the Boys' Brigade was struck a mighty blow when its founder and leader was taken ill at a meeting in London and died of a cerebral haemorrhage on 10th May. Stunned by the loss of its leader, the Boys' Brigade prepared an appropriate memorial tribute with a service in St. Paul's Cathedral on 15th May.

Tributes from many colleagues and supporters, led by King George V, poured in. After the London service, William's body was taken to Glasgow for burial. A massive funeral procession followed Dr. Reith, Chaplain of the 1st Glasgow Company, and the route from Kelvingrove United Free Church to the Western Necropolis was lined with a staggering number of mourners, estimated at 164,000!

William Smith must seem to our modern world to be a very Victorian figure — maybe a bit austere and authoritarian, perhaps even humourless. This is far from the case however. Like many a Scot, he did not exhibit great emotion in public but from his personal writings and the reminiscences of those who knew him, a different picture emerges. In later years, Stanley Smith recalled how 'Our mother died when we were quite young and as we grew up our dad was more like an older brother than a father. We seemed to be three boys together'! Kate Mathieson, a family friend, recalls William Smith as a guest in her home displaying 'natural charm' and taking valuable time out to sit on the staircase with her as a little girl asking to be introduced to her favourite teddy! Perhaps the most moving tribute to William Smith's influence on others comes from the late Arthur Reid who was the colour sergeant (i.e. the senior boy) in Smith's own 1st Glasgow Company in 1914 when he died. Arthur was drawn aside when the news broke in Glasgow and told before the other boys. Sixty years later this strapping 17-year-old could still recall — 'I cried bitterly.'

Sir William Smith's life was bound up with the movement he initiated. His significant achievement in pioneering voluntary youth organisations is often unacknowledged. This Scot, however, gave to the world a conception of what could be done for the adolescent and his ideas have influenced the lives of countless numbers of young men. One of William's colleagues in the North Woodside Mission many years later pinpointed the man's great gift: 'He could see a boy through and through. He knew the difficulties of mind and body that beset a boy entering upon the adolescent period. . . . He placed himself alongside the boy and consciously passed on to him the help and guidance he most

177

needed. . . . His was a manly robust religion which found expression in the common ground of everyday life.'

By any standards William Smith's was an extraordinary life. From the hardship of a one-parent family in the far north of Scotland to the rigours of a Victorian Glasgow business life, his character was moulded to give him total commitment to his life's work — 'the advancement of Christ's kingdom among Boys'. One hundred years on, his singular achievement can be demonstrated in the thousands of boys around the world who benefit from the ideas of this memorable Scot.

AUTHOR

Brian Fraser, who lives in Eaglesham, Scotland, is Director of Personnel at the University of Glasgow and also lectures in Modern History.

BIBLIOGRAPHY

Brian Fraser (co-author), *Sure and Stedfast: A History of the Boys' Brigade 1883—1983*, Collins, 1983.

Series of articles. *Life & Work*, June, July, August 1983 — 'William Smith and the Boys' Brigade', 'The Boys' Brigade in the 20th Century', 'The Boys' Brigade Today . . . and Tomorrow?'

CHAPTER 15

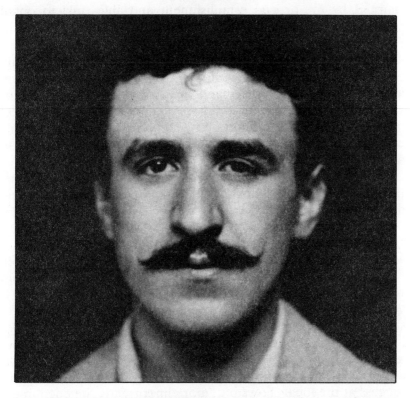

Charles Rennie Mackintosh
An Influential Architect
(1868—1928)

Allan McDonald

When the 20th century was in its infancy the work of a small group of artists from Glasgow was regularly shown at major art exhibitions throughout continental Europe. Illustrated publication in foreign journals increased the influence of the 'Glasgow Style' and the group, led by the architect Charles Rennie Mackintosh, were acknowledged as the leaders of a new artistic movement for the 20th century. The reaction at home to the work of Mackintosh and his circle could not have been in greater contrast. They were spurned by the artistic establishment and able only to obtain commissions from a meagre handful of friends. Given this background it is perhaps not surprising that since 1972 an Italian company, Cassina S.p.A., Milan, has been licensed to manufacture reproduction Mackintosh furniture through legal agreements with a group of private owners and institutions including Glasgow University. Indeed, it is only in more recent times that Mackintosh has been given due credit at home and abroad and his influence can now be detected in the works of numerous contemporary artists, designers and architects.

Charles Rennie Mackintosh was born on 7th June 1868 in a third-floor tenement flat at 70 Parson Street in the Townhead district of Glasgow, the second son in a family of 11 children. His parents were not wealthy. His father, William Mackintosh, was a superintendent of police who hailed from Nairn and his mother Margaret, the daughter of Charles Rennie of Ayr, was a homely woman who loved her children and was greatly loved by them. His father was also a keen gardener and when Charles was 10 years old the family moved to 2 Firpark Terrace in the more salubrious suburb of Dennistoun. Here his father had the good fortune to obtain the use of the large garden of the Dennistoun family home, Golf Hill House, which had been left in the hands of a caretaker. William specialised in growing flowers and met with success at the local shows but, more importantly, he encouraged his children to take an interest in his hobby. They in turn enjoyed visits to his garden so much that they referred to it as the 'Garden of Eden', an understandable sentiment from children who had been raised in the smoke and grime of the industrial city of Glasgow in the late 19th century. As a child Charles did not enjoy good health and he had two physical deformities. He was born with a contracted tendon in one foot which made him limp awkwardly throughout his life and his right eyelid drooped as a result of a chill caught after a game of football. His doctor thus encouraged him to take plenty of fresh air and exercise and Charles loved nothing more than to wander off into the beautiful countryside around Glasgow and to sketch the trees and wild flowers. Neither of his parents were known to be artistically talented and it can be assumed that Charles's love of growing things nurtured his interest in art during his formative years, thus laying the foundation of an architectural vocabulary he was to use throughout his career. Miss Nancy Mackintosh, Charles's youngest sister, recalled years later how family holidays were always an adventure. Charles had a special affection for cats but on one particular steamer trip 'doon the watter' the parents and 11 children were accompanied by a dog, several cats, a hedgehog, a tortoise and a goat which was to provide milk for a sick child.

Charles was a temperamental child who could display fits of rage if things weren't going his way but he also had a gentle, kind-hearted side to his character which gained him many friends. He wanted to be an architect from an early age and, upon completion of his education at Allan Glen's school, at the age of 16, with the somewhat reluctant approval of his father, he entered the office of John Hutchison as an architectural apprentice, studying at the School of Art in the evenings. He was a talented student who consistently won prizes for his work at both local and national level. The young apprentice was a sedulous worker both in the office and at art school but he always found time to ramble the countryside and to develop his growing skills in pencil sketching from nature. He would go to great lengths to acquire specimens whose colour or form caught his eye and would always return from his country walks carrying a bunch of flowers or twigs for further detailed study at home. One can only imagine the derisory remarks and taunts of his peer group on these occasions when he returned to the streets of Glasgow clutching bunches of flowers.

Hutchinson was not an inspired architect and Mackintosh, perhaps feeling that he had learned all that his master could teach him, left in 1889, to join the newly formed partnership of Honeyman and Keppie as a draughtsman. Here he found what he needed. John Honeyman was a scholar, an archaeologist and ecclesiologist as well as an architect, with a great love for mediaeval Scottish buildings which he soon passed on to the new assistant. Any understanding of Mackintosh's art must take into account its underlying – one might almost say its patriotic – Scottishness; but for Mackintosh there was no contradiction between being at one and the same time, a Scot and a cosmopolitan.

In 1890 he won the prestigious Alexander Thomson Travelling Scholarship, a prize of £60, which enabled him to visit France and Italy at a very formative period of his development and gave his confidence an enormous boost. He sent home a selection of his sketches for inclusion in the Annual Exhibition of the School of Art Students' Club and was awarded first prize. It was from this event, and these fine, individual, sensitive drawings of buildings, that his abilities came to the attention of Francis Newbery, the Headmaster of the School of Art. The spark was kindled to fire. From this point on, Newbery's influence as friend and patron had the most important consequences in Mackintosh's career. Indeed, his career, as a graphic artist, as a designer of furniture, and as an architect, can be said to begin with his return from Italy in the later part of 1891.

He continued in his employment with Honeyman and Keppie and, together with his friend and colleague Herbert MacNair, with his evening classes at the old School of Art in Rose Street. Newbery noticed that the work of Mackintosh and MacNair was developing along remarkably similar lines to that of two day-time pupils, sisters Margaret and Frances Macdonald and some time around 1893 he brought them together. They were soon christened 'The Four' through the distinction and similarity of their work. Mrs. Jessie Newbery, wife of the Art School director, recalled some 40 years later that the first epoch-making event in Mackintosh's artistic development was his introduction, through the medium of the new magazine *The Studio,* to the works of Aubrey Beardsley, Jan Toorop, Carlos Schwabe and C. F. A. Voysey. There is no doubt that these influences gave impetus and direction to the work of 'The Four' whose unique style earned them the title of 'The Spook School' – acclaimed by some but very caustically criticised by others.

In 1885 Charles's mother had died and his father remarried. The family moved to a Victorian terrace house in Regent Park Square on Glasgow's south side in 1892 and to *Holmswood,* 82 Langside Road, in 1894. Charles had little opportunity to display his talents in his own home as his father gave him scant encouragement in his artistic endeavours. In 1896 they returned to another house, at No. 27 Regent Park Square and Charles chose a room in the basement which he decorated with coarse brown wrapping-paper and stencilled friezes. His family was horrified but he used this room as a workshop and studio for a number of years and enlisted the help of his sisters for his beaten metal work. His father was doubly annoyed — firstly by the noise and secondly by their habit of working on the Sabbath.

The Macdonald sisters opened their own studio in the city in 1894 and worked on embroidery, repoussé, metal, gesso, illuminating, book illustrating and leaded glass. Here they entertained many interesting personalities such as John Buchan, E. A. Taylor, Jessie M. King and Talwin Morris. Mackintosh and MacNair, fully realising the advantages of such independence, each opened a studio, MacNair's in West George Street and Mackintosh's in Bath Street, where they could work on competitions, meet friends and host parties. Mackintosh became the acknowledged leader of the group and was very popular with the young architects and Art School students. He had great confidence in his own ability, an enormous capacity for hard work and a bold, bravado attitude towards the establishment. To the friends of his youth he was a kind-hearted, warm person who was easily pleased but to strangers, and particularly those not of an artistic bent, he could be cold and even aloof. The ladies were attracted by his dark, handsome features and by his willingness to spring to the defence of any cause which he thought to be unjustly attacked. When he found someone who sympathised with his point of view he could talk with them enthusiastically for hours on end.

The reputation of the Glasgow designers and 'The Four' in particular gradually spread beyond the confines of the Glasgow artistic scene and they were invited to participate in the Arts and Crafts Exhibition Society showing in London in 1896. Their work was not appreciated as it did not conform to either of the two contemporary attitudes to the nature of Art and they were not invited to exhibit there again but one significant benefit accrued by this exposure in London was the interest shown in the work of 'The Four' by Gleeson White, the editor of *The Studio*. He publicly supported the Glasgow artists during the 1896 exhibition and subsequently visited Glasgow to further investigate the work of the group. Two articles in *The Studio* in 1897 entitled 'Some Glasgow Designers and their Work' resulted from this visit. White was amazed to find that these people whose work seemed to be so extremely inventive and innovative did not embrace revolutionary or defiant attitudes but were developing what they considered to be a meaningful iconography for a new age out of the forms of nature and tradition. *The Studio* was widely read in Europe and as a result an article on the Glasgow designers was published by Alexander Koch of Darmstadt in *Dekorative Kunst* in November 1898. This heralded a deep appreciation on the continent which was to encourage the designers and sustain them through many years of apathy at home.

In 1896 an architectural competition was held, limited to 12 Glasgow architects, for the design of a new Glasgow School of Art on a site in Renfrew Street, Garnethill. The brief was drawn up by Francis Newbery and the winners were Honeyman and Keppie with Mackintosh acknowledged as the sole designer. It is not surprising that the result was controversial given the close friendship between Newbery and Mackintosh but the design itself transcended petty jealousies and heralded the arrival of a major architectural talent. The building was constructed in two phases, the first from 1897-99 and the second from 1907-09 and the design was characteristically modified and refined during the two construction periods, which occupied the greater part of Mackintosh's working life. Here we find the culmination of his years of apprenticeship under Hutchison and his expanding skills and ideas for a new approach to architecture which he nurtured as a junior member of staff at Honeyman and Keppie. His vision explodes into every space, every surface and every material. With its huge north-facing studio windows, its towering unbroken wall masses and lack of sculptured ornament the design baffled contemporary critics and yet it is these very qualities which are now admired in the building which is regarded as heralding the Modern Movement in architecture. To enter this building is an unforgettable experience, akin to that of entering the great Gothic cathedrals. Volumes have been written on this magnificent structure and the ideas embodied in it but if one were limited to describing only a part of it then the library, constructed in the second phase, would be that part. It represents the culmination of all of Mackintosh's wide range of talents but most importantly his skilful manipulation of space. It is a two-storey-height volume with an open first floor gallery and three dramatic full height vertical windows on the west gable which must be experienced to be fully appreciated. As in most of his other buildings, Mackintosh was responsible for the design of every last detail including furniture, fabrics, light fittings and fireplaces and often his details were worked out on site in close collaboration with the craftsmen who were to execute the work.

As soon as Mackintosh had completed the competition drawings for the Art School he began work on a design for a Church at Queen's Cross in Maryhill. This building is now the home of the Charles Rennie Mackintosh Society whose 2,000 strong membership is drawn from all over the world.

Another very significant event in 1896 was his introduction to Miss Catherine Cranston who by that time had an established tea-room business which was on the verge of a substantial programme of refurbishment and expansion. Mackintosh contributed to the decoration of the Buchanan Street tea-rooms and the moveable furniture for the Argyle Street tea-rooms and laid the foundation for a collaboration which was to extend over a period of 20 years. It was to provide him with some of the most important and widely recognised of the tragically limited range of commissions that came his way. Of these tea-rooms the most outstanding example is the *Willow Tea-Rooms* in Sauchiehall Street contained in an entirely new Mackintosh-designed building and constructed in 1902-04. There were five separate dining or tea-rooms, a dining gallery and a billiards room. This property which was once a part of Daly's department store has been completely renovated in recent years and is now commercially let as a jeweller's shop. The development of the Glasgow tea-room was no doubt due to the business acumen of Miss Cranston who in a desire to promote good taste created an environment where ladies could gather for an afternoon of gossip in pleasant, tastefully decorated surroundings. Mackintosh was able to design these rooms to the last detail including crockery, cutlery, vases, fabrics, carpets, chairs, tables, glass panels worked in iron, and murals. Each space was a total design uniquely of Mackintosh's invention and bearing no resemblance to any contemporary fashions. It is understandable that the Cranston tea-rooms contain much of his best-known works.

Herbert MacNair and Frances Macdonald had married in 1899 and moved to Liverpool, where Herbert had taken a teaching post the previous year, and following their example Charles Rennie Mackintosh and Margaret Macdonald became engaged. Mackintosh had previously been engaged to marry John Keppie's sister, Jessie, who never recovered from the shock of losing him. Thomas Howarth tells of meeting John and Jessie Keppie at their home in Ayrshire in the 1940s and how John was embittered by his association with Mackintosh. Jessie, who had never married, 'could not speak of him and the Art School days without dissolving into tears'. Charles and Margaret were married at St. Augustine's Church, Bowling, on 22nd August 1900, and honeymooned on Holy Island in Northumberland before returning to their newly decorated flat at 120 Main Street (now Blythswood Street). In the same year the couple were invited to exhibit their work at the eighth Secessionist Exhibition in Vienna and there is a tale of them arriving in Vienna to be met by a large crowd of architectural students and being fêted through the city in an open carriage. Not surprisingly Mackintosh considered the visit to Vienna as the highpoint in his life. When Mackintosh went to Italy in 1902 as the leader of the Scottish contingent in the Turin Exhibition of Contemporary Decorative Art, his European reputation had already been made. The German critic Hermann Muthesius had written in 1901, 'If one were to go through the list of truly original artists, the creative minds of the modern movement, the name of Charles Rennie Mackintosh would certainly be included even amongst the few that one can count on the fingers of a single hand.' It is no exaggeration to claim that in the years that followed the Vienna and Turin exhibitions the Scotsman was the best-known living architect in Europe.

On 1st January 1901 Honeyman retired and Mackintosh became a partner of the firm which was re-named Honeyman, Keppie and Mackintosh. The next nine years saw him produce the majority of his architectural masterpieces. He completed a house, *Windyhill,* at Kilmacolm in 1901 for William Davidson, a discerning patron of the arts, and in 1902 he was asked to design a house for W. W. Blackie, the publisher, for a site in Helensburgh overlooking the Firth of Clyde. *Hill House,* as it is known, is now in the care of the National Trust for Scotland and is probably the finest example of domestic architecture by Mackintosh. The external materials are traditional Scottish as are the windows, dormers, chimneys and gables. The exterior is clearly a reflection of the internal layout but displays a maturity which is less evident in Mackintosh's earlier houses and is overtly Scottish. The interiors show further evidence of his development. The showpiece of the house is undoubtedly the white master bedroom. It is extremely simple with a vaulted ceiling over the large bed recess and small touches of subtle colour in the furnishings relieve the whiteness. Once again every detail of this house was designed by Mackintosh even down to the keys for cabinet locks! His client was sympathetic to his intentions; the synthesis of all his skills can be fully appreciated and his true architectural genius is apparent.

In 1903 he began work on the design of Scotland Street School. It is devoid of superfluous ornament which, although omitted for reasons of economy, gives the building a very modern appearance. The three main entrance doors – boys and girls were still provided with independent entrances in those days – are scaled down in size to make the children feel more comfortable with their building. This school was completed in 1906 and during its construction he was still working on the *Willow Tea-Rooms* and designs for interiors of *Househillwood* – a large house for Miss Cranston and her husband Major Cochrane at Nitshill in Glasgow. When one considers how much attention he lavished on each project it can be appreciated that this was a period of phenomenal production and in 1905 he reached his climax when he began the design revisions for the second stage of the Glasgow School of Art.

In 1906 the Mackintoshes bought a new home at 78 Southpark Avenue in Hillhead and furnished it with items which document Mackintosh's work during the previous 10 years. This house has now been reconstructed as part of the Hunterian Art Gallery of Glasgow University and is open to the public. The original house has been described by Mrs Mary Sturrock, daughter of Francis Newbery as 'always joyously attractive and fresh' and the Mackintoshes as 'awfully nice people'. She has emphasised Mackintosh's intense pride in his work and his independence; 'he would allow no one to touch his drawings.' She also reminisced that 'Mackintosh wore hairy tweed suits when everyone else was wearing blue serge' and that Mackintosh and his artistic clique were not acceptable to the ordinary citizens of Glasgow who were outraged.

By the time of the completion of the second stage of the School of Art in 1909 Mackintosh's career had begun to decline. His reputation abroad was in sharp contrast to his lack of status at home but he turned down invitations to work in central Europe because he passionately believed he could lead a revival in Scottish architecture and applied arts with his 'Glasgow Style'. But he was too far ahead of his time for the Calvinistic Glaswegian business community from which he might have expected to find new clients. The attention he paid to every minute detail of his buildings, which is now so admired, had led him into dispute with clients over building costs for their projects and his reputation suffered. He began drinking heavily and his health deteriorated. Keppie and Mackintosh worked almost entirely, in an architectural sense, as individuals – Mackintosh in the vanguard of the 'Modernists' and Keppie upholding the traditional outlook. The profits of the partnership, usually well over £1,000, fell to £204 in 1910 and a mere £77 in 1911. The zealous youth had become bitter and resentful in middle-age when faced with indifference to his art. By 1913 he could no longer cope with his work and he resigned from the practice, ostensibly in protest over a submission by the partnership to a local competition. Mackintosh next tried unsuccessfully to practise on his own in Glasgow and, disillusioned, he and his wife closed their Glasgow home in 1914 and moved to Walberswick, a small village on the coast of Suffolk where there was an artists' colony frequented by their close friends the Newberys. Here Margaret tried to rebuild her husband's self-confidence while they devoted their time to painting water-colours.

When war was declared in August 1914 the Mackintoshes found themselves strangers, speaking a foreign tongue in an area which was under stringent security regulations. Charles's general appearance and the couple's habit of taking long evening walks brought them under suspicion as enemy agents and when correspondence from their Austrian friends was found amongst their papers Charles was summoned to appear before a local tribunal. With the help of influential friends he was eventually cleared of the charge but, outraged, he was only just restrained from filing charges against his accusers.

In 1915 they moved to London, renting two small adjacent studios in Glebe Place, Chelsea. Here they were able to live happily for some years, meeting other artists at the local restaurant, *The Blue Cockatoo* on the Embankment, and playing an active role in the social life of the artists' community. There was little building work in London during the war years but Charles did execute one small commission to alter and redecorate a small terrace house at 78 Derngate, Northampton. The style of the interiors of this house is in marked contrast to the work he did at his peak in Glasgow and suggests that he was continuing to develop as an artist in a way which remarkably forecast the decorative preoccupations of the next two decades. His final architectural works depart from the familiar free-flowing curves of his earlier work and are decorated with hard-edged geometrical patterns in which triangular motifs feature prominently, replacing the ubiquitous squares of his Glasgow period.

The English were, however, no less hostile to Mackintosh's

work than his own countrymen and, apart from a few designs for houses and studios in Chelsea which were never built, he and his wife occupied their years in Chelsea with fabric designing, water-colours and a few small decorative commissions from Miss Cranston and other Glasgow friends. Mackintosh the architect again became frustrated by his inability to build and he lapsed once more into a state of depression. On the advice of friends they decided to take a long holiday abroad and after a brief stay at Mont Louis in the Pyrenees they settled in the small town of Port Vendres on the Mediterranean coast of France near the Spanish border. Here Mackintosh devoted himself to water-colour paintings which were far removed from his earlier architectural sketches and suggest, particularly in the landscapes, that he tried to channel all of his artistic abilities through this medium. This was a happy period for the expatriate Scots couple and Charles completed some 40 water-colours of very fine quality during the next four years.

In the autumn of 1927, however, he complained to his wife of a sore throat and on medical advice he returned to London for specialist examination. They were met by Mrs Newbery who had answered Margaret's call for help and due to her influence Charles was taken to Westminster Hospital where he was diagnosed as having cancer of the tongue. He suffered the agony of radium treatment for some months and virtually lost his power of speech but after making good progress he was discharged from hospital for a period of convalescence. Margaret found them a furnished house in Willow Road, Hampstead Heath which fulfilled Charles's wish of a small garden containing a tree for him to sit under. When they were forced to leave this house Desmond Chapman-Huston, an old friend from Glasgow, let them use the upper part of his own home at 72 Porchester Square. Charles was contented here for a time, walking in the garden or browsing through his host's collection of books and pictures. He soon found the stairs too exhausting and he was given the use of the dining-room which had a balcony so that he only had to use the stairs to go to bed. When, in the autumn of 1928 even this arrangement became too much for him, he was moved to a private nursing home at 26 Porchester Square where, after a brief illness he died on 10th December 1928. Desmond Chapman-Huston arranged for the funeral and a cremation ceremony was held at Golders Green in the presence of a few friends. Margaret was deeply affected by the loss of her husband and returned to Chelsea where she died in obscurity in January 1933.

In a 12-year period of astonishing creative energy Charles Rennie Mackintosh clearly demonstrated that he was capable of the highest architectural achievement. The tragedy of his life is that he was not given the opportunity to realise his full potential in this medium. He demonstrated great strength of character when he withdrew with dignity firstly from Glasgow and then from London to make a serious attempt to start a new career as a water-colourist in France. The growing appreciation of his work in our time is fitting tribute to the timeless beauty of the creations of this outstanding Scot.

AUTHOR

Allan McDonald is a Glaswegian architect living and working in Hong Kong.

BIBLIOGRAPHY

Thomas Howarth, *Charles Rennie Mackintosh and the Modern Movement*, 2nd edn, Routledge and Kegan Paul, 1977.

Robert Macleod, *Charles Rennie Mackintosh*, Hamlyn, 1968.

Filippo Alison, *Charles Rennie Mackintosh as a Designer of Chairs*, Warehouse Publications, 1974.

Newsletters of the Charles Rennie Mackintosh Society.

CHAPTER 16

David Fowler McIntyre
Aviation Pioneer
(1905—1957)

Alan Robertson

David Fowler McIntyre and the aeroplane were children of the same era. Born on 24th January 1905, his formative years coincided with those of the industry in which he was to achieve international stature and which he, above all, was responsible for establishing in his native Scotland.

It was only two years earlier that the Wright Brothers had achieved the first powered flight of a heavier-than-air machine and David McIntyre was already toddling before they could stay in the air for as long as 45 minutes. He was three when the first

British power-driven flight took place at Farnborough and four when Bleriot made the historic first flight across the English Channel. The immense and growing public interest in the aeroplane which followed was reflected in the £10,000 prize which the *Daily Mail* put up for the fastest flight between London and Paris in 1910. This was ten times the figure which it had awarded to Bleriot the previous year.

As always, war provided a powerful stimulus to technical development. By 1918 the British armed services had 20,000 aircraft and their performance by comparison with pre-war flying machines had increased beyond recognition. In 1919, as David was starting to think about his own career, Britain's Alcock and Brown became the first men to fly the Atlantic non-stop and the world's first daily passenger air-service began between London and Paris.

McIntyre's own family background was rooted in a much older transportation industry, shipbuilding. His father, John, was a marine draughtsman when David was born, but by 1908 was managing Mackie and Thomson in Glasgow's Govan and in the following year became managing director of the Ailsa Ship-building Company in Troon.

John and his wife, Louisa Agnes Murphy McIntyre (née Fowler), had seven children, of whom David was the youngest. Moving house was almost part of the McIntyre way of life and having lived in Govan, Bellahouston, Irvine and Troon as well as an unsuccessful sojourn in Canada before David was born, the family finally settled in Ayr in 1911. David's schooling reflected this mobility and he attended Bellahouston Academy, Ayr Academy and Merchiston Castle before finally completing his formal education at Glasgow Academy. He achieved neither academic nor sporting distinction during his school career.

Family, friends and acquaintances alike remember him as having only one consuming interest, aviation. He was, however, forbidden by his parents to fly before he came of age at 21. In the meantime he spent one unmemorable year among the Galloway hills as a 'mud student' or trainee farmer before joining his elder brother James in running a stevedoring business in Glasgow. This was no more to his taste than farming, but experiencing the impact of the Great Depression on Clydeside at first-hand made a deep impression on him. The sight of men queuing forlornly at the dock gates in the hope of being able to sell their labour for a few hours was one which he found demeaning and offensive. The experience does much to explain the emphasis which he was later repeatedly to place on the importance of aviation as a source of employment and consequently as a means of restoring not only industrial prosperity but also human dignity.

His pursuit of a flying career was single-minded. In September 1926 he simultaneously applied for a short service commission in the Royal Air Force and also, as if the dual application would increase his prospects of success, to join the Auxiliary Air Force, which had been founded in 1925 as the 'Territorial Army' of the air. Eligibility for an Auxiliary commission was dependent on achieving the aviator's licence 'A' Certificate. Reluctantly acknowledging his son's determination, John McIntyre put forward the money for a series of private lessons and on 14th December 1926 David first took to the air with Beardmore's Flying School at Moorpark Aerodrome, better known in the subsequent history of aviation as Renfrew.

In those days a basic course of instruction, comprising ten hours dual and three hours solo, cost £115, a sum which was repaid in full by the Air Ministry if the pupil successfully obtained his licence and was accepted into the Auxiliary Air Force, while the Flying School offered a £10 rebate to pupils who completed their training without damaging their aircraft. David learned quickly. After 11 dual instruction flights he made his first solo on 16th January 1927, barely a month after starting his lessons, and on 29th March 1927 he was commissioned in the Auxiliary Air Force as a Pilot Officer in 602 Squadron.

The 602 (City of Glasgow) Squadron had a more than ordinary measure of the enthusiasm and commitment which characterised all the Auxiliary units. Proud of the fact that it had been the first of the AAF Squadrons to become operational in 1925, it was determined to stay out in front. In 1929 it won the newly-established Esher Trophy as the outstanding Squadron in the Auxiliary Air Force for all-round efficiency.

David McIntyre fitted easily into this environment. From the start he was eager to develop his flying skills at every opportunity, although this was an important requirement for all of 602 Squadron's pilots in view of the proximity of the graveyard to the landing strip at Renfrew. It became a Squadron commonplace that 'if you can't read the names on the gravestones, you're too high'. On one occasion he noticed that crows taking off and landing on the airfield made their approach downwind before finally executing an abrupt 180 degree turn and touching down. Thinking that a similar manoeuvre might solve the difficulty of approaching over the cemetery, he promptly tried to emulate the technique. In this instance the aircraftman's results were, however, altogether less gracious than those of the feathered exponents. Having severed the undercarriage from his aircraft in the process, David was heard to mutter that it was time the birds learned the rules of elementary aerodynamics.

His overall ability as a pilot, however, was never in doubt and when the Squadron was reorganised in 1930 into three Flights of three aircraft apiece David McIntyre was a natural choice to become a Flight Commander. It was no coincidence that the Squadron's finest aerobatics came from 'B' Flight under his leadership. For the same reason it was he who was selected to spend a year at Andover attached to No. 12 Tactical Bomber Squadron, one of the premier units in the Royal Air Force, where he took part in experimental blind formation flying using new gyroscopic instrumentation. He completed his course with an exceptional rating.

Seriously as he took his flying, his sense of humour was never far below the surface and seldom more so than in his dealings with parachutes. Once during his secondment to 12 Squadron he was required to carry out a parachute jump from 3,050 m (10,000 feet), an exercise which took long enough for him to allow himself the luxury of smoking a cigarette to pass the time during his descent. He had already made newspaper headlines parachuting. On 15th December 1929 a younger pilot who was being tutored by McIntyre in aerobatics over Renfrew suddenly became aware that his instructor had 'fallen out' of the aircraft while inverted in a slow roll. The pupil successfully returned to base while David walked back with his parachute over his arm from the golf course where he had landed. More than a few of those who knew him believed that his departure from the aircraft had not been accidental, although David never admitted to its being anything else and his log book is characteristically cryptic in its record: 'Aerobatics. Harness carried away. Descended by parachute.' The incident earned him the personal distinction of becoming the first member of the Auxiliary Air Force to be admitted to the Caterpillar Club, the association of those whose lives have been saved by the parachute.

However, as he completed his tour of duty with 12 Squadron in October 1932, a far greater distinction awaited him, for it was then that he learned of his selection to pilot the second of the two aircraft which were about to embark on one of the last great natural challenges left to the aviator — to fly over the summit of the highest mountain in the world, known to English speakers as Mount Everest but to the Nepalese as 'Chomolungma': 'The mountain so high no bird can fly over it'. The Everest expedition had been conceived by Colonel Stewart Blacker, a grandson of the first Surveyor-General of India, and had been taken up enthusiastically by that supreme purveyor of adventure, Scots writer and MP, John Buchan. Searching for a senior pilot, it was Buchan who, in the summer of 1932, approached his fellow MP, Douglas Douglas-Hamilton, then Marquis of Clydesdale and the youngest Squadron Leader in the Auxiliary Air Force. His Squadron was 602.

On Clydesdale's personal recommendation David McIntyre found himself presented with the opportunity to make history. He leapt at the chance. The expedition had three principal aims — to explore and map by aerial photographic survey the virtually unknown southern slopes of the mountain; to produce a motion film of outstanding scientific and educational interest while simultaneously creating a new altitude record for a two-man aircraft; and finally, to achieve these aims with British personnel, aircraft and equipment thereby promoting the international reputation of Britain and her aviation industry.

This final objective in particular appealed to the wealthy and was sponsored by a fervently patriotic woman, Lady Lucy Houston, who had already financed Britain's successful participation in the Schneider Trophy. Thus the Houston Mount Everest Expedition was launched. The expedition left England on 16th February 1933. Behind lay months of painstaking preparation, training, testing and development. Ahead lay a route through Europe, North Africa and the Middle East with all the attendant complications of their various climates and officials, before they reached India, on 22nd March.

McIntyre soon stamped his personality on the expedition, both on the ground and in the air. When they arrived wet and cold in Sicily, David decided that what was needed to warm them up was a rum punch but with no Italian speakers among them he was having difficulty in securing the vital ingredients, despite his best efforts in three other languages, until finally — pointing to some sailors at the bar — he danced a hornpipe and the waiter reappeared with a rum bottle. Over the Libyan desert he demonstrated his abilities as a navigator, following a compass course across the featureless land despite the absence of smoke or long grass on the ground to reveal the difficult crosswinds.

Weather conditions were critical to the success of their assault on Everest. Day after day clouds or high winds held them back. It was not until 3rd April that the winds around the summit fell below 161 km/hr (100 mph). Visibility was hazy but adequate. Previously they had decided not to attempt the flight if the winds exceeded 64 km/hr (40 mph) because of the limiting effect on the aircraft's range and endurance. David McIntyre did the calculations. With a wind from the west estimated at 108 km/hr (67 mph) he reckoned they would be able to stay only 15 minutes in the vicinity of Everest and have enough fuel to return. With the monsoons imminent, it was enough. They decided to go.

With Blacker flying as Clydesdale's observer and McIntyre accompanied by a Gaumont British Film Corporation cameraman they flew for an hour and a half until they passed through the dust haze of the plains at 4,880 m (16,000 feet) and were confronted with the startling panorama of the Himalayan Range rising like another world out of the vapour. They had passed into the unknown and, for all their meticulous planning on the ground, now came the moment that their plans went awry. Only a few minutes from the summit they suddenly realised with horror that the wind had grown stronger and blown them off course with the result that they were approaching the mountain from the leeward side. Now, instead of being able to take advantage of the upcurrents of air near the summit on the windward side, they would have to contend with massive downdraughts of unpredictable speed and strength. No sooner had this realisation dawned than both aircraft were sucked violently downwards. Although pointed at its steepest angle of climb and with its engine at full throttle, McIntyre's aircraft was pulled back 610 m (2,000 feet) by the sudden downrush of air.

Seconds before he had been above the ridge. Now it towered 305 m (1,000 feet) above him. He was hemmed in by the mountains and the wind, since a left turn would have brought him back into the full blast of the downdraught while a right turn would have accelerated the aircraft into the adjoining peak of Makalu at

322 km/hr (200 mph). He kept his nerve, crabbing sideways towards the lowest point of the ridge, not knowing whether they were level with it or below. It was a slow, painful progress until finally: 'A fortunate up-current just short of the ridge carried us up by a few feet and we scraped over.' Even then he had to circle the ridge, venturing three more times into the invisible maw of the downdraught, as he fought to gain the extra height to clear the summit.

To add to their troubles Bonnett, the cameraman, busily reloading his film, accidentally trod on his oxygen pipe and fractured it. As he collapsed he just had the strength to bind his handkerchief around the break before losing consciousness. Having lost sight of the other aircraft, and not knowing that Clydesdale had already crossed the peak, McIntyre pressed on over the summit before commencing an emergency descent. Twisting round to see if Bonnett was still alive, a freezing coldness seized his nose and mouth as the abrupt movement wrenched off his own oxygen mask. After that he had to hold the mask on with one hand and operate the flying controls with the other. At 2,440 m (8,000 feet) his swift actions were rewarded when Bonnett struggled to his feet, green but alive.

They celebrated their triumph with a swim in a pool which had until recently been a home for crocodiles. After the dangers through which they had come, the risk clearly seemed trivial by comparison.

David then flew the expedition's films to Calcutta to be developed only to receive the disappointing news that the survey cameras had not performed consistently and many of the photographs were inadequate for map making. He and Clydesdale were keen to rectify this but in London the expedition committee, the insurers and Lady Houston were all anxious to avoid further risks and permission for a second flight over Everest was refused. Air Commodore Fellowes, the Expedition Leader, duly ordered his team to prepare to return home, but then succumbed to a fever.

While he was bedridden, McIntyre, Clydesdale and their observers took it upon themselves to prepare secretly and make the forbidden second flight on 19th April, by which time David had not only dismantled and adjusted the vertical camera but had personally re-designed the oxygen mask to make it a perfect fit. Despite stronger wind conditions, David McIntyre's aircraft succeeded in crossing the summit again. More importantly the photographic survey, for which they had put themselves at risk a second time, was a complete success and fully vindicated their insubordination.

The most unexpected revelation of the survey was the discovery, at a height of over 5,490 m (18,000 feet), of a lake which experts could only presume was heated by some volcanic source. David McIntyre, keen to mark the Scottish involvement in the expedition, suggested that it should be named Loch Everest, but sadly the authorities chose not to adopt this proposal. In any event, he and his colleagues had achieved international celebrity. In India their movements were followed by huge crowds and the rumour spread that having conquered the 'Armchair of the Gods' they planned next to fly over the moon. Through the *London Times* and Gaumont's film, *Wings Over Everest*, the whole world knew of their exploits.

As the two pilots in this aeronautical triumph, Clydesdale and McIntyre were the centre of attention. They returned as guests of honour and to the award of the Air Force Cross. It appealed to the press that David had once been forbidden to fly and the papers captured the spark within him when they wrote: 'Now he flies everywhere. He thinks, talks and dreams aviation.' Flying at over 9,150 m (30,000 feet) above the highest point on the planet had enlarged David McIntyre's perspective. He returned from Everest with a vision for aviation for which the stage was world-wide and with the determination to put his native Scotland at the centre of that stage.

After Everest McIntyre succeeded Clydesdale as Commanding Officer of 602 Squadron and led the unit until October 1937. At the same time the two men actively pursued their common aim to establish the aviation industry in all its branches in Scotland. Rearmament provided the first opportunity and on 9th August McIntyre and Clydesdale founded 'Scottish Aviation Limited' to undertake contracts which the Government was offering to private firms prepared to bear the capital cost of providing airfields and aircraft to give pilots their first 50 hours of training as civilians before entering the RAF.

From his intimate knowledge of the area McIntyre knew Prestwick in Ayrshire to be a uniquely suitable location on account of its clear weather conditions. An erroneous record to the contrary on Airfields Board files meant that he had to fight to secure approval to proceed. He succeeded but it was the first of the many battles with officialdom which dogged his efforts to establish a Scottish aviation industry.

Flying training began at Prestwick on 16th February 1936, exactly three years after the Everest Expedition's departure for India. The date was more than simply a lucky talisman for the new venture, just as the orange and silver livery of the School's Tiger Moths was more than an expression of David's flamboyance. Both were part of his constant endeavour to reinforce public awareness of aviation in Scotland.

He was a striking figure with his prematurely silver hair, his neat, dark moustache and above all his infectious energy and enthusiasm. Prestwick's natural suitability and McIntyre's leadership made a powerful combination. The initial training contract was completed in barely half the allotted time and others followed in quick succession.

By 1941 Scottish Aviation had trained over half of all the observer navigators in the Royal Air Force and was turning out five times as many aircrew as any other establishment in the country.

Scottish Aviation's next contribution to the war effort arose from one of history's strangest accidents. In November 1940 one of the first aircraft to be delivered to Britain from North America lost its way in bad weather and landed at Prestwick rather than its original destination in Northern Ireland. McIntyre was quick to seize this opportunity to make his airfield the regular terminus for the transatlantic air bridge. For the first nine months until ATFERO, subsequently RAF Ferry Command, was formed, the organisation of the service and a parallel operation to receive flying boats at Greenock and Largs, fell on David McIntyre, by now holding the rank of Group Captain.

He quickly recognised both the revolution in air transport occasioned by the war and Prestwick's potential to become an international civil airport. As early as 1942 he began to publish a series of Target Development Plans detailing his vision for the post-war airport. These included a runway extending into a huge flying boat harbour, freight and passenger terminals with high-speed monorail links to Glasgow, Edinburgh and Carlisle, aircraft research, manufacturing and servicing facilities and even an Air

University. Even without these developments, 37,000 ferry flights and McIntyre's tireless advocacy had made Prestwick the most modern airport in Europe by 1945.

David had been extremely reluctant to hand responsibility for the airport over to the RAF regulars during the war. Characteristically he simply disregarded the first two requisition notices. With the return of peace he was keen to resume control of the airport's development. But it was not to be. On 1st January 1946 the Government took control of Prestwick by compulsory acquisition.

It is a measure of McIntyre's fighting spirit that he battled for seven years to obtain proper compensation for the loss of his airport, but it is equally characteristic that he should simultaneously direct his energies towards establishing yet another branch of aviation in Scotland, this time Scottish Airlines.

He retained a pilot's passion for flying throughout his life and his log books show that he made a point of personally flying, if only once, every type of aircraft handled by Scottish Aviation.

Recognising the transatlantic as potentially the world's premier aviation thoroughfare, he planned for Scottish Airlines a vast network of routes, based in Prestwick, and embracing a score of major cities in the Northern Hemisphere, from San Diego to Vladivostok. The scale of this ambition and the size of the fleet which he had procured came close to bankrupting his company, but principally it was politics which thwarted him again when the nationalisation of the British airline industry in 1946 precluded Scottish Airlines from operating scheduled services.

Undeterred, David transferred his fleet to charter work and made a unique piece of post-war aviation history as the national airlines of Iceland, Belgium, Greece and Luxembourg were all founded with Scottish Airlines' aircraft and personnel. Ironically it was the nationalisation of these airlines in turn which reduced Scottish Airlines' activity to a level that was not economically viable. Yet, while McIntyre was alive he contrived to keep the airline alive.

He did so through a combination of innovation and sheer competitiveness, conceiving the idea of in-flight customs clearance to reduce 'door-to-door' travel time and introducing a fast car service to ensure that despite an additional intermediate stop, his passengers from Scotland were in central London before those of the state-owned British European Airways. Once he even urged his drivers to take to the pavements to beat the traffic jams.

Yet it was manufacturing which became the dominant aspect of Scottish Aviation's activity. McIntyre had been able to develop this side of the business rapidly during the war principally through modification work on aircraft arriving via the transatlantic ferry. This had given his company a unique expertise on American types which it exploited in the conversion of war surplus aircraft to civilian use. He even wanted to combine the wing of the American Liberator bomber with a new Scottish-designed, pressurised fuselage but the British Government would not approve this collaborative venture. Otherwise David McIntyre's 'Concord' would have pre-dated its famous namesake by some 30 years.

Inevitably David wanted to go further and to produce an aircraft wholly designed and manufactured in Scotland. The opportunity came in 1946 with a combined services requirement for a five seater front-line communication aircraft, rugged, easy to maintain and with the short take-off and landing characteristics to enable it to operate in hostile environments. The result was the 'Prestwick Pioneer', an aircraft able to land in a mere 24 m (26 yards) with a stalling speed of 53 km/hr (33 mph) and a top speed of only 196 km/hr (124 mph.)

Motorists around Prestwick soon became accustomed to the unusual experience of overtaking this extraordinary aeroplane, but when it eventually went into service with the RAF in 1953 it fully lived up to its name, providing invaluable support during the counter-insurgency campaign in the jungles of Malaya.

It was followed by the Twin Pioneer, a 16-seat development designed both to open up airline traffic in remote regions without sophisticated airfields and also to operate from short strips close to city centres.

In business David McIntyre's skill was not in design, nor in engineering and least of all in finance. His supreme skill was with people. He charmed and inspired. Never far from the factory floor, he was reputed to know all his employees by name. If 118 men were working nightshift on the prototype Twin Pioneer, it was 'The Groupie' who would appear in the early hours of the morning with 119 fish suppers and as many bottles of beer in the boot of his car. To McIntyre, employees were all part of the family and he treated them in the grand manner, giving foreign holidays for special efforts, arranging anniversary reunions, sports days and huge firework parties where he fired naval maroons because conventional rockets were not spectacular enough for him.

His personality was well suited to the task of selling aircraft and, in the fiercely competitive market he had chosen, it needed to be, particularly after 30th August 1957, when a Twin Pioneer crashed into the sea off New Guinea, the only witness a native fisherman who reported that a wing had fallen off. As a result an intensive programme of modification was promptly instituted to change the material of the wing strut fittings in all the existing aircraft.

By the beginning of December only one aircraft remained to be modified, G-AOEO, the demonstrator in which McIntyre was due to embark on a sales tour of North Africa. The aircraft had completed fewer than 600 hours flying. The safe life of the suspect material had been calculated at 2,500 hours. Nevertheless colleagues urged him to wait. The modification would take only two days. But David was impatient to depart, eager to be extending Scottish Aviation 'the world o'er' in line with the company's motto.

He left Scotland on 3rd December bound for Libya. On 7th December the aircraft failed to return from a demonstration flight and the following day the wreckage was finally discovered in the desert some 483 km (300 miles) south-west of Tripoli.

The particular stresses of low altitude demonstration flying coupled with the loads imposed by the aircraft's short take-off and landing characteristics had caused the wing brace fitting to fail prematurely. The port wing had come off and the aircraft had plunged out of control. David McIntyre, and five companions, were dead.

He is buried, not amid the heat of the North African desert nor in the frozen reaches of the Himalayas, but in the tranquil green of an Alloway churchyard, in Scotland where his pioneering ultimately had most meaning. There is an appropriate memorial window in the church, gifted by his family. Surrounded by Everest, by aircraft and by the dove of peace, which together represented McIntyre's fervent belief in aviation as a means of improving the human condition, the central figure is Moses, the visionary, the leader, the man whose commitment attracts fierce enemies and devoted followers, the man who persists through years in the wilderness in the pursuit of his goal.

The real legacy, however, is where David McIntyre himself planted it, at Prestwick, and in the people of its thriving aerospace industry, who, over half a century on, continue to design, manufacture, sell, support and teach others to fly aircraft 'the world o'er'.

AUTHOR

Alan Robertson is a personnel director for British Aerospace.

BIBLIOGRAPHY

Clydesdale and McIntyre, *The Pilot's Book of Everest,* William Hodge and Co. Ltd, 1936.

James Douglas-Hamilton, *Roof of the World—Man's First Flight Over Everest*, Mainstream Publishing Co. Ltd, 1983.

Douglas McRoberts, *Lions Rampant—The Story of 602 Spitfire Squadron,* William Kimber & Co. Ltd, 1985.

Alan Robertson, *Lion Rampant and Winged—A History of Scottish Aviation Limited,* LRW & Co., 1986.

CHAPTER 17

James Wilson
Editor and Statesman

(1805—1860)

Ruth Dudley Edwards

James Wilson was a manufacturer, a writer on finance, founder and editor of *The Economist*, and finance minister in both Britain and India. He has never received the recognition he deserved. As a politician, his outstanding work was carried out behind the scenes and his potential as a statesman was just being realised when he died at the age of 55. In his journalistic life, his reputation was swamped by that of his son-in-law, Walter Bagehot, editor of *The Economist* for 17 years and a man of genius.

Yet if Bagehot was, as he has been described, Victorian Britain's most versatile genius, Wilson was the embodiment of her most striking virtues. He was self-reliant, self-made, successful, diligent, strong-willed, thorough, dogged, honourable, genial, tolerant and charitable in human relations, a loving family man and a loyal friend.

Wilson was born at Hawick, Roxburghshire, on 3rd June 1805. His mother, born Elizabeth Richardson, died after the birth of the 15th of her children, of whom five boys and five girls survived into adulthood. James, the fourth son, was too young when she died to retain but the barest recollection of his mother, whose place was filled for him by his greatly loved eldest sister, Catherine.

Despite the loss of Mrs Wilson, the environment in which James spent his early childhood seems to have been happy. His father, William, was a well-to-do woollen manufacturer and a well-known Quaker (the family used the 'thee' and 'thou' convention). Within the family, a strong ethical sense went along with a belief in the merits of hard work. Throughout his life James always was to remember his father with great respect.

In 1816, aged 11, James was sent to the Quaker School at Ackworth, Yorkshire. Although scholastically successful and popular for his good nature, he had a well-concealed but deep-running shyness that was never to leave him. Discipline at the school was firm: for instance, talking at mealtimes was banned and the children conversed in deaf and dumb language. Yet Wilson was happy there and rose to the demands made of him. Standards were high: Wilson won a prize for the best essay on three great attributes of God – Omnipotence, Omniscience, and Omnipresence.

He left after four years, by then top of the school and a boy so studiously minded that he wanted to become a teacher. His father, who gave his children virtual freedom of choice about their career, sent him to a seminary at Earl's Colne in Essex. After a very short time he wrote home: 'I would rather be the most menial servant in my father's mill than be a teacher' and he was summoned home immediately.

He would have liked to study for the Scottish bar, but indulgent though his father was, he could not agree to his son taking up an occupation frowned on by the Quakers. There was nothing for it but to go into business, and so, at the age of 16, James was apprenticed to a small hat manufacturer at Hawick. During the next few years he spent his spare time in reading a great deal, often late at night, a habit he dropped in early adulthood when he became too busy. Bagehot observed that Wilson never learned how to skim reading matter. Even with a newspaper article, 'if he read one at all, it was with as much slow, deliberate attention as if he were perusing a treasury minute.'

His first months at Hawick were spent in mastering his trade with his habitual concentration and thoroughness, whereupon his father bought the business for James and an elder brother, William. They ran it successfully for a couple of years, but Hawick was too small for their ambitions. In 1824, when James was only 19, they moved to London where, with a gift of £2,000 each from their father, they set up the hat manufacturing firm of Wilson, Irwin, and Wilson. By mutual consent it was dissolved in 1831, but under the name of James Wilson and Co., Wilson stayed in the same line of business. He later calculated that by 1837 he was worth £25,000: he believed those years to have been invaluable in teaching him about the middle and working classes and about international trade.

By the mid 1830s his domestic circumstances had changed dramatically. Until January 1832 he and his brother had lived with two of their sisters; on the 5th of that month he married Elizabeth Preston of Newcastle-on-Tyne and they moved into a house he had built for them in Southwark, near his factory. On his marriage Wilson became a member of the Church of England.

Wilson had a considerable aesthetic sense, and his wife shared his interest in music (he had played the flute as a boy) and art. Their letters show them to have been a devoted couple, although Elizabeth's recurring ill-health caused him worry and led to enforced separations. They were to have six daughters – Eliza (1832), Julia (1834), Matilda (1836), Zenobia – known as Zoe – (1838), Sophie (1840), and Emilie – Wilson's future biographer (1841).

In 1836 they were affluent enough to move to Dulwich Place, a substantial mansion in extensive grounds, but in that same year Wilson began to speculate in indigo. He invested most of the capital he had built up through 20 years of hard work and lost it when, following the economic crisis of 1837, the price of indigo fell. Having invested more than he could easily afford, he was unable to hold on until better times. By 1839 his personal and business finances were in a critical state.

In his marvellous memoir of Wilson, Bagehot wrote delightfully of the temperamental failing that led Wilson into trouble on this occasion: 'It may, however, be admitted that Mr. Wilson was in several respects by no means an unlikely man to meet with, especially in early life, occasional misfortune. To the last hour of his life he was always sanguine. He naturally looked at everything in a bright and cheerful aspect; his tendency was always to form a somewhat too favourable judgment both of things and men. One proof of this may be sufficient; − he was five years Secretary of the Treasury, and he did not leave it a suspicious man.'

Wilson reacted to financial catastrophe with characteristic moral courage and dogged determination. Bagehot was later to remark that Wilson was never to show 'greater business ability, self-command, and energy' than during this crisis. He was able immediately to pay off his personal creditors and to pay half of the demands against his firm. Through negotiation he avoided bankruptcy and in due course voluntarily paid all his creditors in full. He was to remain in the hat business until 1844 when he retired and concentrated his money and energies on *The Economist.*

Wilson was a man of far too much vitality to be satisfied by a life of business and domestic activity. Despite his shyness (which few people noticed) he loved intellectual society and conversations about economics, politics, statistics and other public concerns. It was one of his remarkable peculiarities, noted Bagehot, 'to be a *very animated* man, talking by preference and by habit on *inanimate* subjects. All the *verve,* vigour, and life which lively people put into exciting pursuits, he put into topics which are usually thought very dry. He discussed the currency or the Corn Laws with a relish and energy which made them interesting to almost every one.'

His company was much sought after, and among the important friendships he made during the late 1830s was one with his Dulwich neighbour George Porter, Permanent Secretary of the Board of Trade and author of *The Progress of the Nation*, whose mind Wilson later described as the most 'accurate' he had ever known. Porter, like Wilson, his brother George (who became Chairman of the Metropolitan Anti-Corn-Law Association), and most of his other close friends, was passionately in favour of free trade.

In March 1839 (the year in which Richard Cobden and his

associates founded the Anti-Corn-Law Association), at the height of his negotiations with creditors, Wilson published his first pamphlet, 'Influences of the Corn Laws' – a forceful argument in favour of free trade. Its novelty and particular value stemmed from his rebuttal of the usual divisive class arguments on the issue: that the Corn Laws helped agricultural interests at the expense of the consumer. Wilson demonstrated lucidly and calmly from a basis of facts and figures that protectionism was against the interests of all. Many years later Cobden was to admit that he 'never made any progress with the Corn Law question while it was stated as a question of class against class'.

Wilson could have chosen no better time to embark on a career as a writer on economics. Protectionism was a matter of great public debate; emotions ran high and issues were only half-understood. The free trade issue was admirably suited to Wilson's eminently practical intelligence. Bagehot believed that he had been probably the most effective of all writers on the principles of free trade, that he thought his arguments out for himself from first principles, that they transformed free trade from a class to a national question and that in due course they were proved to be true.

The reaction to the pamphlet from the thinking public was almost universally favourable; although 130 pages long, it was published in instalments within the *Leeds Mercury*. Among its admirers were Richard Cobden and three influential men who were to become lifelong friends of Wilson's: the distinguished and independent-minded Whig politician Lord Radnor, the indefatigable free trade campaigner Charles Villiers (MP and barrister), and his brother Lord Clarendon, who was to be in time Lord Lieutenant of Ireland and later Foreign Secretary.

Within a few months Wilson was a public figure. Reluctantly he made speeches for the Anti-Corn-Law League, but he always disliked that kind of activity, preferring the patient work of constructing and developing an argument on paper. In 1840 he published 'Fluctuations of Currency, Commerce, and Manufactures' and the following year 'The Revenue; or, What should the Chancellor do?', both of which added to his reputation as a financial writer of clarity and integrity, whose beliefs were firmly rooted in broad principles and hence always consistent: as a thinker he was ever unaffected by fashion.

Simultaneously Wilson was writing articles for the *Morning*

Chronicle and was looking for a satisfactory platform from which to declaim at some length on the issues of the day. He offered his services free to the *Examiner* and was reluctantly turned down by an editor who could not afford the costs of extra printing. Wilson thereupon decided to found his own journal.

In September 1843, he brought out the first issue of his weekly paper, *The Economist: The Political, Commercial, Agricultural, and Free-Trade Journal.* Its purpose was to stimulate 'every man who has a stake in the country . . . to investigate and learn for himself' about public affairs. Wilson believed strenuously that abundant facts were a prerequisite for the forming of sound opinions, so the basis of the paper's contents was the systematic weekly survey of economic data. As with his first pamphlet, his timing was impeccable, for there was just beginning a period in which the economic aspect of social, political and international relations was to be the dominant theme.

The paper quickly became invaluable as a source of trade and financial statistics: it was particularly useful on the subject of the booming railways. Wilson's ideal was unfettered competition; he was violently against regulations and controls. But he was as violently against uninformed investment. Perhaps mindful of his own mishap over indigo speculation he was motivated to try to save businessmen from their own enthusiasm. At the height of the railway mania, in 1845, he added a nine-page Railway Monitor to the paper, giving weekly figures on companies, lines, finances and traffic, with warnings about the limitations on available amounts of capital, labour and materials for railway construction. (Railway Monitor lived on in title, until 1934, when *The Economist WEEKLY COMMERCIAL TIMES Banker's Gazette and Railway Monitor A Political, Literary and General Newspaper* was renamed *The Economist*). He was proud that he saved the fortunes of many would-be investors at a time when dishonest or ill-informed railway journals were fanning the flames of lunatic speculation.

Slightly oversimplifying, a later editor of *The Economist,* Geoffrey Crowther, described it in the early days as being 'virtually a house organ of the Anti-Corn Law League', a cause which triumphed in 1846. But Wilson's paper was much more than that. It covered all important political and financial news, at home and abroad, for Wilson was always internationally minded. One of his closest friends was a Belgian parliamentarian, and during the 1840s and 1850s he was to forge close links with other

Continentals. It was only logical that a free trader should be an internationalist.

The success of the paper in the early years was wholly dependent on Wilson. No abstract thinker, he saw political economy as the science of buying and selling, and he wrote about it in a way that made sense to businessmen. One of his great gifts was what Bagehot called 'business-imagination', which 'enabled him to see "what men did," and "why they did it;" "why they ought to do it," and "why they ought not to do it." ' He had an instinctive understanding of statistics. His habit, wrote Bagehot, 'of always beginning with the facts, always arguing from the facts, and always ending with a result applicable to the facts obtained for his writings an influence and a currency more extensive than would have been anticipated for any writings on political economy'. Added to all that, Wilson was what Bagehot called a *belief producer* – his cogently-argued articles made converts, and as many in the ranks of politicians as among businessmen (one of his more unlikely admirers was the Duke of Wellington, ever a man to respect inspired common sense). The paper soon became influential abroad.

Wilson was a man of great energies but even he was almost exhausted by the first months of the paper. He was writing the bulk of the copy, as well as continuing to carry on his business. Added to that was the nervous strain of again having invested all his disposable capital in a risky venture, and his misery at having to live without his family, who had been sent to live in Boulogne for a time to improve his wife's health as well as to save money.

In the event, the paper was a solid success; its circulation during the 1840s was in the region of 3,000, and within a few years Wilson was able to repay fully the money loaned to him by others (principally Lord Radnor). By 1846 he and his family were settled in a country house in Westbury in Wiltshire where he intended to stand as a Liberal in the next election. He captured that Tory stronghold in 1847 by assiduous canvassing and through the patronage of influential politicians, who respected his gifts and independence while liking him for his agreeable personality. He was by now the trusted confidant of many senior public figures, who gave him inside information frequently and requested information or advice.

Wilson's successful maiden speech in the Commons concerned the currency and he soon secured a reputation as a useful and interesting speaker and a good parliamentarian. He attended the House, edited *The Economist* and enjoyed the warmth of his family. As the girls grew up they were sent in turn to study music and languages in Cologne, almost always accompanied there and back by their father. Although there were no feminists among the Wilsons, the girls were encouraged to develop their intellects and two of them occasionally wrote book reviews for the paper.

In the spring of 1848, the Prime Minister, Lord John Russell, offered Wilson a secretaryship at the Board of Control (the India Board). He addressed himself to his new job with his customary assiduousness and made a great personal contribution in the inspired work he put into introducing railways to India. Additionally, he was an immensely effective government representative on a number of committees, spent long hours in the Chamber and made a number of distinguished contributions to debates. It was he who persuaded the Duke of Wellington to go along with the repeal of the protectionist Navigation Laws. As well as all this, of course, he continued to edit and largely write *The Economist* and lead an active and enjoyable family and social life both in London and Wiltshire.

Russell's government resigned in February 1852, and was replaced by one led by Lord Derby, with Disraeli as Chancellor of the Exchequer. The latter was one of the politicians most antipathetic to Wilson, who could never abide inconsistency especially if he suspected it sprang from political expediency. In July of that year he won Westbury narrowly after a hard contest.

Derby's government was defeated in December, and Lord Aberdeen formed a coalition in which Gladstone was Chancellor. A brilliant appointment was that of James Wilson to the Financial Secretaryship to the Treasury, a post he was to fill with great success for five years. It was, as Bagehot discussed at length in his memoir, an office peculiarly suited to Wilson's special gifts. His judgment was consistent; his sheer common sense meant that he decided the straightforward bulk of cases correctly; his clarity of thought and exposition – so evident in his *Economist* writings – made his position on even the most complicated cases strikingly clear in the minutes and memoranda that flowed effortlessly from his pen. Moreover, he had a most unusually efficient memory, able to remember after several years any official transaction in person or in writing, and considerable physical stamina. He worked as harmoniously with two Chancellors – Gladstone and

Sir George Cornewall Lewis, a great and highminded friend – as with his colleagues and subordinates. And in explaining the minutiae of financial measures in the House of Commons, his faculty for lucid exposition was of incalculable benefit.

Wilson's work was unglamorous but vital – the nuts and bolts on which the whole financial conduct of the nation depended. His office gave him (as Bagehot put it) 'substantial power' without 'legislative fame', a matter of no concern to a man whose eternal preoccupation was with doing a worthwhile job well. For that reason he turned down the Chairmanship of Inland Revenue. A promotion to the Vice-Presidency of the Board of Trade he also eschewed – partly because it would reduce his power over events, but also because he would have had to refight his seat, which he was by no means sure of holding.

For Wilson 1857 was a momentous year. He stood successfully for Devonport, gave up the editorship of *The Economist* to Richard Holt Hutton and met Walter Bagehot, who was to be his protégé, his son-in-law, his surrogate son, his dear friend, his intellectual inspiration and his greatest successor as editor. He also lost his brother William, who drowned with three of his children off the coast of Dunbar, and provided the occasion for one of the grown-up Wilson's few visits to Scotland. His life did not contain enough leisure to travel much, and when he did he preferred to see friends in Paris or Belgium: he had few strong links left with Scotland.

Early in 1858, however, he was asked to visit Edinburgh to investigate a long-running dispute over the Royal Institute's refusal to recognise fully the Academy of Scotland. The Treasury Minute that Wilson wrote subsequently embodied what was generally accepted as the just view, survived the collapse of his government in February 1858 and forms the warrant upon which the Academy's position is now based. In gratitude the Academy presented Mrs Wilson with a portrait of her husband by its President, Sir John Watson Gordon, and a replica of a marble bust displayed in the Scottish National Gallery.

A further visit he made to Scotland in December 1858 affords us glimpses of his distancing from the society of his youth, and of his ferocious appetite for work. To Sir George Lewis he wrote: 'A Sunday in a Scotch Hotel is the best of opportunities for getting up any amount of arrears of correspondence . . . if you have scores of friends in the Town and on every other day of the week asked to dinner three deep, you have no chance of seeing anyone suited to the job.' Along with that went his internationalism and his intellectual curiosity. All those considerations overrode the many good domestic, professional and financial reasons for remaining at home.

In the months before he left for India Wilson spent his time in travelling around the United Kingdom to consult authorities on India. A pleasant interlude came in September in Hawick, where he was made an honorary Burgess. On 20th October 1859, accompanied by his wife, three of their daughters and the husband of one of them (his future private secretary, William Halsey), he set off for India. The family's supplies included two horses, a cow, sheep, geese, ducks and fowl. Wilson found the six-week journey immensely relaxing and arrived in Calcutta in December in fine shape and happy to follow the suggestion of the Governor-General, Lord Canning, that he immediately follow him and join his tour of the upper provinces of India.

Observers of Wilson during his short time in the sub-continent speak of his delight in it and his optimism and enthusiasm about its future. 'He probably,' wrote a colleague, 'learnt more of the Country in a very short time, than any person who ever landed on its shores, and his general information extended daily.' As early as 18th February 1860, he presented his Budget in Legislative Council at Calcutta. He had done his homework so well that although he was proposing quite heavy taxation, he gained widespread support from the majority of all sides. For yet again, Wilson's clarity of mind and exegesis proved deeply reassuring. Communities united only by suspicions about government intentions found themselves converted to his point of view by the sheer logic of his position. They appreciated his directness and fairness.

It was an ex-colleague of his, Sir Charles Trevelyan, President of Madras, who undermined Wilson's work and made his last months harder than they should have been by protesting publicly against his taxation plans. Although he was recalled to London as swiftly as possible, much damage had been done and Wilson had perforce to put a great deal of extra work into achieving the implementation of his budget.

Two further measures he achieved before he fell ill in the summer. The first was the introduction of a rational system of

213

public accounts and the second a plan for the introduction of a government paper currency. Among the admiring letters was one from Prince Albert.

Wilson's last few months were spent in immense labour, for little of his work could be delegated. With the start of the rainy season, and not long after he had sent his family to a healthier climate, his health began to deteriorate. A combination of overwork, anxiety and an unhealthy climate led to his rapid deterioration. On 11th August he died and his funeral was the largest ever seen in Calcutta, where in due course a statue was raised to him.

The main reaction to his death, notes Bagehot, was 'That he should have left a great English career *for this*!' Yet Wilson's record in India makes such a reaction inappropriate. India gave him the opportunity to prove himself a great statesman; while it was tragic that his life was cut short, he had already performed a great service for the country.

At home he had founded a paper that still flourishes. It now has an international readership of well over a quarter of a million. Wilson had made it good: Bagehot made it great.

The Economist stayed true to Wilson's basic principles: in 1943 Crowther wrote that the paper's policy was still the same as in 1843 – 'to hold opinions, to hold them strongly and, if need be, to express them strongly; but to have as few prejudices as possible and certainly no party prejudices.' It has survived to this day supporting the central things it has always supported. Again, as Crowther put it, *The Economist* is 'the same river, coming from the same source and moving towards the same sea' as that of Wilson and Bagehot. In essence it believes in two principles: liberty and the common interest. It sees the purpose of life as the fullest development and expression of human personality. And it attempts to measure policies against the notion of international common interest. Its passion for free trade is part of its dream of universal cooperation – the dream for which James Wilson died nobly.

It remains to Bagehot to provide the epitaph: 'he was placed in many changing circumstances, and in the gradual ascent of life was tried by many increasing difficulties. But at every step his mind grew with the occasion. *We* at least believe that he had a great sagacity and a great equanimity, which might have been fitly exercised on the very greatest affairs. But it was not so to be.'

214

AUTHOR

Ruth Dudley Edwards is a biographer and historian.

BIBLIOGRAPHY

Walter Bagehot, 'Memoir of the Right Honourable James Wilson' in *The Collected Works of Walter Bagehot* (ed. Norman St John Stevas), volume III, pp. 323—364.

Emilie I. Barrington, *The Servant of All,* 2 volumes, Longmans, Green and Co. Ltd., 1927.

Mrs Russell Barrington, *Life of Walter Bagehot,* Longmans, Green and Co. Ltd., 1914.

The Economist 1843—1943, Oxford University Press, 1943.

The Economist, 1843—1857, *passim.*

CHAPTER 18

John Clunies Ross
King of the Cocos
(1786 — 1854)

Billy Kay

The first time I heard of Clunies Ross was in the spring of 1976 at the home of the renowned Gaelic poet, Sorley Maclean, in Skye. There a Portree man, David Forsyth, told a far-fetched tale of how he had a claim to the throne of the Cocos Islands because he was descended from the first king, a chap called 'Cluny' Ross, who had settled there with nothing but a bevvy of Malay beauties for comfort, in the middle of the previous century! Now Highlanders rarely let truth get in the way of a good yarn, and I'll never forget the humorous twinkle in Sorley Maclean's eye when he suggested that on Forsyth's ascent to the throne, he himself could become '. . . *an Bard . . . an Bard Coconagh*' — the Gaelic bard of the Cocos. *Gaidhealtachd!*

Cluny remained an hilarious yarn and a pleasant memory of warm Highland hospitality until he surfaced four years later in the very different landscape and culture of Shetland. Tom Anderson was driving me across the mainland to conduct an interview for my *Odyssey* programme on Shetland's whaling tradition, when he casually pointed to a hamlet called Weisdale and told me it was the birthplace of a man called John Clunies Ross, King of the Cocos. The semi-mythical subject of the Skye yarn was obviously very real to a great many Shetlanders, and he was apparently held in the same esteem as Shetlanders such as Arthur Anderson, founder of the P and O shipping line and Sir Robert Stout, Prime Minister of New Zealand. Cluny was feted as a local boy made good in no less a publication than *The Shetland Book,* the education committee's textbook for schools. No mention of Malay harems or tall tales here, just factual material of Ross's 'enlightened' rule on his island paradise!

The final impetus which whetted my appetite to find out the truth about this fascinating character and his island kingdom came in 1978, when the *Scotsman* published a little syndicated notice announcing that the Australian government had taken over jurisdiction of the Cocos-Keeling Islands which until then had been under the sole rule of the Clunies Ross family. What I present now is, I hope, a reasonably objective sifting of the myths, fantasies and facts surrounding John Clunies Ross who was born the son of a schoolteacher in a cottage on the shore of Weisdale Voe on 23rd August 1786 and died 'King' in the Cocos-Keeling islands in the Indian Ocean in 1854.

> To begin, then, at the beginning, I am a native of Zetland descended maternally from a Norwegian family and lineally on the paternal side from one of those ignorant and therefore misguided men who, in the last century, led forth many of the tribes of N.W. Scotland to assert with their sword — hundreds opposed to millions — Royal Hereditary pretensions against National Constitutional rights, and were in consequence mostly ruined, cut off and expatriated.

Thus John Clunies Ross begins his own version of his settlement on the Cocos Islands in a letter to Rear-Admiral Sir T. Bladen Capel, an important British official in the East Indies in the

1830s. The letter is very much an appeal for recognition of Ross's legitimate ownership of the islands, and is therefore very selective in the history it chooses to relate. The pejorative description of his Jacobite ancestor here, for example, is influenced by the fact he wants to appear true-blue and loyally British. Elsewhere in the letter he rails against the Dutch. When expediency demanded it, however, he sent his son to Java to ensure the family would enjoy his privileges as a Dutch national, and he himself was for a time quite content to sail his trading vessel under the Dutch flag. Possibly the Shetland background had taught him that his first loyalty was to his islands, and that international politics were only of interest on the rare occasions they could be exploited for the benefit of the locality. In Clunies Ross's case, the benefit of the locality was, first and foremost, the benefit of himself and his family. He and his family down through the generations would maintain that what benefited the family would automatically benefit the rest of the people — and more frequently than not, benevolent paternalism characterised their rule on the islands. But when any ruler has almost absolute power, abuses frequently occur — as the experience of Shetlanders and Highlanders at the hands of the lairds and landowners in the same period reveals.

Although Clunies Ross portrays himself as a penniless seaman, there was much in his family history which placed him on the side of lairds rather than native peasants. His mother, Elizabeth Ross of Lund, was descended from Laurence Bruce, the half brother of the infamous bastard son of James V, Robert Stewart, Earl of Orkney. Much of the Shetland mistrust of the Scots dates from the excesses of the Stewart earls and their henchmen in the late 16th century. Laurence Bruce engaged in a campaign of 'extortion and oppression' until the islanders successfully petitioned the Privy Council to have his powers curbed. On his father's side, Ross was the great-grandson of Alexander Cluness, a Rosshire laird who had fled to Shetland via Orkney following the defeat of the Jacobite cause in the 1715 rising.

Clunies Ross recounts the family story that the old clansman is said to have broken his sword over his knee when he heard the news that his son was stooping so low as to marry a native Shetland girl. In his writing, Ross appears proud of the Jacobite hauteur, yet is anxious to play down its political and social implications. Despite his pride in his father's family it is the name of his mother's family — Ross — which John used throughout his adult life. Again this is probably due to his social aspirations — the Rosses of Lund were still an eminent land-owning family in Shetland, albeit one which gave little preferment to John's mother. A possible reason for this may lie in the fact that the girl was pregnant and the marriage hastily arranged. The wedding was far from popular with the bride's family, and John must have been brought up with an awareness of his generation's fall from grace in Shetland's social hierarchy. He may also have resented it, for his personality shows a tension between what he was and what he felt he should be — a tension that was eventually resolved when he fashioned his own social hierarchy on the Cocos Islands.

The route to the Cocos was a long one, but one which had origins rooted in the Shetland experience: 'I may almost say that I was born at sea, the walls of my parents' bed chamber being often wetted by its spray. Most of my waking hours were spent in and on its waves from the age of towards three at most to 13 when I proceeded to serve apprenticeship to the Greenland whale fishery.' With all the ships from the Scottish and English whaling ports stopping at Lerwick to make up their crews for the Arctic run, as many as 900 Shetlanders would enlist for a whaling season, earning hard cash to supplement their subsistence crofting/fishing economy at home. For John, though, the whaling took him away from Shetland at this early age, and he never came back.

It was on a return voyage from an expedition to the Antarctic region in 1813 that John's life began to focus on the East Indies, then a semi-barbaric pirate-infested region where local despots presided over slave-states, and where the maritime superpowers of Britain and the Netherlands vied for supremacy. In Timor, fortune suddenly raised him from third mate and harpooner on the *Baroness Longueville* to commander of the brig *Olivia,* then hired as a coastal vessel by the British Javan government. His first voyage took him to Batavia, where he met the brig's owner, one Alexander Hare, a friend of the legendary Sir Stamford Raffles and at that time England's man in Borneo. And quite a man he was, scouring the Java Sea all his life for a peaceful haven where he could have his women and slaves in peace! For the next 18 years the lives of these two very different characters would intertwine. So much so that, as we have seen, by the time their story reached Skye, the identities of the two had been switched around, with Hare's 'harems' being unfairly attributed to Clunies Ross.

219

As a moral Christian, Clunies Ross would have been outraged at this calumny. At least, he would have shown outrage if it was the thing to do. For Ross worked happily for Hare for over a decade and does not seem to have been unduly repulsed by his sexual proclivities, nor his treatment of the natives. It was only when the two men vied for control in the Cocos Islands that the Shetlander's moral indignation was publicly sparked. Hare had been an official British Resident in Banjarmassin in Borneo, had friends in high places, and when he settled his people in the Cocos before Clunies Ross, the latter resorted to character assassination to consolidate his claim to the islands. As a character, it was open to assassination. This is how Ross describes him to Rear-Admiral Capel:

> He was the eldest of four sons of a watchmaker in London, a man of most excellent character and moral conduct, but who, on being a free-thinker on matters of religious belief, did on principle leave his children to form opinions for themselves on that subject: a liberty which, however harmless, or even valuable in result it may prove to those whom nature may have furnished with intellectual powers superior in strength and activity to the merely animal propensities of humankind, is certainly the reverse for those in whose mental constitution the latter has received the predominance as was the case in MR HARE's composition . . . [he was] licentious in all respects of corporeal indulgences.

This righteous 'unco guid' tone pervades all of the Scot's writing, especially when referring to the licentious Englishman. It must be said that in sexual mores, he appears to have been a saint compared to Hare, and the countless other Europeans who abused their power by indulging their sensual gratification. In this, his Calvinist Shetland background may have come into play. However, as we shall see, the high moral stance he appears to have held successfully on sexual matters was not always carried through to other areas of life, and there are justified claims that he was content to keep the native population in a state of near-slavery.

In the years before settling in the Cocos Islands, he was happy to turn a blind eye to Hare's excesses. The overall moral climate at that time and place, however, could only be described as perverse. Political expediency overruled humane moral considerations. After the local Sultan had granted Hare the lands at Banjarmassin, his friend Raffles had the British authorities sanction the transportation of convicts as settlers there from

Java. Many died on the ships or working in the jungle in Borneo, and as the demand for more people, especially women, increased, it is thought that innocent Javanese were rounded up and transported . . . 'nearly 3,167 subjects of the British Crown were kidnapped and sent into slavery'.

From 1813 until the Dutch takeover in 1818, Clunies Ross was in effect the principal manager of the colony and its unfortunate inhabitants. In a letter to Raffles in 1825 he states his conviction . . . 'that the plan of colonising that country was highly politic, the object in view invaluably interesting to the British Empire, and that the means adopted to effect it were both humane and well calculated to obtain the desired end. . . .' Here we see the determined vision, some would say the tunnel vision, of the Empire builder — who believes that the end always justifies the means. Ross would show the same single-minded purpose when establishing his own little Empire a few years later.

The ship he had built in the colony, *The Borneo,* was used to carry Hare and his slaves to the Cape of Good Hope in 1820, as Ross made his first voyage to England since 1811. Adventure again followed him, for according to family lore he escaped from a Press Gang in London by sprinting round a corner and running into the nearest open door. The havoc wrought on Shetland by the forced removal of many of its sons by the Press Gang would no doubt have quickened Ross's dash for freedom. As luck and the best romantic fiction would have it, the open door he entered was to change his life in an unexpected way; for the daughter of the house, Elizabeth Dymoke fell in love with this wild colonial boy and their first child, John George was born a year after they were married.

Conducting further voyages to the East on behalf of Hare, and witnessing the steady increase of his family, the idea of settling in some remote trading spot took root in the adventurer's head. The Falklands, Melville Island, the Pagi Islands in Sumatra, Christmas Island, Australia all crossed his mind and were rejected before he resolved to examine the uninhabited Cocos-Keeling Islands. His trip to the Cocos in 1825 was possibly undertaken at the instigation of Hare, for he too was on the lookout for a place to settle, far from society's disapproving gaze. Ross, however, had decided in advance that the place would be his, and the report of his four-day reconnaissance reveals a man with an unswerving purpose: 'On concluding the examination I found reasons for deciding on adopting the place for settlement, and in commencement proceeded to take formal possession and to clear a space on each of the entrance-bounding isles, wherein I placed the seeds, roots and plants which I had provided at Sumatra for the purpose.'

Incidentally the irony of the 'holier than thou', 'unco guid' side of his personality comes out in his rejection of the idea of settling in Australia because it is ' . . . a country that had the taint of convicts'. He himself had of course no such taint on his leadership of the convict colony in Borneo, nor did his son John George who imported convict labour to the Cocos from Bantam in western Java throughout his lifetime as the second 'King'. The 'taint' of convicts was nothing to the taint of slaves and C. A. Gibson-Hill, by far the most accurate historian on the settlement of the Cocos, reminds us that ' . . . John Clunies Ross himself kept the slaves that Hare left behind him when he went from Cocos in 1831 under conditions close to slavery, and defended himself on the grounds that he dare not give them complete liberty in case Hare's heirs claimed against him for their value.' When he got on his moral high horse in the writings of his later years, the first King was apt to have bouts of amnesia about certain aspects of his reign.

Cluny was undoubtedly a courageous, thrawn man who had no trace of doubt in his head when he departed for the remote atoll with his pregnant wife, children and a handful of settlers, including at least one fellow Shetlander called Leisk. The Scots word 'thrawn' aptly describes the stubborn strength of purpose which is engrained in some types of Scottish character. In certain circumstances the blinkered stubborn will to succeed is an attribute worthy of praise; if it goes too far, however, the will can become perverse — and that is another meaning of thrawn. Both meanings could be applied to the behaviour of Ross after he landed in Cocos and realised his worst fears — Hare and his harem had got there before him.

Ross 'hutted his family' on another island and resolved that he would overcome this temporary setback in the long run — that away from the world of privilege and patronage the stronger individual would gain the upper hand. His only fear was that the outside world would recognise Hare's claim as sole owner before his own. Hare probably did not see Ross as a threat initially, thinking that the old social structure, in which he was above Ross, would prevail.

When he had first mooted settling in the Cocos, he wrote to Ross saying he preferred to import skilled settlers from the continent, rather than rely on the natives or the British. The Englishman's reasons for rejecting the latter are interesting, especially his naively prophetic views on the Scots: 'The English are, I fear, too delicate, the Irish are so given to drink and quarrelling that there is no doing anything with them, and the Scots are always for pushing on and would merely make a stepping stone of me on their way to Java or India.' After his experience with the Scots on the Cocos, I bet you he wished his antagonist had been one of his delicate fellow countrymen instead of a thrawn Caledonian with an indomitable 'will to power'. Yet it was a will softened, at least for public consumption, by a streak of romance. It is to the pseudo-romantic past of Scotland that he dedicated the name of his island capital, Selma being the name of the capital of ancient Scotland invented by James MacPherson in the fake 'ancient Gaelic' poetry of *Ossian*. This was possibly the greatest literary spoof of all time and it created a vogue for Scottish romanticism worldwide. Clunies Ross, with his Jacobite ancestors and noble lineage, was not immune from the style.

'We have named our settlement New Selma, in memory of the most Ancient Capital of our unconquered and, we trust, unconquerable country, the capital of our ancestors who compelled the proud Romans . . . not only to desist from attempting to subjugate them, but even with their own hands to limit their dominion in Britain. . . .' His patriotic cry for legitimacy is always backed up with a strong moral and religious appeal.

In the eyes of his Presbyterian God, and most others too, Ross undoubtedly won the moral argument over Hare hands down. Visiting the islands in 1829, a Dutchman, H. van der Jagt, described how the brutality of Hare was driving his slaves to seek refuge with the Ross colony. This resulted in Hare placing many of his slaves on a more distant island, while keeping their children semi-imprisoned close by, so that they could be used as emotional pawns to bring any escapees back: 'These children are confined separately in special huts on Rice Island where Mr. Hare lives. These small structures which scarcely deserve the name of huts, are walled in with a double palisade of which the openings are filled up with stones, so that it is impossible for the children to escape or for their parents to see them.' With sexual abuse of

223

mothers and daughters common, Hare could quite accurately be described as having 'set up a concubine manufactory on the Cocos.'

Violent brutality towards the men and boys was also the norm, and it is hardly surprising that over the months and years, more and more of Hare's followers escaped to Ross's camp. The escape of the women was undoubtedly facilitated by the British men who had accompanied Ross, and lacked any other source of wives. By 1831, the diaspora from Hare's colony was such that he could no longer survive and he shipped himself and those loyal to him to Indonesia — where apparently he died trying to set up another harem at Batavia a few years later.

With total power Ross set about running the islands on sound lines and bringing discipline and order into the coconut industry. How successful this was in his own lifetime is debatable, for those few visitors who came from the outside world often presented contradictory evidence on the Ross régime.

In 1836, for example, H.M. surveying vessel *Beagle* called in at the Cocos and both Charles Darwin and Commander Fitzroy described what they saw in fairly negative terms. Darwin, as reliable a witness as one could hope for, gave this impression of New Selma. 'Captain Ross and Mr. Leisk live in a large barn-like house open at both ends and lined with mats made of woven bark. The houses of the Malays are arranged along the shore of the lagoon. The whole place had rather a desolate aspect, for there were no gardens to show the signs of care and cultivation. . . . The Malays are now nominally in a state of freedom, and certainly are so, as far as regards their personal treatment; but in most other points, they are considered as slaves.' Fitzroy is even more condemnatory, suggesting that the situation of the Malays 'shew the necessity that exists for some inspecting influence being exercised. . . . A visit from a man o'war, even only once in a year, is sufficient (merely in prospect) to keep bad characters in tolerable check . . . ' Ross had been absent from the islands at the time of the visit, and in counterblast to these criticisms, he later asserted that Fitzroy and Darwin had been taken in by Leisk, who at the time was stirring up and exaggerating native unrest and hatching a plot with an American called Raymond. Their ultimate aim was to take over the islands for themselves and convert them to an emporium for visiting American whaling ships.

Ross put down the aborted insurrection himself and his version of the story alleging Leisk's 'stirring up' the Malays was given some vindication when Commander Harding of HM sloop *Pelorus* investigated the turmoil for himself in December 1837, interrogating 'each individual to discover if any just ground of complaint could be substantiated against the resident. I gave them a patient hearing, and I esteem it praiseworthy that not one of the number could substantiate the slightest act of injustice or oppression on the part of Mr. Ross, tho' their excited feelings dictated many silly and imaginary wrongs. . . . Nevertheless, a great many were restless and dissatisfied. . . .' The 'restless' — Malay and European — were transported almost immediately to Bencoolen in Java by Ross himself. The brave certainty of the man in his actions is revealed in the fact that he declined the offer of an escort by the British ship, confident in his ability to dominate the malcontents until he was rid of them. Harding summed up the action: 'Thus were these islands weeded of the indolent and worthless characters, and Mr. Ross well satisfied that the greatest benefit would accrue, not only to himself and family but also to those that remained.'

And so the unique way of life of the kings of the Cocos was established — hardly any of the original Europeans remained and he held total control over the destiny of the people of the islands. From the departure of the original Europeans, it can be surmised that the islands were not big enough for any other figure of authority apart from King John. Given the extraordinary power he wielded, however, he does not appear to have abused the position beyond the exploitation of cheap labour common at the time. Remember that he died in 1854, before the United States was engulfed in a Civil War caused by the South's demands to continue its 'states rights' of holding slaves. Ross's rule on Cocos I liken to that of an authoritarian plantation owner of the Old South — inventing for himself a noble present and a patrician past to legitimise his slave holding. Provided that everyone knew their place the régime was benign, but woe betide anyone who stepped out of line.

F. Wood-Jones, who wrote of the history of the islands in his book *Corals and Atolls,* described Ross as 'a man with a firmly settled belief in divine justice; but situated as he was in an isolated coral reef 700 miles from land, he by no means underrated his ability to be its successful instrument.' Little is known of Ross in his later years, but we do know that he increasingly devoted himself to reading and writing. Captain Duintjer of the brig *Dankbaarheid* visited the islands in 1842 and described him as having 'a healthy and venerable aspect, intelligent, acute and deep thinking'. He had a library of over 1,000 books, and wrote articles on subjects ranging from the formation of coral reefs to a critique of Malthus's work on political economy.

His reign in the Cocos had lasted 27 years by the time he died aged 68 in 1854. Ironically the legitimacy of British Dominion status he sought for his islands was not achieved until three years after his death. Even in death, however, Ossianic romance accompanies the man on his last journey. Wood-Jones recounts the tale that the morning after his death, his grandson was sent to tell the news to the crew of a schooner lying in the bay, but when he got there, they were already in mourning . . . 'It seems that at sundown — when the spirit of Ross fled — a sound had rushed through the air, and to each listening man upon the schooner had come the wail of the passing spirit of his beloved chief. The schooner lay far out in the lagoon, but the news came clear and unmistakable, and the boy rowed back a troop of silent men who had needed no telling of the loss which they and the little kingdom had suffered.' The grave of Ross and his wife is marked by a large Celtic cross of Scottish granite, imported by his descendants.

Those descendants continued more or less in the tradition of benevolent paternalism established by John. By far the majority of visitors to the islands — from the Scottish naturalist Forbes to the American mariner Slocum — were full of praise for the unique society which had developed, Slocum describing it as a 'paradise on this earth' in 1897. This despite unsavoury facts of Cocos life such as the truck system where the imported convict labour and the native-born Malays earned Clunies Ross tokens which could only be exchanged for overpriced goods in the company store! Martin Dowle has argued that the truck system was possibly based on the one used by the lairds in Shetland, but I would imagine it was in widespread use all over the East Indies.

This kind of exploitation was becoming unacceptable by the 1970s when Australia bought out the Ross interests for a reputed £4 million. The thrawn independence of yesteryear had become the perverse exploitation of the modern age. The islands are now in the democratic control of the Malays, except for the area around the Ross mansion. It is outwith the island council's jurisdiction and the family in turn are not allowed a vote.

Is there any permanent Scottish heritage? Well physically, apart from the Celtic cross, there is only the mansion Oceania House, almost entirely built from materials shipped from Scotland; the glazed tiles and bricks, for example, originated in Kilmarnock. On the cultural level, the third 'king' George and practically all of his eight brothers and sisters were sent home to Scotland to be educated — Madras College, Dollar Academy and then Glasgow and Edinburgh Universities appear in most of their stories. It was probably this generation which established Scottish country dancing as part of the island culture. Linda Hargreaves, a daughter of the last 'king' who now lives in England, tells me that it is still going strong.

Another Scottish characteristic influencing the history of the place is the total lack of racism. The Clunies Ross kings frequently married Malay women, and the intermarriage undoubtedly resulted in mutual respect for the different cultural traditions of the islands.

Writing an account of island life in the 1940s, a former military administrator, Lieutenant-Colonel J. A. Harvey, described the character of the people. 'They have a keen sense of humour, and as a result of the Ross influence they have a solid Scots habit of industry and pride of craftsmanship grafted upon the natural courtesy and charm of manner which is common to all races of the Malay archipelago.'

Finally, John Clunies Ross could be described as the definitive 'lad o' pairts' — one of that kenspeckle band of Scots worthies who make their mark in far-flung corners of the world, but never let themselves or their descendants forget where they came from. In 1933, 134 years after Clunies Ross left his native parish, the committee charged with raising the money for the first Whiteness and Weisdale Public Hall sent off an appeal to the current King of the Cocos. They received £100, a good part of the money required. The hall was built and stands as a reminder to the local people of the very different islands where a Shetlander was king.

AUTHOR

Billy Kay is a writer and broadcaster who devotes his work on radio, television and books to the advancement of awareness of Scottish culture.

BIBLIOGRAPHY

C. A. Gibson-Hill (ed.), *Journal of the Malayan Branch of the Royal Asiatic Society*, volume 25 (parts 4 & 5, December 1952), Malaya Publishing House Ltd., 1953.

J. S. Hughes, *King of Cocos*, Methuen, London, 1950.

F. Wood-Jones, *Corals and Atolls*, L. Reeve, Kent, 1912.

Newspaper article by Martin Dowle in *The Scotsman*, 10th July 1978.

CHAPTER 19

Sir Thomas Johnstone Lipton
Message Boy to Millionaire
(1850—1931)

J. E. Walker

> Lipton's Butter and Ham
> That's the stuff you should cram
> If you want to get stoot
> Just tak' a blaw oot
> O' Lipton's Butter and Ham

This popular jingle sung in Glasgow was one of Tom Lipton's publicity stunts in attracting business to the first shop he opened in Glasgow in 1871.

With US $500, his savings from working four years in America, he started what was known as his 'Ham and Egg' shop in Stobcross Street, putting into practice some of the advertising gimmicks he had seen in use in America. He revolutionised the rather staid methods of selling that existed at that time in his native city.

By 1898 he had established strings of shops in every town and city in the United Kingdom, his main area being London. From grocery goods he expanded to the purchase and management of estates in Ceylon (Sri Lanka) of tea, coffee and cocoa, fruit farms in Kent, meat packing companies in Chicago, refrigerated wagons on the railways of the United States, curing stations in most conurbations, the manufacture of biscuits and other bakery goods, and the bulk-buying and bottling of wine.

He made the selling of tea one of his most specialised spheres of interest. His slogan, 'Lipton's Tea — Direct from the tea gardens to the teapot', became commonplace. The United States was his biggest target, and at the peak of his career he was selling 200 tonnes of tea a week and employing 5,000 agents throughout the world to sell it. Currently Lipton is the biggest seller of tea in America.

Through his later yachting exploits, which brought him into association with the Prince of Wales, later King Edward VII, he moved into the society of most of the crowned heads of Europe. An invitation to be his guest on his steam yacht was much sought after.

In business he went on to compete for Government contracts and on one occasion supplied provisions for 70,000 men on manoeuvres on Salisbury Plain. In 1888 he visited Russia to arrange for the supply of rations to the entire Russian Army of 1,000,000 men.

In 1898 he crowned his efforts by the successful flotation of his vast concerns into a limited liability company. The issue of £2,500,000 was enormously oversubscribed.

How did this man, who left school at nine years of age to work for 2/6d (12½p) a week, achieve such an astounding success in such a short period of time?

Thomas Lipton was born of Irish parents who arrived from County Monaghan, fleeing from the disastrous effects of the potato famine. They settled in Glasgow, as thousands of others did, and opened a small shop in Crown Street, selling mainly butter and eggs which they obtained from contacts in Ireland.

Their first dwelling was on the fourth floor in a tenement building in Crown Street, and on 10th May 1850 Tom was born.

Glasgow at this time was burgeoning with industrial development in coal, iron, engineering and shipbuilding. The streets alongside the docks were Tom's first playground. The income from the little shop barely paid the rent and Tom, when nine years of age, had to earn his keep by working, part-time, as an errand boy for a stationery shop in Glassford Street for 2/6d (12½p) a week. At 10 years of age, he obtained full-time employment at 4/- (20p) a week in a shirt-making factory, his first job being the gumming of shirt patterns into sample books for travellers. Ultimately dissatisfied with his meagre wage he asked for a rise and was told: 'You're in a devil of a hurry. Four shillings is all you are worth.' He kept looking for more remunerative employment and obtained a job as a cabin boy with the Burns shipping line whose vessels traded between Glasgow and Belfast. It was in this job that his first love of ships and seafaring was nurtured and led ultimately to his great yachting exploits.

At 17 years of age he shipped steerage to America — the great Eldorado — to make his fame and fortune with 18 pence and 4 threepenny bits in his pocket, and instead found hunger and hardship.

In an article in the *Weekly Scotsman,* 1928, Sir Thomas recalled, 'I found lodgings at a boarding house in Washington Street, New York, and was lucky enough to be boarded for nothing for a whole fortnight until I got my first job. This was my reward for inducing a dozen or so of my fellow immigrants whom I had got to know on shipboard to patronise the house.' He travelled widely, living rough, often sleeping in the open, taking any work offered and always seeking a better opportunity. After working in the stockyards of Chicago butchering pigs, on a tobacco plantation in Virginia and on a rice plantation on Coosaw Island, South Carolina, where he nearly died of fever, he stowed away on a sailing schooner to Charleston and New Orleans turning his hand to any kind of work but still finding no firm employment. He stowed away again on a cotton steamer bound for New York.

He found New York the most exhilarating of cities and finally secured employment in, of all places, a busy grocery store, where he worked hard to be a success. Over the years he obtained an insight into and studied keenly the American methods of business and the means taken to attract and retain customers.

Towards the end of his fourth year in America he suffered a tremendous bout of homesickness and an overwhelming desire to return to Glasgow to see his parents. He had a close family connection particularly with his mother to whom he had always promised he would return and see her driven in a horse and carriage. He had managed to save US $500, equivalent at the exchange rate of the time to £100 which in 1871 was a goodly sum.

The gifts he returned with for his parents were not exotic treasures from the New World but perhaps indicative of his Scots upbringing — a barrel of flour and a rocking chair.

After working for a short time in his parents' shop, Lipton was eager to launch out on his own and try out some of the ideas of salesmanship he had picked up in America. So at the age of 21 he commenced a grocery business in a small shop in Stobcross Street, Glasgow. His working capital was £100, part of which he immediately spent in making the shop attractive. The lighting was made to be brighter than in any of the shops around and served as a beacon in the street. People, like moths, flock to bright lights. While serving he always wore a white jacket and apron (all his subsequent employees were required to do the same). He worked early and late doing all the jobs from window cleaning to message delivery. Often he was so engrossed with his affairs that he could hardly leave the shop and on many nights slept under the counter so that he could greet his early morning customers. Taking a tip from Benjamin Franklin, he put a big sign in his window letting people know he did this. When business was quiet he set out a sign 'Delivering orders. Back in 13 minutes.' Then business soon picked up. He put all of his profits back into the business.

Lipton decided on a super publicity campaign — what he called 'bold advertisement' — the main message being: 'Give good value. Be civil to all. Treat rich and poor alike.' He retained the affinity with his parents' roots by buying largely from Ireland, making personal trips, purchasing in bulk, cutting out the middlemen, and undercutting his rivals. His head was buzzing with ideas and though aggressive, he always leavened his approach with humour, a rare quality in those days. He turned the most mundane of sales material — what could be more mundane than butter, ham and cheese — into a joyous crusade. None of his contemporaries anywhere ever employed such imaginative business methods.

He employed a cartoonist to paint pictures of fat jolly pigs being driven to market, 'Going to Lipton's!' Children flocked to see his 'Lipton's Orphan', a baby pig led through the streets at the end of a length of rope by a man dressed as an Irish farmer. They snarled up the traffic and created great fun. Every sales ticket on the goods in the windows had a funny picture or comment so that the windows were always crowded with interest. In one instance he had a mirror with a concave curve showing the customers as thin going in and a convex mirror on the exit showing them coming out stout — a novelty at the time. This side-show attracted people from all over. It became the thing to do when visiting Glasgow.

He had promissory coupons printed in a facsimile of the current £1 note, that for every five shillings spent he would give £1 worth of goods. They resembled the authentic notes so closely that after several police court cases of them being passed as genuine, Lipton had to make them less similar. One of his most ambitious schemes was to import jumbo-sized cheeses from America with the ballyhoo of them being made from six days' milk from a herd of 800 cows. One such cheese was recorded as weighing 625 kg (1,375 lbs). The unloading of cheeses by crane from the ships was a spectacle, and their conveyance by a well-decorated steam traction engine through all the main streets created a carnival atmosphere. Like the Christmas dumplings of our childhood when silver threepenny and sixpenny pieces were secreted in the succulent mixture, he had gold sovereigns hidden in the cheeses and competitions to guess their weight. He himself would cut the first segment with a silver trowel. On one occasion the entire cheese was sold within two hours. He had a balloonist drop thousands of telegrams addressed to his shops and offered rewards to the first 20 people to arrive with one of them. His shops swarmed with claimants. He was also very generous in offering well-labelled hams as prizes at all kinds of charity functions.

Lipton shops spread 'like an amiable epidemic' throughout the country. A record of eight new shops opening in one day was recorded. In a very short time he had shops in every district of Glasgow then in almost every town in Scotland, England and

Ireland and eventually in his ultimate target, London. He established his main central depot in City Road, London. The offices alone were a grand advertisement for they were constructed in the latest style of accommodation and efficiency. Lipton himself resided in a fine house in Highbury and came to his office early every morning in a fast trotting cab, remaining till late.

As soon as he was able he rehoused his parents in a seven-roomed villa in Cambuslang, then a residential suburb of Glasgow, and on their death, that of his mother particularly being a very sad occasion for him, he converted the house into a 'Lipton Memorial Nurses Home'. Speaking of this house Sir Thomas is reported in a 1923 newspaper to have said, 'The place where my mother lived is sacred to me. She was my sole inspiration in my efforts to get on in the world.' At this time he also owned a few horses which he exercised himself when he visited Glasgow, and which were used to give his mother coach trips around the district as he had always promised her.

In 10 years the ex-errand boy had an army of 10,000 employees and, still in his thirties, Lipton was a millionaire.

Why Lipton came to specialise in tea merchandising is uncertain. However, the story goes that, by chance, he met a man in London who was in difficulties with his mortgage payments on a tea plantation in Ceylon (Sri Lanka). Sir Thomas paid off the debt and bought the plantation. On visiting Ceylon, en route to Australia he found that many of the coffee estates were in depression, so he purchased a number of them. The same happened with cocoa.

The famous 'Lipton's Tea' slogan was born. On entering the tea business Lipton found he had to compete with well-established cartels with massive investments but with his now familiar tactics supported by numerous outlets he was soon making inroads. His master-stroke was the packaging of tea in units of 1/7d (8p) per 0.45 kg (1 lb.) Until that time tea was sold loose by weight. He cut the established price by 3d (1p). Other tea merchants sold tea from chests and drawers but the tea was exposed to dust and dirt and grew stale. Lipton's attractive packeting, labelled with variety and weight, became the popular way to sell it. Never a man to miss a possibility of advertisement Lipton made much capital of the fact that one of his tea-tins left by Peary's expedition to the

North Pole was recovered 49 years later and had not lost its quality.

America, with its traditional coffee drinking habit, was his next target and it was not long before tea sales were firmly established there. Today with tea bags, tea leaves, iced tea mixes, decaffeinated teas, flavoured teas, herbal teas, fruit teas, teas in cans, Lipton is now the best-selling tea in the United States. It is reckoned 10,000,000 cups of tea are drunk daily.

In the sale of tea he again broke new ground by engaging men to go out and sell to other retail outlets which did not normally retail tea. W. H. Scott, who at 20 years of age was the assistant manager at Lipton's Dublin store earning £1 per week, tells how Lipton sent for him and gave him three samples of tea, a map of Scotland and £15 ($25) expenses and said: 'We haven't enough agencies in Scotland, establish some. Send the money back with your orders and I'm going to pay you 10/- (50p) extra a week.' 'It was one of my happiest moments,' Mr. Scott says.

For a week he toured Scotland. He had no trouble opening agencies but he could not get the money in return. At the end of the week Lipton cabled: 'You're no good, come back.' But the next day in a 'dry goods store', whose manager had never thought of carrying tea, he got a big order and a big cheque. After that he toured Europe for Sir Thomas, opening up new agencies. Lipton always referred to him as his 'Great Scott'.

Scott also relates how Lipton had signs painted and displayed all over London but had to wait until the arrival of his first crop from Ceylon. Two weeks before it arrived he dressed 150 men as Tea Packers and headed by a Ceylonese girl, paraded the streets daily. When the tea arrived, four tons of it, every ounce was sold. Lipton was considered to be responsible for changing popular choice from China tea to Indian and Ceylon tea.

One of Sir Thomas's favourite stories relates to a friend, Lord Dewar, who enjoyed hunting big game in Africa. On one trip Dewar telegraphed Lipton to let him know how popular his tea was there. 'For three pounds, I can buy six wives.' 'I immediately telegraphed back that I was sending out several three pound parcels but so far I haven't received any samples of the wives.'

Lipton never married and despite having many social engagements in his later years, he also remained a teetotaller and a non-smoker.

It was not until 1898 when his business had been made into a limited liability company and he had less personal responsibility for it that his thoughts turned to his boyhood passion for ships and sailing. He purchased the Clyde-built steam yacht *Aegusa*, renamed it *Erin* and sailed many cruises around the Clyde area. His enthusiasm increased and it was the Prince of Wales, later to be King Edward VII, who directed his attention to the ignominious defeats suffered in trying to recover the America's Cup from the United States.

The America's Cup competition commenced in 1851 when a yacht named *America* sailed across the Atlantic under a Commodore Stevens and challenged the yachtsmen of the Royal Yacht Club to a race for a hundred guinea cup. In the subsequent race, round the Isle of Wight, the *America* beat the British entry *Aurora* and the cup was handed over to the New York Yacht Club. The event has become the supreme yachting competition. Any challenger has to repeat the feat of the original *America* and win in the defender's own waters. When Sir Thomas came on the scene, nine unsuccessful attempts had been made. As a gesture to his parents' love for their native land he tried to get a suitable yacht designed and built in Ireland and to have a skipper and crew of Irishmen to sail in her but was unable to get an Irish yacht designer at this time. His first yacht *Shamrock I* (all his yachts were named *Shamrock* to keep the Irish connection and he also entered the challenge as a member of the Royal Ulster Yacht Club) was designed by the famous Scottish designer William Fife and was built on the Thames by Thornycroft & Coy. The arrival of *Shamrock I* in 1899 after successful trials against the then recognised fastest yacht, *Britannia*, coincided with Admiral Dewey's triumphant return from the Spanish-American War and the two competing yachts were preceded by Dewey's flagship *Olympia* up the Hudson river. The whole event became a great carnival, the more so for the Americans as their entry, the *Columbia,* designed by Nathaniel Herreshoff and owned by three American businessmen, won the race with convincing ease. Lipton returned disappointed but determined to try again. He realised that his yacht had not been raced sufficiently and the crew not trained enough for the contest.

Shamrock II was designed by George Watson of Glasgow, built by Denny Brothers, Dumbarton, and skippered by Edward Sycamore of Brightlingsea, the top skipper of the time. Her trials were remembered by the exciting incident in the Solent when the Prince of Wales narrowly escaped injury when sailing in her when her steel mast was carried away. At Sandy Hook the *Columbia* was again the winner. *Shamrock II* did, however, win the first of the three legs of the race. This took place in 1901.

The third attempt was made in 1903. Again the design was entrusted to Mr. Fife and the vessel was again built by Denny Brothers. The captaincy was given to Robert Wringe of Southampton who had been the second in command on the *Shamrock I*. The trials proved this boat to be very speedy but despite the betting odds being lower in America once again the British entry was comprehensively defeated.

It was not until 1914 that Lipton made a further challenge. *Shamrock IV* was designed this time by C. E. Nicholson of Messrs Camper and Nicholson, Gosport, where the ship was built. It had been arranged that the competition should start on the 10th September 1914, and was to be the best ship in three out of five races. *Shamrock IV* was on her way over the Atlantic when World War I was declared and she was laid up in Brooklyn until 1920 when the race finally took place. *Shamrock IV,* skippered by Sir W. P. Burton, an amateur yachtsman, won the first two races and actually crossed the line on the third race ahead of the American entry, named *Resolute*, but lost the race on handicap. The *Resolute* won the two remaining races.

The last challenge took place in 1930. *Shamrock V* was again designed by Nicholson and built at Gosport.

The rules of the race were again altered in that both yachts had to conform to similar dimensions according to Lloyds scantling standards and raced on level terms.

Lipton was now 80 years old and his endeavours to win, in his one remaining passion, caught the imagination of the world and he received phenomenal good wishes from all quarters. The Americans designed and built four contenders and raced them against each other in exacting trials. The yacht *Enterprise* was considered the best of the four and was entered for the race. This vessel incorporated all the latest equipment. It had a duralumin mast with mechanical aids to work the sails and a controversial triangular boom. *Shamrock V* was skippered by Captain Ned Herd and had proved herself to be the fastest of her class in British waters. The *Enterprise* was owned by a syndicate headed by Harold S. Vanderbilt and captained by him. Once again Lipton was defeated, the *Enterprise* winning the four first races. Lipton had been defeated in his greatest ambition and announced that this was to be his last race.

The *Enterprise* cost £150,000 to build and equip and the *Shamrock V* £30,000. The cost of competing was more than one man alone could sustain and Lipton stated it would require, as the Americans had done, a syndicate of interest.

The tremendous sympathy and admiration for Lipton in his unavailing attempts to win this trophy prompted the Americans to present him with a similar trophy which was called 'a loving cup'; standing 18 inches high on a silver base with the design of the original America's Cup in relief with the inscription 'This symbol of a voluntary outpouring of love, admiration and esteem is presented to the gamest loser in the world of sport.' The 'loving cup' was provided by public subscription. The Utah miners provided the silver base and even children contributed their pennies for the purchase. Lipton may have lost his races but he won the hearts of America in his pursuit of winning. He was a household name.

The New York Yacht Club kept the trophy for 132 years and were eventually defeated in 1983 by an Australian yacht from Fremantle. In 1987 Dennis Conner of the NYYC, the losing holder in 1983, regained the trophy at Fremantle, Australia. The next event is likely to be held in the 1990s, and is likely to cost each entrant over £10 million.

On the declaration of war in 1914 Lipton immediately offered his steam yacht *Erin* for service. He had it converted into a hospital ship and despatched it to the assistance of Serbia which had suffered more than most from the ravages of the war and diseases. The *Erin* was torpedoed in the Mediterranean and several of the crew lost. In 1929 Sir Thomas found a replacement by buying the steam yacht *Albion* and renaming it *Erin*. This yacht acted as tender to his yacht *Shamrock V* on its voyage across the Atlantic to challenge for the America's Cup in 1931.

Lipton's popularity and acclaim brought him many honours. Queen Victoria conferred a knighthood on him in 1898 and four years later he was made a baronet. He was also made a Grand Officer of the Crown of Italy and of the Order of St. Sava (Serbia); Hon. Colonel of the 6th Volunteer Battalion Light Infantry; and H. M. Lieutenant of the City of London. In yachting circles there were few clubs in England and America in which he was not made an honorary member. In Britain he was elected as a member of the very exclusive Royal Yacht Club for his services to British yachting. In 1923 he was elected a Freeman of the City of Glasgow. At a banquet to honour 'Pioneers of American Industry' he was flanked by Firestone, Rosenwald, Edison, Schwab, Ford, Chrysler and Eastman.

Sir Thomas retained his enjoyment of life, taking pleasure in recounting many a humourous incident. Apropos his appointment as Hon. Colonel of the Light Infantry he tells how he was asked to lead the battalion in a Royal Review in Edinburgh on horseback in front of 40,000 troops and 100,000 spectators. A friend had told him not to bother bringing a horse as he would provide him with one. It turned out that the horse had not been trained for such an occasion. It took four men to hold it until he got mounted and then it dashed ahead of his battalion nearly mounting the grandstand. When the massed bands began, the horse bucked so fiercely that Sir Thomas was shot into the air and he says, 'When I came down it wasn't there.'

Although Sir Thomas was such a keen sportsman he states that he only made one wager in his life. 'It was with Sir Harry Lauder (the famous Scots comedian, singer and noted pinch-penny). We were both going to America, he in the S.S. *Mauretania* and I on the S.S. *Baltic* and to please Harry I staked 9d (4p) against his 4½d (1½p) that I would be in America first. Harry beat me but it gave him some terribly anxious moments. The *Mauretania* ran into thick fog for about three days and Harry got so excited that he went down into the engine room to urge on the stokers. Then he discovered that he had lost a 6d piece (2½p) and all the stokers stopped to look for the coin. Harry finally found it in his shoe. Anyway I lost and weeks afterwards I got a postcard from Honolulu asking me to let him have the 9d (4p) and the accrued interest. I wrote back to say that I had invested it for him and that he would get it and the dividends when he returned.'

In 1915 his financial affairs advanced further with the formation of Thomas J. Lipton Inc. of America. In 1983 it recorded a billion dollars of sales and in 1986 its net income was $91,458,000.

In character Lipton was a singular combination of shrewdness and simplicity. He prided himself on rarely forgetting a name or face and he was constancy itself in his attachment to old friends and servants. Two of his maxims in business were never to take a partner and always decline a loan. He used to tell his staff that corkscrews had sunk more people than cork jackets would ever save. 'Treat rich and poor alike,' he said to them. 'The poor man's 20 shillings are as good as the rich man's £1.'

In all the associations of his career, commercial, sporting and social, Sir Thomas contrived to be genial, considerate, courteous and entertaining, with the inevitable result that few men have been so generally liked and respected by all classes of society.

On his business empire going public he found himself a very rich man and was very generous in bestowing gifts to the friends he had made throughout his struggles. As an example, he sent a gift to the police constable who had patrolled the beat in Stobcross Street when he opened his first shop.

It is now apparent that almost all his most generous gifts were to the poor and always anonymous. In 1897 the Princess of Wales scheme to feed poor children in London benefited from £25,000. Later he gave £100,000 towards the building of a huge working-class restaurant in City Road, London, administered under the Alexandra Trust. In the year of his death in 1931, in the midst of the great industrial depression he donated two gifts of £10,000 to the Lord Provost's Fund for the poor in Glasgow. These sums were tremendous amounts of money at the time.

Today the company, through the Thomas Lipton Foundation, carries on this tradition and supports a variety of causes such as the United Cerebral Palsy Foundation and the Boys' Clubs of America and has donated £1.5 million to Second Harvest, a national food bank for the poor in America.

On 2nd October 1931, Sir Thomas died at his London home of a heart attack brought on by a chill he had sustained while motoring.

Among the many tributes from Americans was included one from President Hoover: 'He was a fine English (sic) sportsman.' Al Smith, former Governor of New York, said: 'Sir Thomas was an internationally beloved figure.' And Mr. 'Jimmie' Walker, Mayor of New York, commented, 'He was the most popular sportsman of our time.'

On his death the bulk of his estate was bequeathed to the poor of Glasgow. He was buried in the city's Southern Necropolis.

Sir Thomas Lipton achieved success because he cared about quality, value, integrity and creativity. He made the men and women who worked for him care about these qualities too. In his own words 'There is no fun like work.'

AUTHOR

J. E. Walker, a former head of the C.I.D. in Ayrshire, now translates some of his experiences into short stories.

SOURCES

1. From Sir Thomas Lipton's own collection of press clippings bequeathed on his death to the Mitchell Library, Glasgow.
2. From the archives of Sir Thomas J. Lipton, Inc., New Jersey, especially the Company's Presidential Progress Report for 1986.

CHAPTER 20

Jane Haining

Devotion Far From Home
(1897—1944)

Elizabeth Walker

Perhaps the most significant thing about Jane Haining's birth was its location. She was born on 6th June 1897 in an unpretentious Dumfriesshire farm called Lochenhead which stands near Ellisland Farm, famous because *Tam O'Shanter* was penned there by Robert Burns. Her death, some 47 years later, in wretched circumstances in the foul Nazi den the world knows as Auschwitz is paramount. But it is for her life between these years that her devotees, at the mention of her name, will remember her with love, and be inspired by her courage and commitment.

Jane, or Jean as she was called at home, was the fourth child and second daughter born to John and Jane Mathieson Haining. Her sister Helen, born some five years later, was to bring joy and sorrow as Jane's mother died in childbirth, and little Helen, a weakly child from all accounts, died 18 months later. Jane's parents were deeply religious people and she grew up in an atmosphere where religion was as much a part of life as breathing. Her father hid his grief in hard work on the farm and fulfilled his duties as parish councillor and an elder of the Kirk. Jane proved an able pupil at the village school, and in the upper school managed her work with eagerness and ease. Even at this tender age, she gave the impression of being 'a little mother', often taking charge of her elder sister, Margaret.

At 12 years of age, she was entered for a scholarship to Dumfries Academy and scored well in the bursary competition. Jane was one of the first to attend the Moat Hostel for Girls which adjoined the academy, and boarded there for the next six years. Apart from her promising academic successes, 41 prizes in all including Dux of the Modern School, higher grade passes in English, Maths, Latin, French and German, she is remembered during these years as a shy, retiring girl, but one who delighted in and excelled at taking charge of newcomers and making them feel at home. This quality above all others would be the one to colour and consume her life.

At 18 she embarked on a business course at the Atheneum in Glasgow, and at its successful completion two years later, she took up an appointment with the thread combine, J. and P. Coats Ltd at Paisley. Her boss, Mr. M. L. Peacock was later to write of Jane, 'Her ability and qualifications soon marked her out for something definitely better than the ordinary clerical work of an office. Well do I remember her saying to me when she was about 28 to 30 years of age, that she had a desire, an urge indeed, not to continue in office work, but rather to give her life in service which would bring her in contact with other lives, particularly young lives in the formative years.' She gained rapid promotion at Coats, and stayed 10 years. Her life was filled by her many church activities, being a devout member of Queen's Park West Church in Glasgow. Here she elected to work with young people, and her special spheres were the Sunday School, and later, the Band of Hope. It was during this time that her interest in foreign missions began to emerge. She was never open about herself or her innermost feelings, but was perhaps influenced by another family member, Miss Margaret Coltart, who had been a missionary in India for many years.

The passing years made singularly little change, outwardly at least, to the life of Jane Haining. Her sister Margaret came to Glasgow and they helped each other through the trying times after the death of their father and the selling of the farm. Their companionship continued for about five years until Margaret left Glasgow, and shortly after this, Jane's missionary interest was re-awakened with greater fervour. At a meeting of the Jewish Mission Committee of the Church of Scotland, probably the only one she ever attended, she told Dr. George Mackenzie, 'I have found my lifework.' This Church of Scotland organisation had been established in 1925 to convert the religiously adrift Jews of Eastern Europe. Some were initially attracted by the opportunity of learning English, but not a few were led by a much deeper interest in the message of Christianity.

Good at languages, a committed Christian, free from family ties, Jane Haining in her early thirties was ready to receive such a calling — the spark had kindled to flame! She immediately took steps to realise her vocation. Back to school she went, this time to the Glasgow School of Domestic Science, to secure the desired diploma and a housekeeper's certificate as well. Thus equipped, she accepted the post of matron in a radium institute in Manchester, but kept close ties with her old church and enjoyed the regular delivery of *Life and Work* the Missionary Record of the Church of Scotland. It was fitting that in one such copy the eagerly awaited call came to justify Jane's existence, to serve with her heart, mind and soul. A matron was required in the Girls' Home of the Church of Scotland's Jewish Mission Station in Budapest — a far cry from her life in rural Dumfriesshire. But that part of her life was over and with characteristic unruffled efficiency, she tackled the Hungarian language and mastered it.

After a period of training at St. Colms, the Women's Missionary College in Edinburgh, she was ready to go to Budapest. At 35 years of age the waiting was over, the preparation had been done, and her Dedication Service was held in St. Stephen's Church, Edinburgh on the 19th June 1932. It was officiated by the Reverend T. B. Stewart Thomson.

She felt at home in the fine city almost at once, from Buda, with its royal palace and rolling hills, to where Pest spread itself out on its flat sandy plain, with the Danube flowing between. Jane soon familiarised herself with the Jews of Budapest, and quickly recognised that any worries Jewish parents might have had about their offspring being in a totally Christian atmosphere were worth risking for the exceptional academic training they would receive. Tragically, some of the girls came as 'unwanted children' from homes broken by divorce, and for these little ones, Jane would show particular patience and understanding. To the daughters of Israel she became a mother and their mutual love would help them endure the dark days to follow. At the end of January 1933, Adolf Hitler became Chancellor of the German Reich. As he brutally trod down the Jews in his demonic rise to power, Jane spent her time calming the uncertain lives of her charges.

At the end of three full and happy years at the mission, she took her entitled home leave. She was willingly granted re-appointment and to mark the committee's satisfaction with her running of the home, her salary was increased from £100 to £125 per annum. Back at the mission some months later, Jane combated the menace of Nazism with increased work and managed to have a happy, frivolous Christmas with her girls. Her tireless spirit was physically tested at this time, as she constantly tended girls sick with scarlet fever, debilitating influenza and some orphaned children who needed 'heaps and heaps of love'. One of those children, Eszter Balazs, still living in Budapest today, remembers Jane with the following anecdote:

> From half past two we had a play period — piano lessons, hobbies, talks and plays. During this time she would see to it that newcomers always got involved. A rather big and clumsy girl arrived one December. She did no reading, approached nobody, hardly answered questions and was inclined to sit alone. Miss Haining called her to give a hand at the distribution of sweets. This happened regularly at four o'clock. Mothers sent or brought these for their children but Miss Haining arranged that the lot was pooled and equally distributed amongst all of us, so there should be no distinction between rich and poor, between the well cared for and the abandoned children. Miss Haining did this to save us from envy. The new girl soon got involved and found friends.

1938 saw the German annexation of Austria. As oppression followed, Jane found herself with several Austrian refugees to take care of. The accumulation of work and worry was wearing her out, and she began to long for her leave. The trip was duly planned, and she was happy and revitalised to be among her ain folk once more in the summer of 1939. She and her companion Miss Prém, headmistress of the mission school, addressed meetings in Glasgow, Aberdeen and Galashiels on the daily persecution of the Jews, but their 'holiday' came to an abrupt end when the Germans invaded Poland and the Second World War began. Jane's surviving sister Agnes writes of this time, 'I remember seeing them onto the bus in Dunscore village — it was pouring of rain.'

Immediately, they began the nightmarish journey back to Budapest, amid chaos and confusion caused by people frantic in their efforts to avoid the Nazi war machine. In the ensuing months after a bitterly cold winter, Denmark and Norway were struck down before Hitler turned to Holland, Belgium and Luxembourg. It was evident that Hungary could not enjoy quasi-neutrality much longer. In the light of the steadily worsening situation, the Church instructed its missionaries to return home. Jane decided to remain. As her sister wrote, 'If the children needed her in peacetime, they had much more need of her in war-time and she would never have had a moment's happiness if she had come home and left them.'

The next four years were increasingly austere. Hungary became an enemy country and the diplomatic staff of the Allied nations all eventually left. Staying on, Jane quietly looked after her girls and despite police surveillance continued her work without hindrance. But when the German army took possession of Budapest in March 1944, the lot of the Jews became considerably harder. While the world was in turmoil life under Jane Haining's aegis went on in a practical way — she cheered the girls' spirits and impressed them by cutting up her genuine leather luggage to provide decent soles for their shoes. Food was scarce so she made regular trips to the market at 5 a.m. and loaded and carried the heavy rucksacks herself. A war bonus was offered to teachers in the state schools and in the mission to augment the increased cost of living. Jane, of course, refused to take more than her original salary.

The Mission school at this time had 335 pupils of which 224 were Jewesses. In the Girls' Home under the direct control of Jane were 48 boarders, 31 being Jewesses. It was one of the saddest moments of her life when the order came that all Jews must wear the conspicuous Star of David. She put the yellow star on her girls' clothing and wept bitterly for man's inhumanity to man. A report in 1944 from the Budapest mission to the Church of Scotland headquarters in Edinburgh states,

> The Committee is under a very deep debt of gratitude to Miss Jane L. Haining, matron of the Girls' Home, who has acted for the Committee in all negotiations required for the maintenance of our missionary work. By her personal influence and faithfulness she has inspired such loyalty in all workers that the Budapest Mission has maintained its former high standards. Recent events have seriously altered the situation, and the thoughts of the Church will be with Miss Haining and her colleagues in the new difficulties that have arisen.

It was not until the spring of 1944 that the German military machine formally occupied Hungary. Until then it was a satellite axis state and as such, had escaped the wrath and the more evil aspects of Nazi rule. The advances of the Soviet forces from the east, however, prompted the German resolve to purge Hungary before it was too late. Beginning in early April under the direct orders of the notorious Gestapo chief, Adolph Eichmann, they started to round up all Jews and other people deemed undesirable by the authorities. Jane, like many foreigners living in Hungary at that time was not immediately targeted for arrest.

Earlier in the year Jane had discovered that the daughter and son-in-law of the mission cook were 'using' school accommodation against her strict orders. She had forbidden this practice, and sacked the cook for condoning these activities. This was a dangerous thing to do, because, as Jane knew, the young man in question was a member of the 'Arrowcross', the Hungarian Nazi party.

On the morning of 4th April, two Gestapo men appeared in her office. They searched this and her bedroom and after giving her 15 minutes to gather a few possessions, they took her away. After questioning she was charged with eight offences, all too ridiculous to be taken seriously. These were as follows:

1. She had worked amongst the Jews.
2. She had wept when putting yellow stars on the girls.
3. She had dismissed her housekeeper, who was an Aryan.
4. She had listened to news broadcasts of the B.B.C.
5. She had many British visitors.

247

6. She visited British prisoners of war.
7. She sent them parcels.
8. She was active in politics.

A pupil who witnessed this arrest was later to write, 'I still feel the tears in my eyes and hear the sirens of the Gestapo motor car. I see the smile on her face while she bid farewell.' Representation via the Swiss Consul, who looked after British interests, was made, but to no avail. It was only through the efforts of Sophie Victor (now Mrs. Benes), a young helper at the mission, that Jane was eventually tracked down to a prison cell in Budapest's Föutcu Gaol. Sophie and the Revd Nagy visited Jane twice in this prison taking food and a change of underwear on each occasion. She was held there for 17 days and during this period shared her cell with another British female, Miss Frances Lee. Of Jane, Miss Lee writes, 'She endeared herself to all her fellow prisoners and everybody wept when she left. As for me, I feel her loss more acutely every day — it is rarely one finds such a dear, good, unselfish friend.' She also details that when Jane left from Föutcu she was, 'In very good health and spirits. Little did I dream I would never see her again on this earth.'

Recent research now reveals a great deal about Jane's movements in that fateful summer of 1944. On or about 22nd April, Jane was transferred to a holding camp 25 km (15½ miles) east of Budapest at a place called Kistarcsa. Jane sent a postcard to her friend Miss Prém. She asked for food and this was sent immediately. Sometime around 12th May, she was placed in a cattle wagon with 90 or so other human beings. The wagon was originally designed to carry eight horses. It took her to the small town of Oświecim, 60 km (37½ miles) south-west of Kraków in southern Poland. The English translation of Oświecim is Auschwitz. Jane Haining arrived there between 13th and 16th May, 1944. Auschwitz had once been a small town in the Austro-Hungarian Empire, a place of no special interest or significance. Under its Polish spelling, Oświecim, it appears on a 1905 guide to Austria-Hungary, as a junction on the Vienna to Kraków railway, with a branch line to Breslau. Forty years later it was to become the most terrible railway terminus of all, to which trains from every corner of Nazi tyranny brought Jews, gipsies and others to their death, some killed while working in nearby factories and labour camps, others shot at random, but the majority, possibly as many as two million, gassed within a few hours of their arrival.

Two Hungarian women who also arrived at the concentration camp around that time have since written of their experiences — Olga Lengyel's *Five Chimneys* was published in English, in 1959, and Gracia Kerényi's *Book of Songs* in 1982. From the accounts described in these two books and from data provided by the Auschwitz museum, we now have some idea of the privations a woman prisoner would have experienced. Of the train journey Madam Lengyel wrote. 'The cattle car had become an abattoir. More and more prayers for the dead rose in the stifling atmosphere. But the S.S. would neither let us bury nor remove them. We had to live with our corpses around us, the dead, the contagiously ill, those suffering from organic diseases, the parched, the famished, and the mad must all travel together in this wooden Gehenna.'

When everybody left the train, men and women were separated into two groups. From then on all had to pass in front of an S.S. doctor who decided his or her fate by a mere movement of the finger. People were divided into two categories — those who were able to work and those who were not. The number of people unfit for work was always much greater than the number of people considered fit for work. On average 70-75 per cent of new arrivals were considered unfit. These unfortunates would be surrounded by the S.S. men, then led to the yard of one of the gas chambers. Jane, at 47 years of age, passed this first selection. This we know because she sent her first of two letter cards from Auschwitz, again to Miss Prém.

Auschwitz consisted of a number of camps and work areas. The women's camp was called 'Birkenau' and its deplorable conditions marked it as the most infamous extermination centre in Auschwitz. In the middle of 1944 it housed around 35,000 prisoners. Between 800 and 1,000 *select* women were crammed into stable barracks by the S.S. These buildings were originally designed for 52 horses. The new female inmates who passed this selection were processed first by being herded into a large hangar-type wooden building. Olga Lengyel describes this scene thus:

After waiting about two hours in front of a vast but coarsely constructed building, we were thoroughly chilled. Then a troop of soldiers pushed us inside. An officer began to bark orders. 'Undress! Leave all your clothing here. Leave your papers, valuables, medical equipment, and form rows against the wall.' The interpreter translated this into all languages. At that moment, our last doubts

249

vanished. Now we understood that we had been horribly deceived. The luggage we had left at the station was lost to us forever. The Germans had expropriated everything, even to the smallest souvenirs that could remind us of our past lives. But our hour of shame had begun. I lined up in my row, completely naked, my shame engulfed in terror. At my feet lay my clothes, and on top, the pictures of my family. Around me the frightful agitation, the weeping and the cowering, continued. Now we were compelled to undergo a thorough examination in the Nazi manner, oral, rectal and vaginal — another horrible experience. We had to lie across a table, stark naked while they probed. All that in the presence of drunken soldiers who sat around the table, chuckling obscenely. We were then pushed into another room where men and women, armed with scissors and clippers waited for us.

The prisoners were then issued with pyjama-type uniforms and given a prison number. Jane, being non-Jewish, would have this tattooed on the inside of her left forearm. Her number was 79467. Prisoners also had identification numbers sown on the left side of their jacket and the right leg of their trousers. Triangles of different colours were displayed above the prisoner's camp number. The colour denoted the reason for arrest, nationality or category. A white triangle adorned with the letter 'P' signified the prisoner was Polish, the letter 'R' Russian. A green triangle was reserved for common criminals. Jewish inmates had their triangle trimmed with a yellow band and the added stigma of a painted red stripe on the back of their clothing.

They would then be marched to their barrack-type accommodation of which Olga writes in *Five Chimneys*, 'To make matters worse, the roof was in deplorable repair. When it rained, the water leaked in and the internees on the top bunks were literally inundated. But those on the ground level were hardly better off. There was no floor except the beaten earth, dirty and wet, which the lightest rainfall turned into a sea of mud. Besides, at the lowest level the air was absolutely suffocating. The filth in the barrack surpassed imagination.'

At this time the Nazis were exterminating thousands of people every day. The official statistics were May: 360,000; June: 512,000; and from 1st to 26th July 1944: 442,000. In less than a quarter of a year the Germans had liquidated more than 1,300,000 men, women and children at the Auschwitz complex! In this hell hole, Jane Haining survived. We know this because on 15th July 1944, she wrote her second letter card to Margit Prém. The following is the transcript. All prisoners were obliged to write in German in order that censors could cut out any disturbing or embarrassing details.

Auschwitz 15th July 1944

My Dear Margit,

I still have no reply to my first letter, but I know it is not your fault. I shall briefly repeat what I'd already written in case you haven't received it. You are allowed to write twice and I once every month.

Parcels are neither tied, numbered or named. I asked you also to register my name with the Red Cross. But still send a few parcels until the Red Cross can begin. However, if possible, continue sending apples or other fresh fruit and biscuits, rusks or similar kinds of bread. Naturally the Red Cross does not send such things.

Margit, what do you intend to do with the flour? Sell it? What is on the top is the best I think, but you know that one should not disregard anything that is left over. Have you used up all the eggs?

How are you all? I think of you day and night with love and longing. I wait for news to hear how everybody is, also your dear family, Margit. Is the old aunt still with us?

There is not much to report from here. Here on the way to heaven are mountains but not as beautiful or high as ours, but nevertheless . . . .

Greetings to all the family. Love and kisses.

Your Loving Jean

This last letter from Jane is all that remains to mark her presence in that terrible place. The letter is held in safe-keeping in the archives of the Church of Scotland's headquarters, 121 George Street, Edinburgh. What happened to Jane after its writing can only be speculation. The most probable scenario is that she would not be passed fit for work at a later selection inspection. To keep the camp population within tolerable limits these selections were held when new, healthier and stronger slave labourers arrived. Weakened by barely adequate feeding, the inmates were easy prey for debilitating illnesses such as dysentery, smallpox and typhoid. From certain surviving camp records we now know a number of Hungarian women, admitted around the same time as Jane, died on the 16th August 1944. This group was gassed on that day and it is this form of death that Jane most probably experienced. How, exactly where and exactly when Jane died we will never know.

So ended the life of a Scottish woman whose only crime was that she wanted to help others. Her stated date of death as intimated to Swiss authorities is 17th July. Jane's last letter is postmarked 21st July. A death certificate sent from the German Legation in Budapest to the Church of Scotland Jewish Mission in Budapest stated that 'Miss Haining was arrested on justified suspicion of espionage against Germany. She died in hospital on 17th July 1944 of cachexia following intestinal catarrh.' Cachexia is the general collapse of the body systems due to insufficient food or some chronic malady. How accurate a record this is, no-one can know. All we do know is that Jane lived in that place for over three and a half months, and we can suppose that in the midst of this carnage she continually inspired others with the qualities of courage and determination that had marked her entire life.

The last gassing at Auschwitz was in late November 1944. Russian troops of the First Ukrainian Battalion liberated the camp on 27th January 1945 — they found some 7,000 prisoners.

Two beautiful stained glass windows now adorn the entrance to Jane's old church in Glasgow. They are simply named *Service* and *Sacrifice,* a fitting tribute to a missionary with a plain Scottish sense of duty informed by a deeply religious mind. Jane's courage and commitment is shown in her return to Budapest, her valour in remaining there, and in being uncompromising in her devotion to the Jewish children of Hungary. She was the only Scottish person slain in an extermination camp and her devotees hope that her name will soon be officially recorded at the Holocaust Museum in Jerusalem. Her ambition was to help others, and in particular to oppose anyone who would distinguish between the child of one race and another. She did this with her heart, her soul and her life.

AUTHOR

Elizabeth Walker was born in Lanarkshire, brought up in Ayrshire and now lives in Hong Kong with her husband and four children.

BIBLIOGRAPHY

Olga Lengyel, *Five Chimneys*, Granada Publishing, 1972.
Martin Gilbert, *Final Journey*, George Allen and Unwin, 1978.
Thomas Keneally, *Schindler's Ark*, Cornet Books, 1981.
Elie Wiesel, *Night*, Penguin Books, 1981.
Gerald Aston, *The Last Nazi*, Sphere Books, 1986.
Revd. David McDougall, *Jane Haining of Budapest*, The Church of Scotland, 1949.
Oświecim State Museum, *Selected Problems From The History of K. L. Auschwitz*, 1979.
Issues of *Jewish Mission Quarterly*, The Church of Scotland, 1944—48.
Various letters from people who knew her.